Second Language Students
in Mainstream Classrooms

PARENTS' AND TEACHERS' GUIDES

Series Editor
Professor Colin Baker, *University of Wales, Bangor, Wales.*

Other Books of Interest
A Parents' and Teachers' Guide to Bilingualism
 COLIN BAKER
Becoming Bilingual: Language Acquisition in a Bilingual Community
 JEAN LYON
Building Bridges: Multilingual Resources for Children
 MULTILINGUAL RESOURCES FOR CHILDREN PROJECT
Child-Rearing in Ethnic Minorities
 J.S. DOSANJH and PAUL A.S. GHUMAN
Curriculum Related Assessment, Cummins and Bilingual Children
 TONY CLINE and NORAH FREDERICKSON (eds)
Encyclopaedia of Bilingualism and Bilingual Education
 COLIN BAKER and SYLVIA PRYS JONES
Foundations of Bilingual Education and Bilingualism
 COLIN BAKER
Language Minority Students in the Mainstream Classroom
 ANGELA L. CARRASQUILLO and VIVIAN RODRIGUEZ
Mainstreaming ESL
 JOHN CLEGG (ed.)
Making Multicultural Education Work
 STEPHEN MAY
Multicultural Child Care
 P. VEDDER, E. BOUWER and T. PELS
Teaching and Assessing Intercultural Communicative Competence
 MICHAEL BYRAM
Teaching and Learning in Multicultural Schools
 ELIZABETH COELHO
Teaching Science to Language Minority Students
 JUDITH W. ROSENTHAL
The Guided Construction of Knowledge
 NEIL MERCER
Working with Bilingual Children
 M.K. VERMA, K.P. CORRIGAN and S. FIRTH (eds)

Please contact us for the latest book information:
Multilingual Matters, Frankfurt Lodge, Clevedon Hall,
Victoria Road, Clevedon, BS21 7HH, England
http:/www.multi.demon.co.uk

PARENTS' AND TEACHERS' GUIDES 2
Series Editor: Colin Baker

Second Language Students in Mainstream Classrooms

A Handbook for Teachers in International Schools

Coreen Sears

MULTILINGUAL MATTERS LTD
Clevedon • Philadelphia • Toronto • Sydney • Johannesburg

Library of Congress Cataloging in Publication Data

Sears, Coreen
Second Language Students in Mainstream Classrooms: A Handbook for Teachers in International Schools/Coreen Sears
Parents' and Teachers' Guides: No. 2
1. Education, Bilingual–Handbooks, manuals, etc. 2. Students, Foreign–Education (Elementary)–Handbooks, manuals, etc. 3. Second language acquisition–Handbooks, manuals, etc. 4. English language–Study and teaching (Elementary)–Foreign speakers–Handbooks, manuals, etc. 5. Mainstreaming in education–Handbooks, manuals, etc. I. Title. II. Series.
LC3719.S43   1998
370.117'5–DC21   98-13163

British Library Cataloguing in Publication Data

A CIP catalogue record for this book is available from the British Library.

ISBN 1-85359-409-1 (hbk)
ISBN 1-85359-408-3 (pbk)

Multilingual Matters Ltd

UK: Frankfurt Lodge, Clevedon Hall, Victoria Road, Clevedon BS21 7HH.
USA: 325 Chestnut Street, Philadelphia, PA 19106, USA.
Canada: OISE, 712 Gordon Baker Road, Toronto, Ontario, Canada M2H 3R7.
Australia: P.O. Box 586, Artamon, NSW, Australia.
South Africa: PO Box 1080, Northcliffe 2115, Johannesburg, South Africa.

Typeset by Archetype-IT Ltd (http://www.archetype-it.com)
Printed and bound in Great Britain by WBC Book Manufacturers Ltd

Contents

Acknowledgments

In the course of this project, which changed its nature over time, many people and institutions have given their time to helping me and to providing invaluable professional support.

I should first like to thank the Board of Trustees, the Director and the Heads of Schools of the International School of Brussels for the award of a six-month sabbatical leave. This allowed me time to travel to some of the countries that many of our students come from and to begin writing what I planned to be a very short handbook for teachers in international schools. As I visited schools and talked to teachers it became clear that few schools offer this opportunity for teachers to expand their professional horizons. My sabbatical leave not only made possible a unique professional opportunity in the writing of this book, but also enabled me to return to my students in Brussels, refreshed and reinvigorated.

Next, I should like to thank the European Council of International Schools for their award of a Fellowship in International Education. This award was used to fund part of the cost of my travel and provided a context for my visits to schools. I should like also to thank Jennifer Henley, Executive Officer for Information and Resources at ECIS, for her time and professional advice. My conversations with Jennifer at various stages of the writing have helped me to assemble my thoughts in an organised manner.

With the award of ECIS funds comes the appointment of a mentor to oversee the project. In my case, Richard Hall, Director of the International School of Brussels accepted this task. It could not have been a more happy choice from my point of view. Dick Hall is a linguist and has a real understanding of the issues of second language acquisition as well as a wide knowledge from his own experience of the needs of mobile international families. In his busy life he has found time to be a kindly, humorous and stimulating mentor. He took the time to read the earliest version of the text in the Christmas vacation and to make extensive and helpful comments. He has been a prime mover in urging me to extend the project along more ambitious lines. I am very grateful to him for his consistently positive and encouraging support.

Someone else I would wish to acknowledge is Edna Murphy, formerly Head of the Elementary School of the International School of Brussels. Edna has always shown a special interest in the needs of second language children in international schools and was the initiator and editor of the book, *ESL: A Handbook for Teachers and Administrators in International Schools*, published by Multilingual Matters, to which I contributed a chapter. I should like to thank Edna for the time she has given in reading through a later version of this text, particularly the pedagogical sections. Her editorial comments are always spiced with a rich dollop of humour, and she too has been very positive in urging me to extend and expand on the original project.

I should like to thank Marjukka and Mike Grover of Multilingual Matters, and my editor Professor Colin Baker. Their supportive dealings with a novice author have encouraged and energised me while I worked through the stages of bringing a book to publication. Colin Baker began by describing himself as a stuffy academic. This could not be further from the truth. He has shown sensitivity and kindness in steering me in directions that have, I believe, immensely improved the quality and readability of the book.

A further key contributor to this project has been my husband, David. He has helped me above and beyond the call of duty. His humour, enthusiasm, map-reading skills and professional contacts throughout our six-and-a-half weeks of travel added greatly to that experience and brought us many friends. He has also contributed generously with time and knowledge in the area of technology, and I should acknowledge a debt to him relating to Chapter 11 and Appendix B.

There are two further groups of people whom it is a pleasure to thank. The first is made up of colleagues at the International School of Brussels who have given their time so that I could ask questions about specific pedagogical areas. I should especially like to mention Jeffrey Brewster, Librarian of the Early Childhood Literacy Center at ISB. Jeffrey is someone who has given me valuable insights into the education of young children and has been consistently generous in sharing his knowledge of young children's literature. The second group comprises all the people who helped me in arranging school visits and who gave their time so willingly during my visits to schools. I include country by country the names of further kind people who gave information and insights into expatriate and national life in those places. These lists of names are a practical demonstration of the rewarding connections and professional goodwill I experienced throughout this project.

Colleagues from the International School of Brussels

Early Childhood Center

Jeffrey Brewster, Librarian, Literacy Center.
Sarah Scheele, 2nd Grade teacher.

Elementary School

Frances Bekhechi, ESL teacher
Veronica Bourke, 6th Grade teacher
Barbara Campbell, Language Arts team leader and 5th Grade drama coordinator
Christine Laphkas, 5th Grade Teacher
Mary McGeary, Mathematics team leader and 5th Grade teacher
Eileen Rodgers, 4th Grade teacher

People and schools by location

My thanks go to all of them. I am aware that some of these people, as is the way with international educators and professionals, have moved on to take up other posts. I give their role at the time of my visit.

Belgium

Mrs Hadas Ben-Porat, Israeli parent contact at the International School of Brussels.
Mrs Yoko Matsumoto, Japanese parent contact at the International School of Brussels.
Mr Akira Hiramatsu, Director, **Japanese School of Brussels.**

China

Sheila Macdonald, Head of ESOL Department, **International School of Beijing.**
Mr Ian Rysdale, Director, and Barbara MacDonald, ESL Coordinator, **Western Academy of Beijing.**
Ms Jane Drake, Executive Director of the **American Chamber of Commerce in the People's Republic of China**, Beijing.

Japan

Mrs Sono Okabayashi, member of **ISB alumni committee, Japan**, and counsellor at **Kawaijuku International Education Center**, Tokyo.
Mr Kenichi Kamiya of **Japan Overseas Educational Services**, Tokyo.

The Director and staff of **Fukimidai Elementary School**, Yokohama.
The Director and staff of **Miyamaedaira Junior High School**, Yokohama.
The JFL coordinator of **Kawasaki-shi Comprehensive Educational Center.**
Ms Jeanette Thomas, Headmistress, and Dianne Nisita, Head of Language Acquisition Department, **Saint Maur International School**, Yokohama.
Mr Hiroshei Sakai, Public Affairs Manager, **Exxon Chemical Japan,** Tokyo.

New Zealand

This was the personal part of my travel, and unfortunately took place when schools were on holiday. I should like to record, however, numerous conversations I had with family, friends and total strangers about their experiences in the New Zealand education system. What was illuminating for the purposes of this handbook was talk with and concerning members of the Maori and Pacific Islander communities.

Singapore

Mrs Margaret Levers, Head, **ISS International School.**
Mrs Colleen Lee, Elementary School Principal, **Overseas Family School.**
Mr Laurence Basapa, Public and Environmental Affairs Manager, **Exxon Chemical Asia Pacific.**

South Korea

Mr Y. H. Yoon, President, **Exxon Chemical Korea Limited,** Seoul.
Ms Tami Overby, Executive Director of the **American Chamber of Commerce in Korea,** Seoul.

Thailand

Mr Graham Sullivan, Principal, Mrs Stella Counsel, Head of First School and Jean Kingham, ESL teacher, **Bangkok Patana School.**
Rodney Bueschlen, ESL Coordinator, Elementary School, **International School Bangkok.**

United Kingdom

Dr Ibtissam al-Bassam, High Mistress, **King Fahad Academy**, London.

Introduction

The Need for This Handbook

This handbook is designed as an aid to teachers of mainstream classes in the elementary sections of English-medium international schools. Teachers of these classes are faced on a daily basis with managing the education of children from diverse language and cultural backgrounds. Most international schools contain a majority group of students from one of the English-speaking countries of the world; however, it is the presence of the second language children that gives such schools their unique flavour. It is also the presence of these students that offers a major challenge to classroom teachers.

In the early days of international schooling, a pioneering spirit was evident. This arose out of the challenge of founding and developing schools to meet the needs of an entirely new group of students. This group, continually expanding in number, was made up of children from mobile expatriate families with high educational expectations. The oldest of the English-medium schools designed to meet these students' needs were founded in the 1950s. At this time teachers largely drew on their prior experience in national school systems. Schools were small, and parents, teachers and administrators frequently felt part of a joint enterprise, united by a common purpose.

Things have moved on. It is fair to say that international schooling has come of age. An assignment overseas is now considered a normal move in the course of many business and professional careers. Parents expect to find an appropriate education for their children in the new location and international schools exist in most major cities of the world in order to answer this need. Professional bodies such as the regional councils of international schools now monitor developments in the world of international education. Non-profit making trusts such as the European Council of International Schools and International Schools Services offer recruitment services and may be called in by large companies or organisations to set up international schools. Governing boards of individual schools recognise the value of receiving accreditation from ECIS or from one of the nationally based accreditation and inspection services. Post-graduate courses in international education have been established in universities in the United Kingdom (for example at Bath and Oxford Brookes Universities) and in the United States (at Michigan State University and The College of New Jersey among others). Frequent in-service opportunities exist to serve the specific needs of international educators, among them the annual Administrators' Academy run by International Schools Services and the International Seminars organised by the British Council.

It remains true for teachers in international schools, though, that there is no single source of professional knowledge and experience to answer their needs in catering for this mobile student population. In general, teachers in international schools must base their practice on evidence and experience gathered from a variety of sources. One of these sources is the body of information and research based on minority school populations in national schools.

There are important differences in the circumstances of students in international schools, however, and these differences require teachers to develop new understandings to inform their teaching in the unique circumstances of an international school. The purpose of this handbook is to collect together the theoretical findings and practical applications that are relevant to mainstream teachers in international schools. In all cases this material has been interpreted in the light of 18 years' experience of international education.

This handbook is not designed to be read from cover-to-cover in one sitting. Readers should feel free to look up sections that seem immediately interesting and later to consult chapters that answer a need at the time. After a certain amount of trial and error, it has been decided that anecdotal and personal comments are better placed in separate textboxes. This decision was reached because it seemed inappropriate to present such personal experiences as general findings. Extracts from children's writing and other sources that give a fresh and vivid insight into life in international schools and expatriate communities have also been included. The aim is to make the handbook more readable and relevant as well as to offer a variety of viewpoints.

It has been decided that large numbers of academic references should not be included in the body of the text. This handbook is essentially designed to be a practical document. However, some acknowledgments of sources are included within the text where appropriate, and lists of books that supply the source material are provided, along with further suggestions for useful reading under topic headings, in the bibliography.

The handbook is constructed so that teachers move through general background material relating to second language students in international schools before they come to the chapters that describe everyday life in the classroom. Thus Chapter 1 provides information on the nature of international school students and their families, Chapter 2 deals with issues associated with intercultural adjustment, and Chapter 3 offers an outline of relevant second language acquisition issues. Chapters 4 and 5 provide information and suggestions relating to the presence of second language learners in mainstream classrooms.

Finally, Chapters 6 to 11 offer detailed suggestions relating to the subject areas of the curriculum. These suggestions include the following topics: How to modify general grouping and teaching strategies to allow more effective participation by second language students in the mainstream programme, how to adapt subject area material to allow second language children access to the content, and how to exploit the potential of the content areas themselves as vehicles for language learning.

A summary of contents is included at the end of each chapter, however the form of the summary varies according to the nature of the material presented in a given chapter. Chapters 1 to 3 are discursive in nature and cover a wide spectrum of information and opinion. It seemed more helpful in these instances to summarise the contents in the form of a list of salient points. Chapters 4 to 11 include more practical material broken down under headings that give a clear indication of the material that follows. The summaries for these chapters, therefore, take the form of several paragraphs giving an overall picture.

Explanation of Terms Used in This Handbook

Children who speak more than one language are described in a number of ways. These include the terms **bilingual, speakers of other languages** and **speakers of English as an additional language.**

For students in international schools, however, English is the second major language in their lives after their preferred home language, despite the possible presence of third and fourth languages deriving from home or previous schooling. It has been decided, therefore, to use the term, **second language,** to describe both the students and their families throughout this handbook. For the sake of simplicity, the symbols **L1** and **L2** are used in the pedagogical sections to replace the terms **first language** and **second language.**

The terms, **elementary school** and **elementary level,** are used throughout the handbook to describe schools and classes that cater for students between the ages of five to 11 or 12 years. This terminology, used in the American system, has been chosen for two reasons. First, many international schools offer an American-style education and their schools and classes are named according to the system generally used in the United

States. Second, other terms, such as **primary school** and **first school,** are used in different systems to describe different age levels. It therefore seems least confusing to use the single term, **elementary,** to describe education for children of five to 12 years, even though many international schools use other terms to describe the education of this age group.

The term **young children** includes students up to the age of six years old. Chapters and sections of the handbook described as relating to young children refer to students of that age. Where the term **older children** has been used, it refers to children aged between eight and 12 years. The group in between, aged seven, the American second grade level, may fall into either category depending on the developmental age of the child and the nature of individual international schools. Teachers of that age group will find useful material, it is hoped, under both headings.

Chapter 1
Setting the Scene

Introduction

The aim of this chapter is to provide a context for the detailed comments of later chapters. New teachers in international schools frequently have little experience of the expectations and way of life of mobile, expatriate families. They may be unprepared for the exceptional demands of teaching in international schools, although many teachers in the school systems of English-speaking countries now have experience of working with diverse classes.

International schools vary in the make-up of their student bodies, but they have a common mission. This mission is to serve the needs of international families with high educational expectations for their children. In many schools the majority of students come from mobile, expatriate families. These families may experience only one posting outside their home country or may relocate frequently. In other schools, many of the students are the children of local families who have an international outlook, or international connections, and who wish their children to be educated in English. A third group of students is made up of children who have previously been educated in English outside their home country. On returning home their parents prefer that their children continue to be educated in English.

The material that follows aims to give teachers an understanding of the families, way of life and nature of international school students. With the aid of this understanding it is hoped that teachers will feel more confident in their relations with parents and better equipped to work with children in international schools.

The Distinct Nature of International School Students

Teachers in many national systems are now used to working with classes of students from diverse countries and cultures. The potential underachievement of these incoming children has become a matter of concern to politicians, academics and educators in the countries concerned. Consequently, much research has been carried out in order to arrive at an understanding of the nature of second language learning and

5

cultural adjustment among minority language school children. This research has, in turn, guided the creation of a body of materials and teaching strategies to help cater for these students. Children in international schools, however, are distinct from children in national systems in a number of important ways. These differences are significant in the daily life of a classroom teacher and require a new approach to materials, social interaction and communication with parents.

Up to this point, very little research has been carried out on this unique group of students who gain their education in a number of countries. However, several terms have been coined to describe mobile children from higher socio-economic groups; these include, **Third Culture Kids, Overseas Brats** and **Global Nomads**. It seems the case that young people who have experienced this form of life-style feel themselves to be different from their peers who have stayed in one schooling system. A strong impression of these feelings is given on Internet sites such as the **Overseas Brats** and **Global Nomads International** home pages.

What are the chief differences that teachers will find among their new students? The two major factors that distinguish these children are mobility and the nature of their families. Although a proportion of international school students experience only one posting outside their home country, many experience a series of moves every two or three years. These moves are the result of their parents' relocation to take up a first overseas job, or a fresh assignment in a series of postings. It is not surprising in these circumstances that many non-English-speaking families choose to place their children in English-medium international schools, since English-speaking schools now exist in most of the major cities in the world. In this way, they can minimise the disruption caused by frequent moves.

For many parents, a further attraction of English-medium international schools is the opportunity for their children to acquire English. English is not the most spoken first language in the world, but it is the world language of business, international diplomacy and numerous technical areas. Parents who send their children to international schools are typically employed in organisations that require the use of more than one language. Such parents place a high value on their children becoming bilingual, if not multilingual.

These families have high expectations for their children, often including the possibility of higher education in one of the English-speaking countries. The parents tend to be well-educated themselves, to travel widely and to speak a number of languages. They retain a high sense of esteem in relation to their own culture and language and expect at some time to return to their home country. On their return, they expect their children to re-enter their national school systems. They choose an English-medium education for their children as a way of better equipping them for the sort of world in which they will live and work.

In theory, at least, the high esteem which such families feel for their own culture and language makes the lives of second language children in international schools rather different from those of minority language students in national systems. The schools themselves aspire to make second language children feel at home in an English-speaking world without affecting their esteem for their own language and culture. International schools accredited by reputable organisations declare this explicitly in their mission statements. The following example is typical of such statements where the school in question 'accepts the duty to create an educational environment in which students can take pride in their own cultural roots, whilst developing an appreciation of, and sensitivity to, other cultures'. (See pp. 30–6 Maintaining cultural identity, for a full discussion of this area.) It is one of the chief aims of this handbook to suggest ways of ensuring that second language students leave international schools enriched by the experience of living with two cultures and languages.

Varieties of International Schools

International schools develop in response to the needs of the expatriate communities that exist in a particular location. They vary in size, facilities, methods of funding, mode of administration, type of programme and in the make-up of their student body.

International schools are founded by a variety of bodies including groups of companies, international organisations, charitable trusts and private owners. One typical pattern is for a school to start its life in a private house or in part of another building, such as a hotel or office block and to expand as student numbers rise and funds can be found. Thus, many international schools in major cities today are housed in purpose-built premises in pleasant settings.

Most international schools derive the majority of their students from expatriate families with diplomatic, international civil service and business backgrounds. Not all students, however, are necessarily from managerial or professional families. Many embassies and other organisations offer the chance of an international education to the children of all members of their staff.

Schools in certain countries tend to have a high proportion of host country students. Italy, Spain and the countries of South America come to mind in this connection. Local families with international business

backgrounds in these locations often opt for an international education
for their children. These parents view the opportunity to learn English
and to acquire an understanding of a wider world as an investment for
the future. Finally, some schools have scholarship or bursary schemes
designed to offer places to children of families unable to meet the cost of
the usually high fees. Such children add a further dimension to the life of
the school since they frequently bring a diversity of experience. This group
may include refugees and the children of less well-off groups of
expatriates.

International schools vary in their entry criteria. In full and associate
member schools of ECIS (the European Council of International Schools),
the type of child accepted into the school is directly related to the school's
mission statement. Many schools accept all children whatever their
educational or linguistic profile, and offer ESL and learning support
programmes that meet these students' special needs. A few schools also
make the major social and financial commitment of providing places for
children with mental or physical handicaps.

Other schools opt for selection. Some accept only children whose
English has reached a certain level of competence. Others feel unable to
provide adequate help for children with learning difficulties. In theory,
this type of selection should lead to a student body with a more consistent
learning profile. This is not always the case, and even in international
schools with rigorous selection policies, there exist classes with a high
degree of diversity.

In most English-medium schools, the greater part of the teaching staff
comes from the countries of the English-speaking world. Most schools,
however, contain some members of staff who are expert English speakers
of other nationalities. These teachers bring a welcome element of diversity
together with a valuable understanding of students' experiences. A third
group on the staff comprises the personnel who teach the host country
and other languages. They are almost invariably native speakers of those
languages.

Among the expatriate staff, the reasons for choosing to teach in a
particular international school vary. A proportion of the staff is generally
made up of so-called 'trailing spouses', who have been posted with their
partner on an expatriate assignment. Other teachers may be married to
host country nationals and make up a core of long-serving members of
staff who provide the school with some continuity and history. The third
major group is made up of teachers who have chosen to teach in an
international school setting as part of a career plan, and as a way to see
the world. Teaching couples are often found among this group. These
teachers tend to be younger and to move on after a comparatively short

time, in order to experience new countries and cultures. Such experience, can, in itself, bring an extra mutlticultural dimension to their teaching.

Textbox 1.1 Extraordinary locations make for memorable experiences

Everything that has been written in this section is as true a description of the general run of international schools as I can make it. These generalities, however, do not adequately convey the sheer variety of international schools. Each has a unique history in terms of its foundation, student body and location and supplies a unique experience for teachers and students. While it is true that associate and member schools of reputable organisations such as ECIS offer an effective education to international students, in every other respect they are distinct. There also exist large numbers of new and transient schools that have yet to become fully established and these, perhaps, offer the greatest variety of all.

Schools are housed in the most varied structures. These range from ex-prisoner-of-war camps in the midst of exotic vegetation to schools in deserts and schools laid out with lawns and water-gardens in tropical cities. Some very effective schools have more modest facilities. One school I visited was in its second year of life at the time. In a hostile political climate, it had been allowed to take over part of a former textile factory, and parents, teachers and students had contributed their time, as well as money, in building-up the facilities and providing extras. One memorable day had been spent by the entire school community in picking-up debris from a flat piece of land prior to its use as a sports field. By the time of my visit a colourful and imaginative play area had been built, a technology centre was in place and student numbers were increasing daily.

A school at this stage in its development might seem a difficult environment for teachers new to international education. I found quite the reverse to be true, due to the special atmosphere that had developed in response to the challenges of founding the school. All elements of the school community were united in their commitment to making a success of this pioneering enterprise and the distinctive and rich culture of the host country was being fully utilised to provide a unique experience for students and teachers. The acknowledged difficulties of living in this particular location contributed to a noticeably supportive and friendly relationship among the teachers. Working in such a school would provide a memorable and enriching experience for any teacher.

The broad range of international schools conforms in a general way to the description given in the previous paragraphs. There are two other groups of schools, however, which serve the needs of different groups of students. These schools differ in their aims from the English-medium schools but can fairly be described as international in outlook and name. They also seek validation from accrediting bodies outside their home countries.

The first group is made up of schools, often with a long history, that have been founded by groups such as missionaries or rich benefactors, for the education of students in a third country. Such schools include the famous schools in Turkey founded during the Ottoman Empire by American Christian organisations. These schools have evolved considerably and now offer a bilingual programme to local students in the local language and English. Some teachers, who are first language speakers of English, are still recruited to these schools. This is sometimes out of a genuine regard for the long historical connection, but also for their value to the English part of the programme. These sorts of schools are invariably rigorously selective and tend to send their students to the most prestigious local universities for their first degrees. It is common, at a later stage, for students to progress to a university in an English-speaking country for further degree work. The local education ministries usually require students in these schools to follow the national curriculum in their own language alongside extensive teaching and use of English.

The second type of bilingual school has a more mobile, international student body. These schools offer programmes in English and another language. Sometimes several different language combinations are offered in the same school. This group of schools is also highly selective, requiring students of whatever age to be proficient in one of the chosen languages. The programmes of these schools tend to be demanding since they frequently require students to cover entire national curricula in both their languages.

Clearly, teachers in bilingual schools are faced with different challenges from those in purely English-medium schools. Many features of working in these schools, though, are similar. The parent body has high expectations and the students may well come from a variety of linguistic and national backgrounds. Families choose these schools from a position of strength because they value the special benefits that a bilingual education will bring their children. And, like the more usual type of international school, successful teachers need to be teachers of language throughout the day as well as deliverers of instruction. With some small adjustments, the contents of this handbook should also be of use to English-speaking teachers who are hired to teach in these schools. (See pp. 61–5, Programmes in international bilingual schools, for a detailed discussion of special issues.)

Despite the sharing of a common language, it is usual to find a wide range of viewpoints and experiences amongst colleagues in the same school. This is due to differences in age, training and national traditions of education. Generally, the programme and prevailing methodology of the school provide a unifying framework, but differences in practice and terminology may at first be unsettling and confusing to new teachers. These differences are a fact of life in international schools, however. Most teachers gradually arrive at an understanding of their colleagues' points of view and, in general, teachers in international schools are a supportive and open-minded group of people.

The impact on the school of its geographical location varies considerably. In some countries, the national Ministry of Education lays down ground rules for curriculum content and preparation for national examinations. This may extend in certain cases to actual censorship of written materials. In other countries, security may be an issue, arising from local causes such as religious fundamentalism or the threat of kidnap. In these locations, practical measures to ensure safety are part of everyday life. According to the locality, emergency procedures for dealing with earthquakes and bomb threats may exist alongside the more conventional fire drills.

For most international schools, however, the host country culture supplies a rich resource. Schools that offer the widest experiences to teachers and students draw on the local language, history, art and traditions to enhance the basic curriculum. In most schools, also, the host country language is often heard. Administrative and maintenance staff, and in many schools, some students, use this language in offices, corridors and playgrounds. In order to be able to interact effectively and courteously with host country staff inside school, and to gain the most from life outside school, new teachers are advised to learn at least some basic words and phrases in the host-country language.

In the early days of an international school assignment, the challenge for new teachers is to be supportive and understanding of parents and students while they themselves are adjusting to the new circumstances. This may seem at times a heavy load. Fortunately, in most schools, a new teacher's colleagues are able to offer understanding and support in this period. All those who have worked in international schools have been through the same experiences and understand the impact of moving. Usually the presence of a group of supportive colleagues changes this potentially draining situation into a manageable and exciting challenge.

International Families

Culture shock

The term **culture shock** is used to describe the potential impact of moving to a new location and a new culture. The fact of recognising the existence of this phenomenon may not make the process of adjustment any less challenging. However, it is helpful to understand the nature of the experience.

International families who move to a new location are faced with the need to come to terms with a new life-style and often with a new language. Even if it is not a family's first expatriate posting, each move involves a period of adjustment. Against an unfamiliar background, the parents are required to make choices about such things as housing, transport, medical provision and their children's schooling. Despite the practical help that many families receive from the employing organisation, the psychological impact of the new culture and location may be considerable.

The process of adjusting to the new circumstances generally follows a recognisable pattern. The first stage is sometimes called 'the honeymoon phase'. During this period, there may be a feeling of excitement and exhilaration, and some people who anticipate a short stay, remain in this state. For them, the time spent in the new location is more in the nature of a holiday; they remain perpetual tourists and thus avoid the realities of facing-up to a longer stay.

For others, the period of excitement may be followed by a sense of loss and lack of identity. There may be a time of depression, frustration and even aggression, as they slowly come to terms with the reality of their new lives. This aggression typically surfaces when expatriates are faced with a situation such as dealing with the local bureaucracy, where lack of language and knowledge about the system place them at a disadvantage. Suddenly, everything about the new location is foolish, misguided and, above all, different. And, of course, not like home where everything was efficient and user-friendly.

This phase may take an extreme form or may pass quite quickly. Generally, there is a gradual acceptance that the new location has some good things to offer, a process that is greatly aided by the making of friends. It is the case with many expatriates, however, particularly those who anticipate a series of moves, that their interaction with the local culture is limited to quite brief forays. They prefer, or are guided by their employers, to live in expatriate neighbourhoods and spend their free time in expatriate clubs and organisations.

It is an important function of international schools to offer an easily accessible and welcoming community where different members of the family can find a place. The spouse at home becomes involved in a range of weekday activities at the school and the whole family uses the sports and indoor facilities at the weekends.

Teachers involved with these families need to be aware of the likely behaviour among both parents and students during the adjustment process. It is not at all uncommon for new parents to appear demanding, anxious and, occasionally, aggressive. Experienced teachers recognise that this behaviour is not aimed at the teacher personally, and learn, over the years, to remain calm and understanding in the face of difficulty. To new teachers the strength of feeling, and the aggressive manner in which some parents express their concerns, may feel threatening. Some families never come to accept totally the differences between the new school system and their home country schools. Most, happily, settle down after an initial period of unease and become active and supportive members of the school community.

Adjustment issues within the family

The move to a new location may bring about a change of roles and relationships within the family. It is helpful for international school teachers to be aware of these factors since they have a direct bearing on their students, and on their own interactions with parents.

It is frequently the case that the 'trailing spouse', (often, in reality, the mother), is left in sole charge of managing the family's affairs while the working partner is away on business. This places a burden on the partner at home who can become, in effect, a lone parent. For this reason it is not uncommon for 'trailing spouses' to feel isolated and resentful. Such resentment may also be connected to the loss of employment caused by the family's move. Some 'trailing spouses' never settle happily until they have replaced that loss, either with a new job, or with voluntary work that carries responsibilities and a time-commitment similar to being in employment.

For some women, it may be part of the normal pattern of their culture to join clubs and organisations and to become involved with their children's school. International schools are well placed both to offer scope to parent volunteers and to benefit from their contributions. However, in cultures where the role of women is viewed differently, it may not be the custom to move around independently or to look outside the home and extended family for social life. Women from these backgrounds are not used to taking part in organisations such as the school PTA or to serving on committees. In expatriate locations they tend to spend much time alone except when venturing out in the company of their husbands and children.

A source of stress for some families is the impact of novel and unexpected influences from school. Children attending an international school for the first time can feel a need to conform to the social customs that prevail. This may bring clashes between parents and children in areas such as clothing, diet, extra-curricular activities, party-going and religious practice. These possible sources of conflict, combined with their own less than fluent English, may give parents the sense that their children are being distanced from them. Generally, these feelings are extreme only in the early days of a new posting. Fortunately, they usually modify as both parents and children move through the process of adjustment.

Concerns related to the new school

Parents of second language students may have concerns relating to their children's academic progress. The source of these concerns is frequently a fear that their children will fall behind in the schoolwork of their national education system. For parents who come from countries with competitive school systems this is a serious consideration, since the options for children's education do not always include a safety net for the less successful student.

Textbox 1.2. New teachers — what they really need to know

The pressures on teachers new to the international school system can be intense. The most extreme instances are where teachers, frequently 'trailing spouses', are hired on the first day of September or even mid-year. Often they have just arrived in their first expatriate posting and their previous teaching experiences have taken place wholly in their home education system. Thus, they are unfamiliar with the nature of international schools and students.

Most schools offer introductions or orientation sessions to new teachers. These take a number of forms and may range from a single meeting to several days of talks and workshops. They usually include a mass of information about finance, insurance and local bureaucratic practices. Often, though, these sessions are restricted to the beginning of the school year, and staff who are hired mid-year may find themselves having to depend on their own resources.

Rarely do such sessions include information that would be of real use to newly-hired teachers. When I sat down to talk to one harassed mid-year hire, it became clear to me that some basic information about the nature of international schooling would have helped her a great deal. In this teacher's case this was the first time she had met with large numbers of second language students in the same classroom as first language speakers. She was unfamiliar with language acquisition issues and had no experience of the strategies useful in diverse classrooms.

New teachers in this situation may find the pressure of answering the needs of second language children almost overwhelming and certainly stressful. A major contributory factor to this stress, as most experienced international school teachers would agree, are the high expectations of both first and second language students' parents. In many cases, fortunately, experienced colleagues are at hand to give support and practical advice. It was for inexperienced and isolated teachers in these circumstances, however, that this handbook was originally conceived.

Teachers need to be aware of the importance to second language students of maintaining their studies in their home language. They should give encouragement in class and, if necessary, moderate their own demands when it is apparent that second language children are tired from doing extra work late at night in their home language. (See pp. 49–52, Maintaining the home language and culture, for a full discussion of this subject.)

In reality, it is sometimes difficult for teachers to reassure parents fully or to give complete answers to concerns of this type. International schools exist to serve the needs of students with a wide variety of educational experiences and school policies are generally formulated to cater effectively for the majority of students. Inevitably, the needs of individual students may not be fully met. Talking frankly and openly with parents is the only satisfactory method of addressing areas of concern. Teachers should explain the school's policies and practice in detail and show how they serve the interests of most of the students. It is possible that even this approach will not wholly convince parents. New teachers should expect this type of discussion with some parents to continue over an extended period. It is a mark of successful teachers in international schools that they seldom feel time is wasted in talking to anxious parents.

Students in International School Classes

The make-up of an international school class is varied. The profile not only changes from school to school, but from year to year in the same school, since the number of expatriates in a location tends to fluctuate. The reasons for these fluctuations are usually political or economic in nature. The relative strength of the dollar is a common reason. So too is a change in the employment policy of big multinational or local business interests, and the state of relations between the host country and other nations. As a consequence, it is common for the number of classes at a year level to alter from year to year.

The mobility factor that remains consistent, however, is the movement of children in and out of the school. Students in international schools frequently stay for only two or three years, so that one-third of the children in a class may be new in September. It is also common for a number of students to move in and out of the class at other times during the school year. Some students regularly enter international schools in April, two-thirds of the way through the school year. These children come from countries such as Japan and Korea, where the school year ends in March. It is thus not unusual for a complete non-speaker of English to arrive in a class late in the school year. These arrivals (and departures) are typical circumstances in the life of an international school teacher and need careful management.

Diversity in an international school class occurs for other reasons also. In a typical class, there is a wide variation in the educational and linguistic histories of the students. And, as with any class, both first and second language children display a range of ability as well as differences in levels of maturity and motivation. There may be students in a class who have acknowledged or undiagnosed learning difficulties and some students who are described as gifted.

A generally held view, among parents at least, is that children in international schools represent the upper end of the ability scale. It is certainly the case that international school students come largely from educated and successful families, and that both students and parents have high expectations relating to further education. Most students in international schools also have the advantage of supportive parents who show an interest in their education and help them with schoolwork. Nevertheless, since the majority of international schools follow an 'open-door' policy with regard to admission, the ability range in most classes is quite wide.

Students in international schools may give an impression of above-average ability because they tend to be confident in their bearing and to converse easily with adults. They can also draw on a wider experience and range of reference than children of a similar age in their home countries. The result is a body of students that may seem rather sophisticated and mature.

Against the possible advantages of international students can be set the reality of a mobile existence. Constant moves, sometimes mid-year, may cause dislocations in the continuity of children's education and interrupt the flow of their learning. Even moves between international schools, where the curriculum and teaching methods are designed to take account of children's varied experiences, do not always result in a consistent and seamless education.

Among the difficulties that arise in the lives of students in international schools is the sense of loss and disruption that occurs when children themselves move on or when their close friends are relocated. It is not uncommon for children to lose their 'best friends' year after year. International school students with strong family support generally learn to adjust to this pattern with resignation and resilience. Many expatriate children who move frequently acquire the social skills that put them on easy terms with their peers and become adept at striking up friendships. However, an important aspect of the work of an international school teacher is to help children deal with loss and change.

Children's linguistic histories vary greatly. Some new second language students may have been raised and educated in only one language. Others have more complex patterns of language use. (See Textbox 3.2 p. 48, What do we mean by a child's home language?, for a discussion of the variety of children's language uses.) The range of languages to be found among students in international schools removes from the teacher the possibility of using the techniques developed in schools with speakers of only one or two languages. In parts of the United States, for instance, the presence of a large number of Spanish speakers enables the schools to employ bilingual personnel and to use Spanish language materials in order to cater effectively for this group. In an international school, teachers are unlikely to be able to speak the languages of most of their second language children.

The pattern and content of each child's previous schooling are other major pieces to add to the puzzle. The length of time spent in school differs among second language children of the same age. Children in Scandinavia, for instance, enter school and begin serious instruction at the age of six or even seven years old. Other children, from British-influenced school systems, begin to learn to read at the age of four. Teachers of young children in international schools have to take these differences into account in planning their strategic approaches in the classroom.

In moving from school to school, it is possible that important stages in the acquisition of basic numeracy and literacy have been missed out. A teacher's first task with a new second language student, therefore, is to establish an understanding of the child's educational history, The limited English of some second language children may make this process of assessment difficult and in these instances, experienced teachers take observations over a period of time. It is wise to wait until students have begun to settle, and a picture of their capabilities and previous learning experiences begins to emerge, before making assumptions. Many aspects of school life other than formal academic assignments are useful in providing evidence of a child's place on the learning continuum. (The early assessment and evaluation of new second language children is discussed on pp. 130–7, Assessing and evaluating second language children in the mainstream classroom.)

Classes of this sort present a continuing and ever-changing challenge even to experienced teachers. Second language children and students with learning difficulties may receive specialist support on a regular basis, yet the overall responsibility for the day-to-day management of each child's teaching and learning lies with the classroom teacher. This sometimes seems an overwhelming task. The level of expectation from a highly educated and articulate parent body may add to the feeling of pressure.

Effective teachers of these complex classes usually exhibit certain characteristics. They are flexible in their approach to teaching and learning. This means that they draw on current thinking about teaching classes of children with differing cultures, languages and educational histories. They are ready, however, to use longer-established methods when useful. They are knowledgeable about the languages and cultures of their students, and are frequently language learners themselves. They understand the expectations of parents who place their children in international schools, and recognise that they must be good communicators to those parents.

Summary

The distinct nature of international school students

- Students in international schools generally have parents who are successful in their sphere of work and who have high educational expectations for their children.
- Mobile parents choose English-medium schools because in this way they can guarantee continuity of education for their children.
- Such parents also view the acquisition of English as an advantage for their children.
- These parents have a high esteem for their own culture and language(s).
- The aim of international education is to give children access to an education in English without diminishing their respect for their own culture and language(s).

Varieties of international schools

- International schools vary in size, facilities, type of programme and nature of their student body.
- Most international schools derive the majority of their students from mobile expatriate families from high socio-economic backgrounds.
- Some schools tend to have a high proportion of host country students.
- Effective international schools accept students according to their mission statement. Some are selective, others take all students and offer them an appropriate support programme where needed.
- Teachers are English speakers; they may be married to host country

nationals, be 'trailing spouses' or recruited from English-speaking countries.

- One type of bilingual school has historically offered a bilingual education to host country nationals in order to allow them to acquire English and later to go on to higher education in an English-speaking country.
- A second type of bilingual school serves the international mobile community. These schools are invariably highly selective.
- It is common to find a wide range of age, training and traditions of education among teachers in an international school.
- The geographical location of a school has a considerable impact on daily life. The most successful international schools draw on the local culture, language and traditions to enrich the curriculum and social activity in that school.

International families

- The impact of a move on families — culture shock — follows a recognisable pattern.
- International schools have an important role to fill in offering a welcoming and supportive environment.
- Parents and children moving through this process of adjustment may display extreme anxiety and even aggression.
- The spouse at home may in effect be a single parent.
- 'Trailing spouses' may feel resentment and a loss of identity.
- Women in some cultures are accustomed to joining organisations; women from other cultures are not accustomed to acting independently and may maintain a home-based role.
- Novel influences from the new school may create dissension and conflict between second language parents and children.
- Parents of second language children are worried that the international school will not equip their children for success in their home schools.
- International schools adopt policies that answer the needs of most children. Teachers need to take time to explain the reasons for these policies to anxious parents.

Students in international school classes

- The number of students in an international school fluctuates in response to the educational and political climate.

- Students generally stay for two to three years, and may enter the school in September or during the school year.
- International school students are not necessarily from the upper end of the ability scale; they display the usual range of aptitude, levels of maturity and motivation.
- Second language students have an extraordinary variety of linguistic histories and educational experiences.
- The role of the teacher in an international school is to deliver a programme of instruction that allows for each child's distinct educational and linguistic profile.

Chapter 2

Cultural Adjustments — Helping Teachers to Understand

Introduction

The aim of this chapter is to describe what happens to parents and their children when they move out of an environment where home and school share common cultural values, and into the complex world of expatriate living and international schooling. Unfortunately, there are virtually no authoritative studies based on the unique student populations in international schools to underpin a description of this sort. (The main source of relevant writing is the **International Schools Journal**, published by **ECIS**, whose location and Website address is given in **Appendices A** and **B**) Existing research on cultural issues in schools largely relates to students from language minorities in national school systems. It is therefore useful and appropriate to draw on personal observation and experience to describe the cultural implications of attending an international school. The primary aim is to offer teachers some practical insights about living and working in an environment where cultures meet and interact.

Adjusting to a New School Culture

International schools, whatever their location and student body, have certain features in common. These features include a lively and friendly atmosphere, an informal relationship between adults and children, and classrooms and corridors that reflect a certain view of teaching and learning. The presence of these elements creates a recognisable international school culture that is largely shared by international schools across the globe.

This school culture is familiar to both students and parents from school systems that share a similar philosophy. Families from these backgrounds understand how the system works and what is expected of them. For other families, this may not be the case. Their home school systems reflect a quite different educational tradition. The first part of this chapter describes the adjustments that must be made by some second language children and their parents in coming to terms with the philosophy, values and daily practice in an international school.

Students and teacher

Adults concerned with education recognise that children take time to adjust when they move to a new school. Even moves within a familiar education system, where the school cultures are similar, may cause distress and educational disruption. For second language students who enter international schools from a variety of educational systems, the impact is likely to be greater and the process of adjustment more difficult. Although each international school is unique in its location and student body, most have a similar ethos that has evolved in response to the needs of mobile children and families. One of the most typical features is a friendly and welcoming attitude to new families, and a generally informal and easy relationship between students and teachers.

The experience of many second language children, new to international schools, has differed from this. Students from school systems in most parts of Africa, East Asia, the Indian sub-continent and the Middle East (with the exception of Israel), and in many parts of Europe, have a different relationship with their teachers. This relationship varies in detail from system to system, but is generally typified by a greater deference to the teacher and a certain distance between adults and children. It is understandable that such students may find the friendly and informal behaviour of teachers in international schools difficult to interpret. They may be unsure how to react until they have had time to observe how other students behave.

Children from these backgrounds find further unaccustomed features in international schools. These include the informal placement of desks and chairs typical of international school classrooms, and the movement and work-related talk that are acceptable for much of the time. Many second language students are used to classes where children sit in rows, and where students only speak when asked a question by the teacher. They may have difficulty in perceiving underlying behavioural expectations in the new school, owing to the informal layout of the classrooms, and the different relationship between students and teacher. A further cause of unease may be the question of discipline. Children who are used to a rule-based system of enforcing discipline, and even in some cases to corporal punishment, may fail to see how order is preserved in a school where there appears to be no obvious system of consequences for misbehaviour. (See pp. 99–101, Discipline.)

Teachers should try to acquire an understanding of the school systems of the main second language groups in their school. With this knowledge, teachers are able to support new students from these groups more effectively during the early days by being explicit about areas of life in an international school that may be unfamiliar.

It is essential that students and parents are made aware of the school's expectations concerning time keeping, discipline and homework. An interpreter should be used, if necessary, to put across this information; many schools maintain a list of volunteers from the main language groups to give this sort of help to new families. A prior understanding of the basic procedures and policies of school life provides second language children with at least some certainties. This is especially valuable for students from 'traditional' backgrounds. (See pp. 96–7, Homework, and pp. 99–100, Discipline, for a fuller discussion of this area.) It is tactful, also, for teachers to display a calm cheerfulness in the presence of new students rather than an overwhelming friendliness. Some second language children take time to adjust to the unaccustomed informality between students and teachers in the new school.

New second language students may also be confused by the marking or grading system in international schools. In many national school systems teachers base grades or marks on the number of errors that students make in a piece of work. Children in those systems tend to concentrate on avoiding mistakes. This practice differs from the approach in international schools where teachers tend to praise children for what they achieve, rather than emphasise their errors. This positive attitude is a feature of the consciously encouraging atmosphere that exists in most international schools. Thus, credit is given for effort in order to reward children whose lack of English or gaps in learning would otherwise earn them low grades. This is done from the best of motives because teachers are keen to build up the confidence and self-esteem of second language children.

Students who are accustomed to this approach understand that there is still much to do and are motivated by the praise to make greater efforts. New second language students from more 'traditional' systems may misunderstand the praise and encouraging comments. They may feel that expectations are low or that that they are performing on the same level as high-achieving children. Teachers need to explain clearly what they expect from an assignment and how students can earn good grades. It is also wise to be honest about the achievements of second language students, although destructive criticism must be avoided. Many second language students feel more secure if they see praise given sparingly and for clearly understood reasons. (See pp. 98–9, Grading policy and pp. 103–4, Assessment and evaluation.)

Textbox 2.1 Intercultural games

International schools are usually generous in allowing teachers to attend conferences, often far away, relating to specific subject areas. The larger conferences arranged by the regional councils of international schools gener- ally cover a wider range of topics. Quite frequently, the programme includes sessions on intercultural issues, and occasionally there is the possibility for teachers to take part in extended intercultural simulations in the form of games.

The purpose of these simulations is to allow participants to experience, if only in a limited and temporary way, the impact of moving into a new culture where the language and social customs are unknown. The behaviour of the participants is itself an insight into the ways that different people cope with the stress of new experiences. Invariably one or two people leave the game after a very short time, all their feelings of insecurity and unease brought to the fore by being placed in a situation where they do not understand the rules.

The usual pattern is for the participants to be divided into two groups and placed apart in separate rooms. These groups represent the members of two distinct societies. Next, each group is introduced to the rules of behaviour that govern their society. These rules include the ways that members of that society introduce themselves, how they thank people, how they acknowledge a positive action, how they show displeasure, and so on. Some of the behaviour is quite physical and may involve stamping a foot, turning away or, even, tapping someone on the shoulder. A few basic words in the home society's language are learnt including numbers and greetings. The basic format is for individuals from each society to make short sorties into the room of the other team. These individuals then report to their home group so that knowledge of the other society and language builds up over time. The rules of such games tend to be extensive and complicated and the simulation is generally constructed to take place over several hours.

The tension among the participants begins to grow even before a few individuals are selected to enter the room of the unknown society. How will they cope without knowing the language and without understanding how things work? Speaking as a participant who made an early visit, I found the experience very unsettling. When I tried to introduce myself, I was rebuffed on several occasions before I realised that I must bow my head before anyone would respond to me. When I tried to exchange my tokens for food, I found that a complicated system of barter was in place. It was only through the intervention of one person who was willing to take the time to teach me some useful words, and who led me through the system, that I was able to buy something to eat. On one occasion, the whole group moved away from me because I had inadvertently put my hands through my hair; something, it became apparent, that was taboo in the new society. As fascinating and revealing were the visits to my own society by members of the other team. Observing their responses it was not difficult to make the leap to imagining how new second language children feel when they enter an international school for the first time. It was instructive too, to see how participants' experiences varied once they understood some of the rules of the new society.

Textbox 2.1 (*cont.*)

They did not feel at ease, but were able to avoid the most painful occurrences, such as being ostracised because of unacceptable behaviour. The lessons for teachers of second language children are clear. Let children know what is expected of them, give them firm guidance in each new circumstance, use overtly welcoming gestures and facial expressions, include them in class activity and provide them with support in the form of a responsible classmate.

Second language students' beliefs and expectations about learning and being taught

Second language students who enter international schools directly from schools in their own countries bring with them the beliefs and expectations concerning education that are current in their own cultures. In some cases these views are similar to those that underpin the approach to education offered in most international schools. This is the case, for example, with children from the Scandinavian countries. It is useful for classroom teachers, however, to be aware that these assumptions are not current in some of the cultures from which second language students come.

It is a practical necessity in international schools, as well as a fundamental belief, that the child is placed at the heart of educational planning. New children, speakers of English and second language students alike, bring a variety of educational experiences when they enter the school. Only by carrying out a careful programme of evaluation and assessment can teachers arrive at an understanding of an individual student's previous experience in school. This understanding is then used to guide teachers in planning that child's future programme. International schools offer real-life reasons why an assessment-driven programme of instruction makes sense. To most teachers trained in English-speaking countries this approach is self-evidently appropriate and effective.

The educational philosophy that drives the choice of programme, classroom methodology and assessment practice in international schools is largely derived from what is current in English-speaking countries. In some cases these approaches have developed in answer to the needs of diverse classes in national education systems and thus provide a satisfactory foundation for work with international school students. It is common to find a developmental approach to the education of young children in international schools. Older children are taught using a variety of teaching strategies and groupings in order to allow for differences in educational histories. Assessment is based on observation, performance-based tasks and portfolios of children's work as well as on standardised tests and formal testing. These practices, however, may be unfamiliar to families from 'traditional' education systems.

An approach that places the child at the heart of the educational process runs counter to what many second language families expect from an education. In so-called 'traditional' education systems, parents send their children to school to acquire a body of knowledge that is accepted and recognised by educated people. The role of the teacher is to impart this knowledge to students, and it is the student's task to copy, memorise and reproduce this information when called upon to do so. At certain times throughout their schooling, students are required to sit examinations that test their knowledge of this body of information. The academic hurdles that need to be surmounted before students emerge fully qualified at the end of their years of education are generally recognised. There is a commonly understood path leading from a successful school career via a prestigious university, to high-status employment.

There is clearly a difference between what some parents and students expect from a school system, and what most international schools offer. Unfortunately, this gulf sometimes makes life difficult for teachers. The recourse for teachers is not to attack or defend particular philosophies of education, but to explain fully the reasons behind the educational policies of the school. Thus they need to be able to show how the programme of studies and teaching methodology cater best, in the school's opinion, for the needs of a mobile student population with a range of cultural, linguistic and educational backgrounds.

Differences in the types of learning activities expected of children in international schools may cause difficulties for some second language students. A typical instance may help to explain the point more clearly. Many students from 'traditional' systems are unacquainted with the approach to a written text that is customary in international schools. In both young and older children's classrooms in international schools it is usual to discuss in age-appropriate terms such features of a text as language, plot, character and outcomes. Discussion of this type involves students in predicting, analysing, making inferences and in forming their own opinions.

Children used to fact-based learning and to memorisation do not understand what it being asked of them. They are not accustomed to open-ended questions, or to questions that require independent thought, but only to questions about facts. It follows that children accustomed to this approach to may have difficulty in carrying out exercises that involve speculative thinking or independent analysis. Effective teachers know they must provide students with continuing support to enable them to understand this different way of thinking and learning. (Detailed suggestions are offered in **Chapters 6 to 11.**)

It is the teacher's task, often with around 20 children in the class, to plan a programme of learning that takes into account variations in students' experience and expectations. Teachers can help new second language students to understand new and different ways of working and thinking, if they themselves have a knowledge of what these children expect from school. Such knowledge offers a useful basis for making decisions about instructional strategies and for offering students the most effective support.

Parents and teacher — the need to communicate

Parents new to the international school system may also find unfamiliar features in the relationship that prevails between parents and teachers. In this area, too, international schools tend to reflect the practices common in many English-speaking countries. Parents in these countries are encouraged to occupy a central role in their children's education. They serve on parent-teacher associations, (PTAs), and are welcomed into the school where they act as volunteers. In international schools the interaction between home and school is likely to be further developed because of the school's customary key role in the expatriate community.

In many cultures, the contact between parents and teachers takes a different form from normal practice in most international schools. In some national school systems, there are a regular series of conferences between parents and teachers and it is not uncommon in many countries for the parents of very young children to have some involvement with the school. From the age of seven or eight, however, parents from many of the cultures from which international school students come, are accustomed to leave the school to manage the education of their children. They are informed of their children's progress through formal, written reports and they have contact with teachers only if they are called to the school to discuss a matter of discipline.

In these school systems there is a divide, recognised on both sides, between the sphere of the teacher and the sphere of home. Teachers are treated with deference and their authority within the classroom is absolute. The parents' role is to support and encourage the child's work at home. Thus, teachers in international schools may need to adjust their expectations about relations between teachers and parents. They should be aware that what is customary for some parents is not customary for others. This variation makes it essential for teachers to find an effective means of communicating vital information to all the parents of students in their classes.

Most international schools have a regular system of formal and informal communication with parents. These include Open Houses at the beginning of the school year when teachers explain the academic programme to parents, class newsletters and conferences with teachers. It is also the custom in most international schools to invite parents to participate in a range of activities. Besides the obvious value of such help, the use of parent volunteers has the added benefit of making parents feel a part of the school community. The activities themselves take the usual forms. These include acting as parent representatives in a classroom, listening to children's reading and volunteering in the library. Other more practical undertakings include making-up children's work in book form, preparing food for class celebrations and the setting-up of display boards. Parents are also asked to serve on all-school institutions such as the school PTA and the Board of Trustees.

Some second language parents, however, do not see the need for this degree of involvement in the school. In the cultures of these parents, neither the school nor families expect parents to participate in their children's school life. The result in international schools is that second language parents tend to be under-represented in the areas that typically involve parents. These include service on formal bodies such as the Board of Trustees and the Parent Teacher Association and informal arrangements such as acting as volunteers. Second language speakers' fears concerning the use of English may be a further element that limits their participation in school activities.

Most schools make an effort to increase the membership of second language parents on school-wide bodies. They consciously seek out representatives from large national groups to serve on the Board of Trustees. They recognise the need for these families to feel that their opinions are given the same weight as those of the English-speaking majority group. Some schools sponsor separate groups for international parents. Such groups often organise coffee mornings for the different nationalities represented in the school and arrange for volunteers to act as interpreters and support people for their language group. Despite these efforts it remains the case in most schools that an element of the second language population is under-represented on all-school bodies and at social occasions.

All sections of the school are responsible for the quality of the relationship with second language parents. The administration sets the tone by welcoming contact with parents and by keeping them informed about school-wide events. The teacher's role is to establish a relationship

Textbox 2.2 Parental involvement in school-life: The PTA in Japan.

The following extract is taken from a pamphlet issued by the **International Students Education Center of Kawaijuku**, Tokyo. This organisation exists to counsel bi-national families and the parents of students returning to the Japanese education system after a posting abroad. (Today a few enlightened prefectures have established returnees sections in some of their schools. For most returning children, though, the adjustment process is a harrowing experience.) This extract explains clearly the differences of expectation in Japan about parental involvement in school affairs.

'In order for Japan to have a democratic education system, the US encouraged Japan to set up a Parent-Teacher-Association in 1946. While the organization is set up so that teachers and parents can discuss various methods to improve the school environment and schools in general, the P.T.A. in Japan has not functioned as it would in the US. Though it has prevented schools and teachers from going in their own directions, the P.T.A. in Japan has struggled to get full involvement from parents and teachers.

The reason behind this is that traditionally the roles of the teachers and parents have always been separated, with parents looking after their children only at home, and teachers being totally responsible for the students at school. Many teachers have not appreciated the partial involvement from parents in school-related matters, and are not necessarily actively involved in the meetings due to the fact that they feel it is more important to focus on class-related materials. Like in the US, the number of working mothers has been on the rise, so currently P.T.A. activities are not necessarily conducted as they were set up to be.'

with second language parents that ensures good communication about everyday matters. This enables parents and teacher to exchange information about children, and allows parents to approach teachers with any questions or concerns. An effective relationship of this type allows small difficulties to be addressed before they become major problems.

The result of this openness is that some new parents take up a great deal of a teacher's time. This is a recognised international school phenomenon. Previously employed 'trailing spouses' find difficulty in adjusting to their lack of employment. Other newly arrived parents have yet to establish a daily routine. The lack of structure in their lives and the reasonable causes for concern about their children in a new school combine to create parents who are often anxious. It is not unusual for such parents to talk to teachers on a daily basis. Happily, for both parents and teachers, in nearly every case, the school offers an outlet for this energy and concern. Parents become involved on a regular basis in the volunteer programme, make friends, and gain a broader perspective on life in the new location.

Teachers may sometimes find the burden of maintaining this degree of communication with parents time-consuming and frustrating. They would frequently prefer to give more of their time to preparing for their work with children. The work of teachers in international schools, however, is as concerned with the families of their students as it is with the children themselves. The nature of expatriate life, with its separation from the wider family and the home culture, leads to greater demands on the school and on teachers from parents. It is essential for teachers to put in place a range of strategies for formal and informal communication and to plan for the regular involvement of all parents in class life.

Maintaining Cultural Identity

This handbook is concerned with international schools that exist to provide an English-medium education for children from a variety of cultural and linguistic backgrounds. Such schools have in common the use of English as the vehicle of instruction, and the fact that the greater part of the teaching staff comes from English-speaking countries. All second language students therefore have to adjust to the use of English.

A further factor with implications for cultural adjustment is the make-up of the student body of the new school. International schools display a great variety in their student populations. However, most schools contain a majority or majorities of students from distinct cultural groups.

A large number of schools contain a majority group of students from one of the English-speaking countries. Some of these schools declare their cultural orientation by including the word American or British in their names. These affiliations lead to the presence of a cultural ethos that derives from the English-speaking group. Obvious signs of the presence of such a group are to be observed in the clothes worn by the students, the street language to be heard in the corridors and playground and the sports played in school.

In other schools, the majority population is derived from a different cultural and language background. English-medium international schools in South America, for instance, typically have a large number of Spanish or Portuguese speakers and many schools in Spain and Italy contain majority populations of host country nationals. Some international schools in East Asia have high numbers of Chinese children of various nationalities. Other schools may have significant populations of students from expatriate groups with historical and business ties in the location, such as the Lebanese and Indian communities of diamond merchants in Antwerp, Belgium. The schools that serve the families of employees of international organisations such as the United Nations are among the few international schools that may have no majority group.

What happens when second language students and their parents encounter the majority culture of an international school is a topic of interest and concern to teachers. It has been emphasised earlier in this handbook that international school students and their families do not, in general, come from groups that view themselves, or are viewed, as minorities. They tend to come from highly educated, well-established families in their own countries and are at ease with their own language and culture. In most cases, their cultural identity is not at issue. As a result, most second language children in international schools experience a more positive outcome than is usual for less advantaged groups in national systems. The process of adjustment, however, remains complex and may bring times of stress and unease to the families of second language students.

The schools themselves are sincere in their desire fully to incorporate second language children into the mainstream life of the school. Most international schools set out in their mission statements their commitment to valuing equally the cultures and languages of all the students. The impact that second language children feel is not the result of discriminatory practices or derogatory remarks. Indeed, international schools are remarkable for their ease in absorbing students from all cultures including groups of children from backgrounds that are traditionally hostile to each other. Cultural difference, however, remains a key element in the areas where new children are required to make adjustments. The first of these areas of adjustment is the fact of the move into a new school and the need to take on the learning of a new language. A second is the need to adapt to the possibly unfamiliar educational ethos. A third is the need to relate to other students and to find a place in the social groupings of the classroom. How children fare is dependent on the attitudes of their families, their own personalities and the type of support they receive from teachers and peers.

The attitude of the family is an essential component in the adjustment process for children living in two cultures. As might be expected, parents vary in their understanding and anticipation of the likely outcomes. This in turn is related to their own or their relatives' previous experience of dislocation and association with unfamiliar cultures. Among the families from which second language students come it is not uncommon for family members to have attended foreign universities or to have worked abroad. The attitudes of parents from this type of family towards new cultural influences are different from those of parents, perhaps from a provincial city, for whom this is a first move outside their home country.

Textbox 2.3 International schools or schools with international students?

The discussion on intercultural issues in this chapter is not quite complete. I have omitted from the main text a sensitive area that is liable to be controversial. A letter discussion initiated by *Newslinks*, the newspaper of International Schools Services, entitled, 'What makes a true international school?' touches on this topic and I have heard teachers and parents express strong views. A further question sets out the issue quite clearly: Are we offering an international education or a nationally based education with an international gloss?

It is a question that must occur to many thinking people when they enter the campuses of international schools that seem to exemplify so much that is typical of schools in English-speaking countries. The superficial signs include the prevailing sports ethos, the terminology current in academic and social life, the soft-drinks vending machines and the display boards advertising graduation items. In other schools, it is possible to find the use of the prefect system and students grouped into 'houses' for the purposes of competition. At a deeper level, many schools draw their textbooks, curriculum development and the larger part of their teaching staff from one English-speaking country. It seems, in some cases, that the students themselves are the only international element.

If it is the case that many international schools offer nationally based programmes, how much does it matter? Parents choose to place their children in these schools and, presumably, are prepared to accept all that they offer. Many international educators, however, administrators and teachers alike, feel strongly that the education provided by a school should reflect at a profound level the many cultures and languages that exist in the student body. Initiatives such as the International Baccalaureate Primary Years' Programme (formerly known as the ISCP) attempt to make international schools more truly international. For my own part, I think it is valuable (and possible) for individual teachers to contribute personally towards fostering a genuinely international spirit. Each teacher has the means to create a classroom that draws on different cultural traditions to inform and enhance the programme. I hope this handbook offers ways of making this possible.

There may be long-standing historical reasons why some families approach an English-medium education with a degree of reservation: families from French-Canadian backgrounds fall into this group, as do some families from previously colonised regions. Present day experiences, or memories from the past, give representatives of these cultures reason to be wary of placing their children in a potentially disadvantageous situation. These families are likely to be acutely sensitive to cultural influences from school. Other families are happy to place their children in English-medium international schools, but are dismayed by the extent that the culture of one English-speaking country predominates.

This variety in parents' expectations and feelings affects in turn the nature of their children's experience in adjusting to their new lives. Parents who are aware that influences from school may entail adjustments within the family are better prepared for the challenges. Other parents are taken by surprise at the way their children change. In some instances, it may seem that their children are becoming absorbed by the new culture and by the English language. It is not uncommon for children at some point during their time at an international school to refuse to speak the home language. It is quite usual for children to go through phases when they reject their family's usual modes of behaviour. Both these ways of behaving occur among very young children as well as older students. Children who have previously worn school uniform or a conservative style of dress may besiege their parents with requests for similar clothing to that worn by the social leaders at school. Other children resent the fact that they do not eat at Pizza Hut and McDonald's and are not taken to see the latest Disney film. These conflicts are unsettling to parents, and may cause friction and unhappiness in the family. This distress may be heightened if parents do not agree between themselves about what it is reasonable to accept, or if grandparents make negative comments about their grandchildren's behaviour and appearance during visits.

The most usual outcome is that parents and children learn to live with both cultures in some sort of equilibrium. After the initial phase of questioning the cultural norms of home, children customarily settle into a pattern that allows them to accommodate both sets of cultural influences. Within the home, they accept the established modes and roles of their culture, including the traditional pattern of social life and religious observance. At school, they adopt the manners and social customs of their peers. The maintenance of the home language and association with compatriots is a vital part of achieving this balance. (See pp. 49–52, Maintaining the home language and culture.)

The nature of an individual child's personality is an essential factor in the process of adjustment. Why should a young girl, newly arrived from Baluchistan, dressed entirely in her country's costume, be immediately accepted into the social heart of the class, whereas a young Swedish boy whose dress is only marginally different from the accepted clothing of the social leaders, remains on the outside of the group for many months? This is partly a matter of the child's personality. Some children are gifted with open, friendly and confident natures that make initial social contact easy. Other children lack the social skills that quickly make them part of the group.

The atmosphere of the classroom is a significant element in the successful integration of new students. Classrooms where difference and variety are accommodated in an accepting and matter-of-fact way contribute greatly to children's ease of entry. There remains a further social hurdle to be overcome; this is the divide between acceptance in the classroom and inclusion in social activity outside school. Quite often, this development does not occur at all. Many second language children socialise only within their cultural group, except for parties to which everyone in the class is invited.

An area of ambiguity lies at the heart of any discussion about the experiences of second language children in international schools. The schools are sincere in their wish not to overwhelm or devalue the diverse cultures of their students. The family is committed to preserving close links with their children and to bringing them up in the traditional ways of their culture. However, for children to be successful in the school environment, they must embrace the educational and social modes that prevail. In order to succeed, children must, if necessary, adopt modes of learning and ways of behaviour that differ from those that are customary in their own culture.

Children, in this situation, live in a complex world. They must balance one set of expectations against another. The most powerful influence in helping them to achieve this balance is the positive support of their families. If parents are accepting of the new cultural influences, while maintaining their own traditions, children come to manage this balancing act without great stress. They are also in a position to gain the most out of both facets of their lives. Fortunately, in international schools, this is the most usual outcome.

How can teachers contribute as a positive and supportive influence in this process of adjustment? They can support parents by being open to their questions and concerns about all matters relating to their children's welfare but especially about issues connected with cultural differences. They can be encouraging and supportive of parents worried about the extreme behaviours of their children related to language and culture during the adjustment phase. They can manage their classrooms so that they become places where difference and variety are accepted and valued. They can incorporate into their teaching, examples and references to cultures other than those usually included in first language textbooks. They can display in their own lives an active interest in languages and cultures other than their own. They can speak out at school meetings if they feel that the school is in danger of offending the cultural sensitivities of certain student groups. (See pp. 79–81, What does being international mean?)

Textbox 2.4 Returning home

The extracts that follow are taken from letters written to teachers in my own school by a Japanese child and his mother after their return to Japan. They willingly gave permission for these extracts to be published, since they hope that the letters will help teachers in international schools to understand more about the lives of mobile second language children. The first two extracts are taken from letters written three months after the family's return home. The little boy was six when he returned to Japan.

The mother writes: 'I apologise for not writing to you earlier, but we have been very busy getting settled. It was more difficult to settle down here than I expected. Living in Belgium for five years was long enough for us to forget Japanese life. Especially for S...., Japan is a strange country. He couldn't accept the Japanese way. For example, he had to sit on a chair for 45 minutes, four times in the morning. He rested his elbow when he was tired, but he was blamed. After a week he refused to go to school and stayed home. In the middle of May, I decided to change him to a school where there are many returnees. There is a special teacher to take care of returnees. She picked up S.... and taught him Japanese as well as the Japanese way, individually. He could take a rest in her class when he was tired. This class healed over his injured heart. Now he doesn't need any special care. He follows the Japanese in his normal class and gets along well.'

The little boy writes: 'Dear everybody, I am sorry to write a letter so late. I did not like the school at first because the person next to me was horrible. She was mean all the time. I did not go to school for a few weeks and I changed the school. I like the new school very much. I still want to go back to ISB. I miss you a lot. Please visit me.'

The last extract is from a letter written by the mother a year later: 'S.... is very fine, having good friends and excellent teachers at the best school in Kawasaki. Imai elementary school where S.... goes is one of the special schools specified by the Ministry of Education. They accept returnees and children from other countries with open arms. The most important thing for a returnee child is to meet a good teacher who understands what he does not understand. If S.... had met a good teacher who introduced him to his classmates by saying that he was from Belgium and was having a difficult time with the Japanese way, if she had asked them to help him in a small way, if she had not said, "I told you that a short time ago!" when S.... asked her what he did not know, if she had dealt with a problem (somebody hid his slippers) without waiting one day, if she had hugged S.... like ISB teachers, S.... would not have refused the first school. This year S....'s teacher is so strict and rigid. She commanded him to stand at the back of the class when he forgot his textbook and to run round the playing field when he talked too much. But S.... does not have any problems. He really enjoys the Japanese school life as a real Japanese boy having an international background. He often has the best scores on the Japanese exams. Can you believe this? Children can accept and adjust to the change because they are so flexible. But, the first day, the first teacher, is so important for them.'

Two points should be made about the lasting effects on children of this need to adjust. It is the case that most children eventually achieve equilibrium between the two sets of cultural influences while they remain in the international school. The next move, particularly if it involves a return to their home system, may bring the need to readjust. If the home system is very different in type from that of the international school, then this process is likely to bring its own stresses. The second long-term outcome is that children may be permanently changed by their experiences in international schools. They may become part of the group of young people known as Global Nomads who never entirely re-integrate into their home culture. For some, this is a permanent cause of difficulty; others feel their lives have been deeply enriched by this experience of different cultures and peoples.

Summary

Adjusting to a new school culture

- International schools tend to have a common culture typified by a friendly atmosphere, informal relationships between teachers and students and a shared educational philosophy.
- Children enter international schools with the expectations about education that prevail in their culture. Sometimes these expectations differ greatly from the philosophy and practice to be found in international schools.

Students and teacher

- Children used to large classes of 40 or more students sitting in rows in front of the teacher are confused by the informal relationship between teacher and student in international schools. They do not know how to behave in this new relationship.
- They do not know what is expected from them in classrooms where the furniture is grouped informally.
- They do not understand how they should behave in an environment where there appear to be few rules.
- They feel insecure in the face of praise for school work that contains many mistakes.
- Teachers can give students a feeling of security by making clear the framework of the school day and their expectations for behaviour in the classroom.
- They should be calm and kind in their dealings with new students rather than over-friendly.

- They should be encouraging about school work, and give credit for clearly specified reasons.

Second language students' beliefs and expectations about learning and being taught

- The families of second language families may have different expectations from teachers in international schools about what teaching and learning entail.
- Families who expect teachers to transfer to children an accepted body of knowledge may not understand concepts such as child-centred education.
- Families who expect students to be tested in a series of examinations may not understand the value of other types of assessment.
- Children who are accustomed to copying, rote learning and reproducing information will not understand teaching that asks them to think independently, to offer opinions or to speculate.
- Students who are accustomed to working in isolation will not understand what to do when grouped with other children for a co-operative activity.
- Teachers need to take time to explain to parents how the educational policies of the school answer the needs of a mobile and diverse student population best. (In their opinion.)
- Teachers can only persuade parents of the effectiveness of assessment-based instruction by showing them that it works.
- Teachers need to give students explicit support in carrying out tasks that involve the use of unfamiliar learning strategies.
- Teachers can help students to be effective in new groupings by giving them explicit, step-by-step directions.

Parents and teachers — the need to communicate

- Some parents of second language students are not accustomed to the degree of involvement with their children's education that is customary in international schools.
- In many cultures, there is a divide between the spheres of home and school.
- In some cultures it is accepted that schools alone have responsibility for managing the education of children.
- Teachers in international schools need to adjust their views of what is normal in the relationship between parents and teacher.

- Many parents of second language students do not at first see the need for a high degree of involvement in their children's school life.
- Schools need to work positively to include the parents of second language students in the membership of all-school organisations.
- Teachers need to ensure that parents of second language students are made welcome in the classroom and are invited to participate in parent volunteer activities.
- Teachers need to be open to parents' anxieties and concerns. In this way, small difficulties may be prevented from turning into major problems.
- The work of teachers in international schools is concerned not only with children but also with their families.

Maintaining cultural identity

- Second language students in international school generally come from well-established, highly educated families. In most cases cultural identity is not an issue. Parents and students feel at ease with their own culture and place value on it.
- Second language students new to international schooling have to make a variety of adjustments. A major adjustment is the need to function in English.
- A further adjustment relates to the impact of the culture of the majority group on the new student.
- Second language students in international schools will not meet with discriminatory practices. Nevertheless, the issue of culture is a key feature in the adjustment process.
- The attitude of the family is an essential component in enabling children to live successfully in two cultures.
- Some families are aware that cultural influences from school will entail adjustment; other families are taken by surprise.
- Children frequently exhibit extreme forms of behaviour during the period of adjustment — they may refuse to speak the home language.
- The personality of the child plays a key role in successful social adjustment.
- The nature of the classroom is an important element in the successful social integration of new second language children.
- A positive attitude towards new cultural influences together with the maintenance of the home language and culture is the best circumstance for children.

- Most parents and children eventually come to live with both cultures in equilibrium.
- To be successful in international schools children have to come to terms with the modes of teaching and learning that prevail.
- Teachers can be a positive and supportive force in the adjustment process. They can offer support to anxious parents, they can create classroom environments in which variety and difference are valued, they can incorporate cultural difference into their teaching, they can safeguard the interests of the various cultural groups.
- Children may have to undergo a stressful period of re-adjustment on returning to their home system.
- Children with experience of international education may become one of the group generally known as Global Nomads.

Chapter 3
Going to School in English — Second Language Learning Issues

Introduction

This chapter has two aims. The first is to present some of the relevant theories and research findings that relate to second language learning. The reasons for including this material are practical. A knowledge of relevant language acquisition theory and an understanding for the reasons behind some of the typical language behaviours to be observed in children as they learn a second language, should, it is hoped, help teachers to make better sense of what they observe. Such an understanding should, in turn, guide teachers to act in ways that foster students' language learning and give them the means to reassure anxious parents. The second aim is to discuss the nature of the provision for second language learning in international schools. The criterion that guided the choice of what to include in this chapter was whether teachers in international schools would benefit from knowing about the topic. In a further attempt to make the material relevant, each section includes a discussion of the practical implications of the topic for teachers and families.

The first section discusses the nature of bilingualism with particular reference to the experiences of international school students. The second section describes the chief factors that affect the learning of a second language. Section three deals with the important subject of maintaining the home language. Sections four to seven offer descriptions of second language teaching programmes and discusses some policy areas associated with language learning that present challenges to international school administrators and teachers.

The Nature of Bilingualism

Parents who place their children in English-medium international schools are committed to the idea of their children becoming proficient in English. Parents of these children are often speakers of several languages and are generally convinced of the benefits to their children of becoming bilingual. They may not, however, be aware of the theoretical and practical considerations that are influential in enabling children to achieve **bilingualism**.

Continuing discussion surrounds such topics as the nature of bilingualism, and the features which typify bilinguals. Helpful definitions take into account the **use** that individuals make of each language and their **ability** in those languages. The discussions surrounding **use** relate to the social and political reasons for being a bilingual, and the circumstances in which each language is used. Bilingual **ability** is concerned with the varying patterns of competence in each language that are to be found in bilinguals.

Much of the study of bilingualism has been concerned with bilinguals from minority language populations. Political, economic and social factors figure largely in a discussion of bilingualism in these circumstances. Among populations such as these, the need to learn a second language is related to economic and social realities. Children are obliged to learn a second language to gain access to the status and economic benefits associated with the speakers of the majority language, in most cases the dominant political group. Second language learning in this situation is likely to have variable outcomes and may pose some challenges to the learner's cultural identity.

As mentioned in previous chapters, children in international schools come largely from families where the home language and culture are not under pressure from more dominant influences. Their families opt for an English-medium education from a position of strength. They place value on the learning of English, in particular, because of its widespread use in world business, commerce and diplomacy. The terms **elite bilingual** and **prestigious bilingual** are sometimes used to describe children from these backgrounds who undertake the learning of a second language.

Children entering international schools arrive with a variety of language experiences. They may come from bilingual homes where from birth they have been accustomed to the use of two languages. The acquisition of two languages in this circumstance is known as **simultaneous bilingualism**. Other children are exposed to new languages in sequence. Such exposure may arise as a result of their parents' relocation, or from changes within the home due to remarriage or the presence of foreign domestic helpers. Some children entering an international school may have already attended schools in languages other than their home language or English. For these children the acquisition of a second or further language is **sequential**.

The ultimate aim for second language children entering an international school is for them to become **balanced bilinguals** with a high level of competence in both languages. It is important to emphasise the level of competence, since, as was mentioned above, the term bilingualism is used to describe a range of competencies in one or both languages.

Additive bilingualism is the term used to describe a positive outcome to the process of acquiring two languages. It also includes a cultural element. Additive bilingualism leads to children being competent users of both languages and at ease in both cultures. In particular, additive bilingualism does not damage children's view of their home culture and language, or their own self-esteem. Children with the backgrounds typical of most international school families are well placed to experience this positive outcome. A negative outcome to learning a second language is termed **subtractive bilingualism**. This arises when children's ease in their own culture and language is diminished as a result of contact with a dominant culture and language. (This circumstance occurs when the first language of minority language speakers in the United States and the United Kingdom, for instance, is replaced by English.)

Children attending English-medium international schools require English for two areas of use. They need competence in informal classroom and social language and they need to acquire the advanced language skills required for success in the mainstream academic programme. Most children immersed in English acquire the means to talk to their friends, to ask for help and to give information quite quickly. In social situations and in general classroom conversation they appear fluent users of spoken English. They can decode and comprehend a narrative text and write correctly in simple sentences. Experienced classroom teachers, however, understand that this level of proficiency is not sufficient to enable students to participate with success in the mainstream academic programme. It is necessary for certain cognitive features and advanced level language skills to be in place before students can work unsupported at the same level as native English and long-term second language users of English.

Jim Cummins' (1984) theory concerning the distinction between the language used in social interaction (**basic interpersonal communication skills**, known as **BICS**) and the language used in situations that require higher level cognitive and academic proficiency (**cognitive/academic language proficiency**, known as **CALP**) relates to these two areas of language competence. This distinction has been used to explain why some minority students fail to achieve fully in majority school systems; they have been given insufficient support in learning their second language to develop the cognitive/academic language proficiency required to perform effectively in a mainstream programme. Experienced teachers in international schools will recognise some of the validity of this much-debated distinction. Academics (see Baker, 1996) in the field argue, however, that the distinction lacks a sound basis in research. They question this neat categorisation of language into two levels. It is likely that there are many competences in language and that many variables are involved in explaining why some second language children never attain sufficient competence to perform effectively in a cognitively demanding academic programme.

Some teachers may feel that what they observe in their students is better described as a language learning continuum. Students move from one stage to another until they reach an appropriate level of competence to work unsupported in the classroom. It is common, however, to find second language students who have failed to make the leap to competence in **CALP**. They continue to struggle with tasks such as drawing inferences or making summaries from a non-fiction text and have difficulty in expressing conceptual ideas orally.

A practical example may be useful to illustrate this abstract and theoretical point. In many language puzzle books aimed at children between the ages of nine and 11, it is common to find tasks where students are asked to fill in the names of the owners of a street of houses, or of people sitting in chairs round a table. The information that allows them to arrive at the correct answer is given in a text phrased in simple English; the facts, however, are presented in a manner that requires inferential thinking from the students. Mr White lives opposite someone who likes animals, (a cat appears in one of the windows), and to the left of Mr Brown who lives opposite someone with a tree in his garden, for example. It is quite often the case, that second language children who express themselves fluently and correctly in spoken English, have difficulty in solving this type of puzzle. It is possible that their difficulty is due to only average ability and aptitude in any language. Another explanation is that they need to develop further their linguistic and cognitive competence in their second language. The distinction between the two types of competence is useful to teachers in international schools, since it underlines the level of English that second language students must acquire to be successful in school.

A further area of debate relates to the possible positive effects of bilingualism on bilinguals apart from the usefulness of being able to function in two languages. The area of cognitive functioning is the focus of much of this research. Despite the difficulty of constructing research studies that exclude the possibility of other influences on the results except the presence of bilingualism, the research seems to show that being a bilingual brings certain advantages. A further area of debate surrounds the degree of competence in both languages that it is necessary for a bilingual to achieve in order to experience these positive effects.

These advantages are generally expressed in technical terms. Put

Textbox 3.1 Educating parents about bilingual issues

It is interesting that the term **bilingual** is rarely heard in international schools except in association with host country language programmes for English speakers. Teachers and administrators refer to speakers of languages other than English as second language or ESOL children, seldom as bilinguals. The very fact that we use the terms ESL, ESOL, EFL (English as a Foreign Language) or EAL (English as an Additional Language), suggests that we think of second language speakers in terms of their command of English rather than as bilinguals. The widespread use of the term, **bilingual**, to describe these children, would bring benefits to students and teachers. Teachers would be reminded that second language students enter the school with a wealth of linguistic experience and skill in language. They would be more inclined to build on children's existing knowledge and experience in teaching them in English. English-speaking students might understand more fully the challenges of learning a second language and offer further support and encouragement.

In fact, native speakers of English in international schools are generally supportive of second language learners at the elementary level. However, it is worth sometimes asking second language students to read to the whole class in their own language, or to exhibit some written work. This frequently has the effect of changing the way they are viewed by their English-speaking peers. A considerable degree of respect is added to the good-natured support and tolerance.

A lack of knowledge about the implications of bilingualism is common among parents despite a general commitment to maintaining the home language and to fostering the learning of English. It appears that many parents of international school students fail to appreciate that the description **bilingual**, with all its associations, applies to their own children. Perhaps they have not understood that being educated in a second language is a very different experience from acquiring a foreign language.

What is the role of the school in fostering a greater awareness of bilingual issues? In my own school, the International Group of the PTA has instituted an annual seminar on bilingualism. These meetings are well attended and indeed some of the same parents return each year for a repeat session. The level of interest and concern shown by the parents who attend them confirms their usefulness. Other schools hold similar sessions in lecture form or with a question and answer format. These initiatives are all valuable, but need to be an integral part of the calendar. Providing a forum for discussion on bilingual issues is a valuable contribution that international schools can make to the well being of their second language students.

simply, it seems likely that bilingualism may lead to a bilingual being a more creative thinker who is also better able to think divergently. Bilinguals may also utilise a greater variety of learning strategies because of their constant need to monitor internally their own use of two languages. They may be more skilled at adapting to different language situations and may have a greater ability than monolinguals to interpret non-verbal cues. The differences that teachers in international schools may notice in practice, are that bilinguals show a greater awareness of the way languages work, and demonstrate an increased ability to learn further languages successfully.

Factors Which Affect Second Language Learning

Much of the content in this section relates to respected hypotheses and theories about the nature of second language learning. Typical of these are Stephen Krashen's (1985) **input hypothesis** (on which is based the notion of the need for comprehensible input) and his **affective filter hypothesis** (1985). These theories and others of Stephen Krashen constitute the basis for much of current methodology in second language teaching. In particular, they underpin the emphasis on communicative language teaching and learning which is found in many international schools. It seems essential to include a discussion of these theories in even the shortest piece about the factors that affect second language learning. Jim Cummins' distinction between **BICS** and **CALP**, and his work (among that of others) on the advantages of maintaining the home language, have a similar force and relevance for teachers in international schools. The focus for this section of Chapter 3, then, is on the aspects of acquiring a second language that apply to the populations in international schools

The factors that affect second language learning can be divided broadly into three categories. First are the factors which are centred in the learners themselves. These include personality, ability, aptitude, and motivation. Second are those external to the learner. These include the quantity and nature of exposure to the target language (in this case, English). A third category includes such factors as the optimum age for learning a second language, and the length of time it takes to reach competence. The final paragraph in this section of Chapter 3 touches on the necessity for adequate linguistic and cognitive development in the home language. This leads on to a discussion in the section that follows entitled, **Maintaining the home language and culture.**

Learners' individual attributes have a key role in the process of acquiring a second language. These areas are by their nature difficult to assess objectively. Confidence, low levels of anxiety and a capacity to take risks are likely to have a positive impact on the process of language learning. The presence of general academic ability and language aptitude, though difficult to measure, are likely also to lead to a positive outcome.

The nature of students' attitudes towards second language learning is a further element in the equation. The circumstances of most international school students ensure that they generally have a **high motivation** towards learning English. The nature of the families from which international school students come ensures that contact with English and the English-speaking culture of the school is perceived as largely advantageous. Such families anticipate, and usually achieve, a positive outcome for their children from the process of acquiring a second language. This has the effect of reducing the emotional barrier of anxiety and wariness that sometimes exists in students who are less fortunately placed. International school students in general have a **low affective filter** (Krashen, 1985); little negative feeling stands between them and a successful outcome to their language learning. Students who exhibit unease and low self-confidence are described as having a **high affective filter**.

The second group of factors that affect the outcome of second language learning relate to the quantity and nature of students' exposure to the target language. **Adequate exposure to the target language** (Krashen, 1982) is a prerequisite for students to succeed in learning a second language. Children in international schools are exposed to language in a variety of contexts. This includes exposure to the contextualised social language of the playground, the corridors and hallways, the classroom, the sports field and after-school activities, as well as to the more abstract academic language used by teachers in delivering the curriculum. For effective language learning to take place, the level of language needs to be at or slightly beyond the level which students can produce themselves. This type of language is described as **comprehensible input** (Krashen, 1985). (See pp. 75–6, Comprehensible input, for a fuller discussion.) In the case of social language, the concrete nature of the circumstances and the need for both speakers in a conversation to make themselves understood, generally lead to an appropriate adjustment in the level of language used. This is why many children in an English-medium school acquire so-called **survival language** quite quickly and with ease. (See pp. 75, Survival English.)

Ensuring that children receive comprehensible input in the subject areas of the academic programme requires expertise and experience on the part of teachers. In this situation students have lengthy exposure to the target language. In order, however, for second language students to gain an understanding of the content and to extend their competence in English, it is essential that teachers present the material in a modified form via strategies that allow access to its meaning. By adapting the content and language of a subject area so that it is comprehensible to second language students, teachers are contributing significantly to these children's acquisition of English. (Chapters 6 to 11 are concerned with giving students access to both language learning opportunities and curriculum content. An important feature is the use of content as a vehicle for language learning.)

The third area that potentially affects the outcome of second language learning is the age that children begin the process of acquiring a second language. The question of the optimum age for language learning is one that has implications for teachers and parents in trying to plan the best outcomes for young students. This topic, however, remains a subject for debate among researchers due to the difficulties of constructing soundly based research studies.

Very young children enter school with the ability to think only in concrete terms. Their acquisition of a second language is dependent on real interaction in authentic contexts. At this age, they have not learnt to read and write in their home language. They must acquire an under-standing of the relationship between meaning and symbols on the page at the same time as they cope with the sound system of a new language. They have comparatively little experience on which to draw in making educated guesses about the meaning of unfamiliar words. These poten-tially limiting features have led to the assertion that slightly older children are more efficient language learners than very young children.

Children between the ages of seven to 11 approach the learning of a second language with certain advantages. As is explained more fully in Maintaining the home language and culture, below, one of these advantages is the level of cognitive and linguistic development in their first language. Their educational experiences enable them to use a variety of intellectual processes in making sense of the second language. They have learnt to read and write in their first language and are able to apply this understanding of the process of reading to the new language. They have a variety of learning and life experiences on which to draw in making sense of what they hear and read. They are likely to be more enthusiastic and less inhibited language learners than students at a later age.

Research findings (Singleton, 1989) related to the optimum age for second language learning are, however, ambivalent. The generally held view that older children make the most efficient language learners is not based on wholly satisfactory evidence. Research studies in this area carried out on various populations of students are unable to eliminate the social and psychological factors that may affect a student's language learning. Some indications are well-founded, however. Students who begin to learn a second language as children often tend in practice to reach a higher level of competence than students who begin at a later stage. It is also well established that young children successfully acquire the pronunciation of the English-speaking group with whom they have contact. Adolescents and adults seldom achieve this level of competence in 'native-like' pronunciation.

It is also a generally accepted finding that the presence in students of **adequate linguistic and cognitive development in their home language** (Cummins, 1986) contributes positively to second language learning. High levels of prior knowledge about the use of language and how a language system works makes learning the second language an easier task. An adequately developed cognitive ability allows students to analyse and to construct meaning more effectively in the second language. It follows that parents and teachers have an interest in maintaining the home language of second language students.

Textbox 3.2 What do we mean by a child's home language?

Many terms have been used to describe the language that occupies the significant place in a child's early language development. These terms include, **dominant language, first language, home language, mother tongue, native language, preferred language and prime language.** The debate about the most appropriate term continues. The discussion arises because the pattern of language use in homes that are other than monolingual is varied. No single term seems to fit all circumstances. In the case of children who attend international schools the pattern of use is likely to be even more varied. They are exposed, because of their parents' life-style, to many linguistic influences. In some cases these languages come to figure significantly within the home.

Among families who send their children to international schools, it is quite common to find marriages between people of different nationalities and languages. Many families employ helpers to clean the house and to share in the care of children. In some cases, children spend a good deal of time with these domestic workers. Very young children starting at an international school quite frequently intersperse the language, (or languages) of their parents, with words from the language of these helpers. As children grow a little older they meet and play with children from the local community. In so doing they may acquire smatterings of a further language. Finally, when they enter an international school, children meet with English. Frequently, if their stay extends over several years, brothers and sisters import English into the home and use it between themselves. It is not uncommon for the children, at least, to feel that English is their most-used language.

This description makes it clear that children's language use alters in response to the circumstances of their lives. This accounts for the difficulty in using a sole term to describe the language that is dominant at any one time. The term **prime language** seems to be in favour at the present time. In this handbook I have chosen to use the term, **home language** to describe the language which bilingual children in English-medium schools use together with English. However, the term, **first language** has sometimes seemed more appropriate when I wished to point out the contrast with second language usage.

Maintaining the Home Language and Culture

Parents who send their children to international schools usually have a strong motivation for ensuring that their children maintain their home language and home culture. Such families have an unforced pride in their home language and traditions. Their family life reflects the nature of the expectations in their home country. Cultural influences from the new school may cause some adjustment in children's daily lives but do not substantially affect the cultural assumptions about family life or the use of the family language. Such families expect to return home and to resume their place in the extended family and in social life.

Most parents also expect their children to re-enter their home school system and to be educationally successful in the terms of their own culture. (Occasionally parents feel that the years at an international school, more often several international schools due to frequent relocations, have changed their children in significant ways. They may feel that an international school in their home country or a school for returnees is more appropriate. They may also have come to prefer the child-centred and supportive approach to be found in international schools.) They are likely, also, to be able to afford to maintain their links with home through visits. In turn, their relations and friends pay visits to the expatriate family. Thus, children in international schools are well-placed regarding the maintenance of their home language and culture.

The value of maintaining the home language and culture has been emphasised in previous sections in this chapter. Academics (Cummins, 1986) and educators advocate the maintenance of the home language alongside the learning of a new language. Cognitive and linguistic development in the child's first language transfers positively to the second language and assists the child in acquiring the second language to an equivalent level. Further benefits follow from maintaining the home language. Cognitive development continues in the first language while the child is learning the second language. So too does the acquisition of vocabulary and of complex written structures. During the early phases of learning English in an international school, even with the aid of teacher modifications, students are unlikely to benefit fully from instruction given in English. As students' mastery of English increases, they can engage more fully with the mainstream programme. The continuation of linguistic and cognitive development in the first language contributes to a seamless continuum of learning.

Parents have a unique role to play in maintaining the home language. They are likely to be the major source of informal input for the child. They are also the managers of their children's continuing formal learning in their home language. Parents maintain the home language by using it consistently in discussing family matters with their children and in conversation about life at school and elsewhere. They contribute to their children's linguistic and cognitive development when they tell them bedtime stories, read together, and talk about books in the home language. A natural reinforcement of the home language and culture occurs when families celebrate the national and religious festivals of their culture within the home and with friends from the same linguistic and cultural backgrounds.

Occasionally some parents who are good speakers of English as a second language switch from the home language or languages to the use of English when talking to their children. They do this in the belief that this reinforces the child's learning of English at school. In these circumstances, teachers should search for a tactful way of raising the issue with parents. (Effective communication between teacher and parents allows discussion of sensitive areas such as this.) It is advantageous for the child if the parents feel committed to the learning of English. However, maintenance of the home language makes a greater contribution to the child's eventual balanced bilingualism. Parents should also feel able to speak to their children in the language that is natural to them. This is despite the possibility that their children may speak English among themselves at home. On the other hand, discussion in the home language about English homework or about a topic being studied at school in English brings benefits to the development of both languages.

At an appropriate time most parents arrange classes in home language reading and writing for their children. The school should make it clear to new parents that this is in the best interests of their child. Some international schools themselves offer classes during or after school in the languages spoken by the larger groups of students in the school. More often, parents make provision for home language literacy tuition in other ways. They may arrange private lessons or send their children to language classes arranged by embassies for their nationals. Many international schools are willing to provide space at the end of the day for the so-called 'mother tongue' classes.

An option for some language groups is for children to attend their own national schools on a part-time basis. Japanese, Korean and other schools exist in some major cities. These offer not only language classes but also a modified version of the national curriculum, usually on Saturday mornings. Despite the heavy load such attendance places on students, this has the advantage of keeping them in touch with their home culture as well as their national school curriculum. These schools act as a focus for their local expatriate community and sponsor or organise themselves the celebration of national festivals.

Support within school for the maintenance of home languages can take a variety of practical forms such as the building-up of a home language collection in the library. Embassy donations as well as school funds are possible sources for a selection of dictionaries, encyclopaedias and guidebooks. (See pp. 252–7, The library or media centre, contains a fuller discussion of the place of home language collections in international school libraries.) A further useful contribution from the school is an up-to-date list of home language classes held in the area. Suggestions for incorporating an awareness of students' home languages and home cultures into all aspects of the school day appear throughout this book. (See chiefly, pp. 79–81, Creating a classroom that reflects cultural diversity.)

An area of interest and concern is the order of the introduction of literacy teaching to young bilingual students. Young children arrive in an international school at all stages of reading readiness in their home language. Certain nationalities, notably children from Asia, may have already begun to read and write in their own languages. Other children, sometimes from the Scandinavian countries, may not yet have begun their formal education. Children who are already learning to read and write are likely to continue to attend classes on a regular basis in the new location. In this case, the teaching of literacy in both the child's languages continues side-by-side.

Parents and teachers have a choice with children whose literacy studies in their home language have not yet begun. In these cases, there are advantages in focusing the attention of children on the reading and writing of English since that is the chosen language of instruction. Two sets of formal lessons may be too much for very young students and may introduce an element of confusion. Formal reading and writing lessons in the home language can begin when children have gained an under-standing, and some mastery, of the process of reading. At this point, knowledge about literacy and the skills of processing and decoding in one language transfer to the other, and children generally learn to read and write in their home language with relative ease. The parents' role before formal home language lessons start is to ensure that children have access to high quality oral input in their home language.

If young students show an interest in learning to read and write their home language, parents should build on their children's interest by involving them in informal reading and writing activities around the home. Some examples include making shopping lists and exchanging notes with grandparents. It is natural and useful, also, to make sound and letter connections and to point out word patterns in the home language.

Textbox 3.3 Adjusting to life as a bilingual

Second language children who enter an English-medium international school for the first time exhibit a range of behaviour during the period of adjustment to their new circumstances. This behaviour may vary at its extreme from complete withdrawal to boisterous, unfocused over-activity. Experienced teachers in international schools are familiar with this pattern and recognise the phases of the adjustment process. For parents who may be coming to terms themselves with a new way of life in a strange city, their children's obvious disturbance may lead to feelings of guilt and anxiety. An aspect of the adjustment phase that may cause parents unease, and also upsets the accustomed course of family life, is the temporarily changed pattern of language use which is common at this time. Quite often, both younger and older children may prefer to answer in English when their parents speak to them, or may refuse to speak their home language to their parents in front of their schoolfriends. Other children temporarily refuse to engage in their normal home pursuits or to speak their home language at all.

Families cope with this situation in different ways. For some parents it is a cause for profound distress and unease, for others who may perhaps speak a number of languages, including English, themselves, the occurrence has a lesser impact. The attitude of grandparents, particularly in families from more 'traditional' societies, can be significant.

I was present, once, at a parent discussion group when a Japanese mother related how her parents would ring from Japan every week to make sure that their grandson was being brought up as a real Japanese boy. When the six-year-old boy refused to speak Japanese to his grandparents on one occasion, the result was, as can be imagined, a great deal of distress and unhappiness on all sides.

At the same session an Israeli parent came near to weeping because her nine-year-old son had announced that he would not be speaking Hebrew in future. Fortunately, parents of older bilingual children were present. They were able to place these events in context. In all cases their children had exhibited reluctance at some time or other in speaking one of their languages. On some occasions they refused to speak their home language, at other times they became resentful about the need to learn English. Eventually, the language use became balanced and relatively consistent. Within the family it became understood when the home language would be used and when it was more appropriate to speak in English. It is quite common, for instance, in many families, for second language parents and children to speak English when English-speaking schoolfriends are present. The pattern in a family and among the students in a school varies greatly, however. In some schools, with a large number of speakers of one language, for example, this group generally feels free to use its own language on all occasions.

Teachers in international schools are able to help parents who are troubled and anxious during the adjustment phase. They can inform them in advance of the likely stages in the development of balanced bilingualism. They can also reassure them at times of difficulty and they can put them in touch with other parents who have shared the same experiences.

The Role of the ESL Department

Accredited international schools make provision for the needs of their second language students within the school day. The support that they offer takes various forms and is usually delivered by specialist teachers of English as a Second Language. (The terminology varies from school to school. In some schools the department is called the ESL department, in others the ESOL (English to Speakers of Other Languages) department.) In large schools there is generally an ESL department with an ESL co-ordinator or head of department who contributes to discussions on school language policies and who represents the needs of second language students in all-school debate. The initial role of ESL teachers concerns the day-to-day language needs of second language students. The aim is to foster the acquisition of **survival language**. This is to enable students to cope with the practical aspects of class and school life and to function socially. (See p. 75, Survival English.) Once some basic structures and vocabulary are in place, the role of ESL teachers is to assist students in acquiring the necessary spoken and written language to function fully in the mainstream academic programme.

The nature of the programme varies from school to school. In some schools, the basic provision takes the form of a pull-out programme of classes for learners at different levels of competence. In many cases, three levels of classes are offered, equating broadly with beginner, intermediate and advanced level learners. The classes themselves may comprise students of mixed ages or serve the students of one year level. In many schools, the ESL provision consists of support within the homeroom for individual students or small groups. The role of the ESL teacher in this instance is to offer language support to the student related to the specific language needs of the curriculum. Many schools offer an ESL programme that combines pull-out classes with classroom support. In some schools with very large second language populations there may also be scheduled times to discuss each student's progress with homeroom teachers and for modifying subject area materials for use in the homeroom classroom.

There is considerable debate about the effectiveness of the different models of ESL programme. The protagonists of the pull-out programme model assert that students have a more effective learning experience in separate focused groups. In this situation it is possible to use only language appropriate to the students' level of English and to foster a personal relationship with students, who, in the early days in school may feel lost and confused. The advocates of home classroom support consider that pull-out programmes diminish second language students' self-esteem and, by separating them from English-speaking students, reduce the opportunities for the meaningful use of English. They also assert that home classroom support enables ESL teachers to target their teaching more effectively to the skills needed by the student. Many experienced homeroom and ESL teachers would argue that second language students benefit from both types of support, and in some schools this is the case.

Increasingly the content and methodology of the ESL classroom reflect and relate to the mainstream programme. In the case of young children, ESL teachers employ the first language reading and writing methodology commonly used in mainstream programmes. Strategies such as process writing, language experience, and shared and guided reading are effective in teaching a second language. They also provide young children with a more integrated language experience. In their work with older children, ESL teachers, where appropriate, try to incorporate or support the content work of the mainstream curriculum. This can be particularly useful before a field trip, when writing reports or planning oral presentations. With both age groups, thematic linking between mainstream classroom content and ESL skills teaching, is effective.

ESL teachers use a range of other strategies in the ESL classroom. With young children, the underlying language curriculum is rarely taught explicitly. The role of the ESL teacher is to provide exposure to, and practice in, useful structures and vocabulary by creating contexts that mimic real life. This approach appears to be more effective in enabling children to acquire English than previous workbook, gap-filling methodologies. Strategies include handwork activities, projects, games, songs, drama and film, together with short field trips where useful. The computer offers further means of incorporating a variety of learning opportunities in an engaging and motivating manner.

With older students, explicit teaching of grammar is appropriate as one aspect of language teaching. Second language children and their parents frequently feel happier when both the structure and sequence of their learning are obvious. Many second language children's previous experience in school leads them to expect a sequential approach based on written exercises. Work with older children does not stop here, however. The opportunity to practise the use of a grammatical item in meaningful contexts is an integral part of effective ESL teaching. The specific language skills required for success in the mainstream programme are also the province of the ESL teacher. The structural underpinning of such skill areas as note taking, summary and the writing-up of science experiments are explained to students and practised in authentic contexts. The language skills needed for studying fiction texts or acquiring information from non-fiction materials are also demonstrated and practised.

The ESL classroom acts as a haven for new second language students.

Textbox 3.4 The early days in an international school — two students remember how it felt

The following extracts are taken from two students' accounts of their first weeks in international schools. They give a vivid impression of the isolation and stress experienced by non-English-speaking students. They emphasise the paramount need for students to learn survival English above all else. Both extracts are taken, with the students' permission, from their graduation speeches at the end of 6th Grade.

Extract From a 6th Grade Graduation speech Given by a Twelve-year-old Japanese Student at the International School of Brussels.

I came to I.S.B. when I was in fourth grade. I couldn't speak any English at that time, everyone around me spoke only English. In Japan, I could talk and talk, shout and shout, but I said nothing here. Nothing was fun at first when I came, but when I began to speak, I felt that this school was great.

The fifth and sixth grade field trips were good. I couldn't speak English on the fourth grade trip so I couldn't do much, but I did speak English in the fifth and sixth grade. Then I felt like I was free. Also when I couldn't speak English, I couldn't get good grades in reports and that didn't make me feel good.

Extract From a Speech Given and Recited from Memory at the Same Graduation Ceremony by an Eleven-year-old Korean Student

ISB's campus seemed huge when I came here. It was very different from my Korean school. It has trees, a chateau, a large playground and four different schools. ISB has a running track and woods, and in PE class we often go running in the woods. It was the first time I had ever seen a place like this before. In Seoul, Korea, my school was a city school with about 3,000 students in it.

At first I couldn't understand anything. I felt very alone. But a few days later I made a friend. He comes from Iceland. He helped me a lot and he showed me how the school works. At that time my English was not good enough so I couldn't understand anything our teacher was saying. Time went by, my English was getting better and I was able to communicate with my friends and teachers. After a few weeks I had found two other friends, one from Japan and one from Kenya. They were both kind to me and I was kind to them. I have been here for only two years, but now I have to leave to go and live in Frankfurt. I am sad about it, because it is such a nice place and I have so many good friends. When I go to the other school I will never forget all the teachers who taught me and were kind to me.

Usually student numbers are small and a close relationship with the ESL teacher develops. Friendships are formed between the students, and jokes and bad times are shared. Targeted and comprehensible language provides children with one place where they know they will understand and be understood. This builds the confidence of second language students. They dare to speak out and to risk making mistakes. In discussions between mainstream and ESL teachers, it often becomes clear that a new child exhibits different, more outgoing and confident behaviour in the secure environment of a small ESL group.

This supportive and encouraging environment is further strengthened if contact between ESL teachers and children occurs outside the ESL classroom. It raises the esteem of second language children if they make presentations in assemblies or take part in a play. It is also valuable for their English-speaking peers to visit the ESL classroom to share in an activity or to view a project.

How Long Do Children Need Support From ESL Specialists?

Many of the second language children who enter English-medium international schools for the first time speak very little or no English. Others have received some teaching in their previous schools. Parents, teachers and the students themselves have a variety of expectations about the length of time it takes to become a competent user of English. Probably each of these groups has a different understanding of what they mean by competence. Parents may assume that fluency in speech and the ability to interact socially are a sufficient basis for children to be described as competent. Experienced teachers in international schools look for competence in the listening, speaking, reading and writing skills that bring success in the mainstream programme.

In practical terms the discussion often revolves around the length of time children receive support inside or outside the classroom from specialist ESL teachers. The early fluency in speech and the ability to communicate socially that many children acquire quickly, lead parents to question the need for further ESL support. It is common for new parents to assume that their children will be able follow the mainstream programme unsupported after a short time in the school. Teachers and parents search for sources of evidence on which to base their decisions.

Research findings provide useful indications concerning the time it takes children to acquire academic skills in a second language (Collier, 1989). In-coming second language students of English in the United States are found to take between five and seven years before they perform on national standardised tests at the same level as native English speakers of the same age. Second language students in international schools may take a shorter time to reach this standard. They do not have some of the social and emotional disadvantages that can hinder the progress of less advantaged students. There are reasons, also, why standardised tests normed on native English speakers are unsatisfactory measures of second language students' competence. (See pp. 104–6, Second language students and standardised tests, for a discussion of this topic.) The findings do, however, provide a basis for useful discussion with parents about their children's progress in learning English. They make the point that the acquisition of academic skills takes longer than acquiring conversational fluency. They also indicate a realistic timescale for mastery of these advanced skills.

Administrators and teachers in international schools search for an objective means of measuring when students are ready to function independently of specialist ESL support. The decision is complicated by the fact that students rarely develop all their language skills at an equal rate. Usually there is an imbalance between their competence in the four skills of listening, speaking, reading and writing. The student's personality also plays a part in this decision. Students who are risk-taking, independent and confident learners may reasonably be moved out of the programme at an earlier stage than timid children who would benefit from continuing small group support.

Some schools use standardised tests and mainstream classroom examinations to provide evidence on which to base this decision. These are only of partial value. Reliable decisions are based on evidence of performance in authentic classroom activities. A variety of assessment evidence is needed to describe adequately how a child functions. The methods for gathering evidence include anecdotal observations, dated check-lists of observed language behaviours, and the collection in a portfolio of pieces of a child's work showing key stages in language development. Systematically administered running records of young children's reading also provide useful evidence. How second language students perform in assessment tasks such as spelling tests, multiple choice questionnaires and extended pieces of writing that are carried out by the whole class are further indicators of second language students' progress.

A last important point needs to be made concerning the time children take to learn a second language. The contribution made by the mainstream classroom teacher in the second language learning of a student is a key factor. Students at the elementary level spend much of their time with the classroom teacher. Effective teachers recognise their role as teachers of language throughout the day. It is their continuing awareness of the needs of second language students that enables these children to make rapid progress. The rate of progress is reduced if the teaching of English is left to ESL specialists alone. Even when students have left the formal ESL programme, second language students need support and specific tuition in the area of language. Teachers need to continue with the use of support

Textbox 3.5 Describing levels of language competency in second language learners

Various terms are used to describe students' levels of competency as they acquire a second language. The same terms are often used to describe the classes that students attend in an ESL support programme. These terms are also used throughout the pedagogic chapters of this handbook (Chapters 6 to 11), in relation to the needs of children at differing levels of language competence.

Beginning learners may not speak, read or write English at all. **Beginners' classes** may, however, include children who speak a few words and have been taught a minimal amount of written English. The phrase, '**false beginners**', is used to describe students who have been exposed to a fair amount of English, or may even have received a number of English lessons, but who can show little understanding or use of English. These students are often difficult to place in an appropriate class since they feel out of place in a beginners' class, but are not equipped to work in an intermediate level class.

An intermediate student is a child who has acquired some fluency in social English and is beginning to read and write at an age-appropriate level. By the time the student is ready to move into an advanced class, she or he can generally read and comprehend straightforward narrative texts and write fairly correctly in simple sentences. The time it takes for this development to occur varies greatly from student to student. Some children pass through an ESL programme in as little as eighteen months, others need support for as many as four years before they can cope with the cognitive and linguistic demands of the mainstream programme unsupported.

Teaching in **an advanced class** is concerned with promoting the language skills and higher order thinking in English that students must acquire in order to achieve CALP, (cognitive/academic language proficiency) as described on pp.42–3. The writing component of an advanced class relates to the use of complex sentences and the creation of a well-argued piece of writing. The reading component deals with those aspects of a text that require inference, and the selection and re-arrangement of information. The oral language needed for expressing a point of view and for discussing a text, as well as vocabulary development, also form part of the content of an advanced class.

It should be emphasised that these terms are broad descriptions rather than objective measurements of students' abilities. They are used for the sake of convenience rather than because of any sound basis in evidence. In any case, children rarely develop at the same rate in all the skills of language. The placement of individual children in an appropriate group is often a matter of debate, and ESL classes invariably comprise students at various stages in different aspects of their language learning.

strategies in introducing new vocabulary areas and new reading and writing skills. They should also expect second language children to work more slowly than their first language peers for some time.

It is a useful practice for schools to include a summary of students' progress in acquiring English in their personal records, including the length of time in an ESL support programme. This acts as a reminder to teachers that students may still need extra help in areas requiring unfamiliar language skills. It is easy for teachers to forget or minimise the continuing impact of working in a second language.

Host Country and Other Language Classes

Parents who choose an international education for their children are frequently competent linguists themselves. They may be able to speak, read and write in two or more languages. They perceive benefit to their children in becoming at least bilingual. They anticipate that one of the advantages of attending an international school will be access to the learning of further languages.

The provision of language classes varies in different locations for several reasons. Some international schools are mandated by the local Ministry of Education to provide classes in the host country language. These are sometimes the schools that attract large numbers of host country children and thus for these students the focus of their language learning is English and their own language. Second language students in these schools who do not speak the host country language are obliged to take both English and the host country language even if both are unfamiliar. If, as it is hoped, their parents make provision for the maintenance of their home language, these children are faced with the challenge of taking classes in three languages at the same time.

Other international schools are free of the obligation to provide host country classes for second language students. In these schools, it is generally the policy to focus formal language learning on the acquisition of English and to advocate the maintenance of the home language. Some schools introduce host country language classes when second language students have achieved a certain standard of English; others, often due to scheduling factors, require that students become thoroughly competent in English before taking further language classes. The situation is made more complex if the host country language has a high status. In this case parents and children are eager to begin classes in this language as soon as possible.

Administrators, teachers and parents are frequently involved in discussions about the timing and circumstances of introducing a third language, almost invariably the host country language.

The research that relates to an optimum time for the introduction of a third language is largely based on student populations in circumstances unlike those of mobile students in international schools. Research carried out on school children in the Basque area of Spain (Cenoz & Valencia, 1994) and in the Duchy of Luxembourg (Baetens Beardsmore & LeBrun, 1991) indicates that trilingualism is the eventual outcome for stable school populations. A distinction is made between oracy and literacy, however. Reading and writing in the third language is generally introduced at a later stage. The population which most resembles the student body to be found in international schools is that of the European schools. These schools serve the families of employees in the institutions and agencies of the European Union. Research carried out on this relatively stable student population (Baetens Beardsmore, 1993) indicates a similar positive outcome with regard to trilingualism. The third language is not, however, introduced until the beginning of the secondary phase of schooling.

What have these findings to tell us about when it is best to introduce formal classes in a third language to second language students in international schools? The significant factor appears to lie in the mobility of international school students. It is common for students to move every two or three years to another English-medium school in a different location. It is likely that a move involves a change of host country language. Thus, there is little stability with relation to the third language in a students' repertoire. Most schools, therefore, opt to focus second language students' attention on gaining a sufficient level of competence in English. Where there is an option, (that is, where host country classes are not mandated throughout a child's stay), most schools wait to introduce formal classes in the third language. Parental pressure is usually only an issue when scheduling dictates that students must attend either ESL or host country classes. Their children must therefore wait until, in the school's opinion, they are ready to leave the ESL programme.

Many schools are able to resolve difficulties with parents and students by offering classes in the host country language to advancing second language students that concentrate on the acquisition of oral skills rather than on literacy. An alternative pattern at the elementary level is to offer cultural studies clubs or activity workshops using the host country language in or after school. These give all children a taste of the language and culture of the host country. Attendance at formal host country classes is arranged once their grasp of English is sufficient to enable them to function effectively in the mainstream classroom.

Textbox 3.6 Cultural studies programmes

Many of the schools I visited contained displays dedicated to the language, culture, history, geography, art, music and cuisine of the host country. Frequently students carried out this work as part of a separate cultural studies programme. The most effective programmes of this type provide a consistent strand relating to language teaching, social studies and science. In locations where travel is feasible, most school arrange a sequence of related field trips; visits from outside speakers are also a standard feature.

In Beijing, for instance, one international school takes its upper elementary grades on trips to parts of the Great Wall, to the imperial summer resort at Chengde and to a farming village. In another international school in Beijing, I saw a unique classroom decorated with Chinese art and students' exercises in calligraphy. A Chinese calligrapher makes regular visits to the school to teach the children the first steps of this great art. The richest and most memorable experiences arise when adequate time is given to the programme as was the case in this school. There is a danger that cultural studies programmes may become merely a series of superficial experiences.

In my own school we have enhanced and refined our Belgian Studies programme based on the outcomes of the first two pilot years. Each unit now comprises several aspects of the same topic and children are given more time to carry out follow-up activities. Belgium being famous for cartoons (Herge, the creator of Tintin was Belgian), we have visited the cartoon museum in Brussels, been visited by a Belgian cartoon artist, viewed some French- and Dutch-speaking cartoon films, and finally, have embarked on creating our own cartoon strips complete with dialogue balloons in both French and English. Not only the classroom teachers, but the French, ESL and art teachers form part of the teaching team.

These programmes are effective and enjoyable for a number of reasons. The best of them offer students real experiences of aspects of the host culture. They provide an integrated area of study that allows students to carry out extensive, in-depth activities. They bring teams of teachers together to work on a single project. Finally, they give beginning and intermediate learners of English effective and meaningful access to the host country language and culture.

Programmes in International Bilingual Schools

Bilingual international schools fall into two groups as was mentioned in Chapter 1. In the first group, a percentage of the student body comes from mobile, expatriate families where the parents are typically employed in business, or as diplomats and international civil servants. The other students come from host country families with an international outlook who choose a bilingual education for their children. Bilingual international schools are usually found in places that have a high status resident population and sizeable expatriate communities. Thus, examples of these schools are to be found in Atlanta, Georgia, and Washington, DC, in Berlin and Paris, in Kuwait and the Gulf States, and certain centres in East Asia.

The second group of schools has a student population largely made up of host country children. Their parents tend to have business links outside the region, or to anticipate a future for their children that involves relocation and the need for further languages. Some schools of this type are to be found in areas which are historically cosmopolitan in outlook. The bilingual schools of the Middle East are instances of this. Founded originally by missionary organisations or benefactors to offer a liberal Christian education in the time of the Ottoman Empire, these schools are now largely managed and funded by the local business communities. One or two retain strong contacts with their founding organisations, members of whom sit on the board and raise funds. In places such as Istanbul and Izmir in Turkey, and Beirut in Lebanon, these schools are some of the most prestigious in the area.

Both types of schools fall within the range of this book. They seek external accreditation from bodies such as ECIS, and from accrediting organisations in the United States, and they employ varying numbers of teachers from English-speaking countries. They attend international recruiting fairs and place advertisements in the magazines produced by international search organisations. The language programmes differ from those of English-medium international schools, and vary from school to school. However, teachers will find that the circumstances of daily life have similarities. The needs of expatriate students and parents require the same sensitive approach from teachers, and the complex language environments require a knowledge of the needs of diverse and multilingual student bodies.

Bilingual schools of both types tend to be highly selective in their intake. In the case of schools serving a mobile population, many require evidence of oral and written proficiency in one of the languages to be studied, even at the elementary level. The eventual aim for their students is further study at famous universities. The schools have found from experience that only gifted students with good study habits and supportive parents are able to meet the heavy demands of a bilingual programme aiming at high standards in both languages. In the schools serving a host country population, there is invariably intense competition among the local community for places in these institutions. Entrance at any age including the very young is by examination. If the children themselves cannot yet read and write the interview is conducted with their parents. Both types of schools offer little in the way of support for learning difficulties, and in the case of most schools, children who fail in the system are eventually asked to leave.

The structure of the programme in the bilingual international schools varies from school to school. The programmes also develop and change in response to local circumstances and rising costs. Some schools offer a choice of languages to be taken alongside English. In many schools at the elementary level there is a divided day, with each language being given a share of the teaching time. It is quite common for the language programme of the afternoon to be taught the next morning so as to allow for continuity in class and homework. In other schools the language teaching and use is weighted at the elementary level in favour of one of the languages. In most schools each language is taught by a native-speaker of that language. Only rarely are the two parts of the programme taught by the same teacher. The John F. Kennedy School in Berlin is an example of this. A bilingual German-English teacher may be responsible for teaching the same class at different times of the day in the two languages, although one language only is used at a time. Schools also vary in their use of the two languages to teach content area subjects. In some schools parallel curricula are taught in each language. In other schools the subjects are divided between the two languages in a variety of ways. There is very little use in any of the international bilingual schools of dual language texts or of bilingual teachers using the two languages to teach the same material at one time.

The schools that serve a local population tend to offer a different type of programme. In the Turkish schools, for instance, the first year is given over to intensive language tuition in English. From the second year, certain subjects are invariably taught in English and others in Turkish. English language tuition continues throughout the school, the methodology being a mixture of first and second language English teaching. Since the Turkish authorities insist on all students taking the Turkish leaving certificate, the curriculum is mandated by the Ministry of Education. The only concession made to the unusual nature of the school is that some of the subjects may be taught in English.

In schools situated in other parts of the Middle East there is a strong emphasis on the acquisition of three languages. Arabic and either French or English are the first two languages taught; the third language is added at the beginning of the secondary programme. The methodology is a mixture of grammar-based traditional language teaching and the literature-based integrated approach to reading and writing. In schools of this type, national history, and on occasion, religious studies, are invariably taught in the local language.

English-speaking teachers in bilingual schools are concerned with the delivery of the English programmes of instruction. They may be required to undertake specific tuition in the English language as well as to deliver a general curriculum. The two types of bilingual school present different challenges to teachers. In the case of the international bilingual schools the make-up of the classes varies according to the entrance requirements. In some schools most of the students are first language speakers of one of the languages; in others, children of many nationalities are accepted on the basis of their proficiency in English or in one of the other languages offered. As with all international schools a number of students enter and leave the school every two or three years. There is generally some short-term provision in the way of extra classes to bring these children up to a certain level of competence in their weaker language. Despite the selective intake, a typical class contains students with a range of abilities, aptitudes and experiences. This variety among the students is likely to be a chief cause of challenge to a teacher charged with delivering a demanding academic programme. Few of the schools offer support programmes to struggling students. The responsibility for resolving the difficulties rests with the classroom teachers. In extreme cases children may be asked to repeat the year and ultimately to leave the school.

In the case of bilingual schools with populations of host country students, the teacher's role is somewhat different. They are likely to share the English language tuition, and the subject area teaching in English, with bilingual host country teachers. This raises a number of issues connected with the use and teaching of English in locations outside English-speaking countries. Bilingual schools of this type owe the presence of English in their schools to the accident of their foundation. Its continuing use is due to the status of English as an international language and its perceived benefit for graduating students. These schools, unlike the international bilingual schools, owe much to the tradition of education in their locality. Their ethos, social language and methods of discipline reflect their geographical situation. The host country nationals who teach the subject areas in English are sensitive to any suggestion of superiority on the part of teachers who are native speakers of English. Teachers from English-speaking countries in this situation need to recognise their role in the school. They have been hired to offer specific expertise in the use of English, not because they are representatives of an English-speaking culture.

It is therefore a sensitive matter for new teachers, in particular, to comment on the practices that they find on arriving in these schools. The teaching of English is almost invariably based on the sequential acquisition of structural competence combined with the use of classic texts. Since the schools are selective and the host-country teachers usually expert in the grammar and vocabulary of English, the students' writing and speaking tends to be correct. The students are generally competent in their use of English when required to deal with matters of fact. Higher-level communication skills in both writing and speech tend to be areas of weakness, although this to some extent reflects the style of curriculum in the school. Pronunciation and intonation on occasion tend to deviate widely from standard usage. Teachers from English-speaking countries may feel that a wider range of teaching strategies and the use of more advanced materials and technological aids would address these areas of weakness. Some schools are open to change and development. Others are not. Teachers need to wait until they are well established and have gained the confidence and respect of host-country colleagues before they make suggestions for change.

Summary

The nature of bilingualism

- Helpful definitions of bilingualism take into account the **use** that individuals make of each language and their **ability** in those languages.
- Most of the children in international schools can be described by the terms **elite** or **prestigious bilingual** . Students of this type approach bilingualism from a position of social, linguistic, cultural and economic advantage.
- The ultimate aim for second language children in international schools is for them to become **balanced bilinguals** with a high level of competence in both languages.
- **Additive bilingualism** is recognised to be achievable by elite bilinguals. These students acquire English and feel at ease in the English-speaking environment of an international school. At the same time they retain their esteem for their own culture and language and use that language competently.
- Second language children need to move beyond the acquisition of **BICS (basic interpersonal communicative skills)**. In order to succeed in the mainstream academic programme they need to acquire **CALP (cognitive/academic language proficiency)**.
- Research suggests that bilingualism may bring positive effects in a child's cognitive functioning.

Factors which affect language learning

- Children's personalities, their general academic ability and language aptitude affect the outcome of language learning.
- A **low affective filter** is a positive factor in second language learning. High motivation and family support for learning the target language improve the likelihood of a successful outcome.
- An **adequate quantity of exposure to the target language** is a prerequisite for successful second language learning.
- **Input at a comprehensible level**, or just above, allows students access to the target language.
- The optimum age for language learning is debatable. However, pre-adolescent children make more uninhibited language learners and are capable of achieving the pronunciation of the target group of speakers.
- The **presence of adequate linguistic and cognitive development in the home language** contributes positively to second language learning.

Maintaining the home language and culture

- The families of most children at international schools have a high regard for their home language and culture.
- Such families expect their children to re-enter their home school systems and be successful.
- Cognitive and linguistic development in a child's first language transfers positively to a child's second language and assists a child in learning it.
- Continuation of linguistic and cognitive development in a child's first language ensures that learning continues during the acquisition of the second language.
- Parents are the major source of informal input of the child's home language and are generally the managers of their children's formal studies in their home language.
- Parents contribute to the learning of the second language by continuing to speak the home language to their children.
- Formal literacy teaching in home languages takes various forms. These include individual tuition, privately arranged classes or part-time attendance at expatriate national schools. Some international schools arrange after-school classes in the languages of large groups of students.
- When very young children have not yet begun to read and write in

their home languages there are some advantages in focusing their attention on the reading and writing of English.

The role of the ESL department

- ESL teachers have two main aims: To foster the acquisition of social language and to assist students in acquiring the cognitive and academic proficiency necessary for success in the mainstream programme.
- Specific ESL provision takes the form of pull-out classes or support within the classroom. Some schools offer both.
- ESL teachers frequently employ first language methodology in the teaching of reading and writing to very young learners.
- With older students ESL teachers incorporate or support the content work of the mainstream curriculum where possible.
- The emphasis in ESL classrooms is on providing opportunities for the real use of English in authentic contexts.
- The explicit teaching of grammar is appropriate as a contributory strand of language teaching. Many second language students and their parents expect a sequential approach based on written exercises.
- Small ESL groups offer an environment where targeted and comprehensible language builds confidence and a willingness to take risks in trying out language.

How long do children need support from ESL specialists?

- Early fluency in speech frequently leads parents and students to question the need for ESL support.
- Research findings indicate that second language students in the United States take between five and seven years to perform on standardised tests to the same level as native speakers of English.
- These findings indicate a realistic time-scale for mastery of cognitive/academic language proficiency (CALP).
- Reliable decisions about the need for continuing specialist support are based on evidence from students' performance in authentic classroom activities.
- Students who have left the formal ESL programme continue to need support and specific tuition in areas of language involving new vocabulary and unfamiliar structures.

Host country and other language classes

- In some international schools the local education ministry mandates host country language classes for all students in international schools. Thus, second language students at these schools are studying English and the host country language at school as well as their home language.
- In other schools classes are scheduled so that second language students focus only on English.
- Stable populations which achieve trilingualism at the age of 18 generally introduce the third language at the secondary stage of schooling.
- Mobile second language students at the elementary level are better served by concentrating on acquiring English and maintaining the mother tongue.
- Cultural studies classes are a positive way of ensuring that all students have access to the host country language and culture.

Programmes in international bilingual schools

- The student population of one type of bilingual international school is made up of mobile expatriate children and host country students from internationally minded families.
- A second type of bilingual school has a student population derived entirely from the host country. These prestigious schools have a long history and are to be found in locations with cosmopolitan traditions related to trade.
- Both types of schools seek accreditation from overseas English-speaking accrediting organisations.
- Both offer bilingual or trilingual programmes including English and other languages.
- Both employ numbers of English-speaking teachers to contribute to the English programmes.
- Both types of school are highly-selective, taking only children with proficiency in one of the languages and a proven record of academic success.
- Little support is offered for struggling learners. Failing children are eventually asked to leave.
- The programmes offered by bilingual schools vary in structure from school to school. One common model offers parallel curricula in both languages. Another divides the subjects of one curriculum between the two languages.

- English speaking-teachers in bilingual international schools may be required to undertake specific tuition in the English language as well as deliver the curriculum in English.
- In bilingual schools with host country populations, English-speaking teachers share the teaching of English and the delivery of the programme in English with bilingual host country teachers.
- The role of English-speaking teachers in those circumstances is to offer expertise in the use of English, not to represent a specific English-speaking culture.

Chapter 4
Day-to-Day Life in the Classroom —
Language Acquisition in Practice

Introduction

This chapter follows second language learners through their first weeks in an international school. It explains how to create a positive language learning environment in the classroom. It gives suggestions for fostering the acquisition of the first essential elements of survival English.

It provides brief accounts of a range of topics related to early language learning. This knowledge is designed to enable teachers to make sense of what they observe and to give them a secure basis for making sound management and instructional decisions.

The Classroom Environment

Layout and appearance

The design and contents of a classroom make a significant contribution to the success of a students' language learning. For all age groups, the aim is to provide an attractive, stimulating and print-rich environment that offers opportunities for the use of meaningful language.

The learning centres and themed play areas, which are customary features of young children's classrooms today, offer effective opportunities for authentic communication. Shopping areas, for instance, with their replicas of fruit, vegetables and other food, together with cash tills, money and weighing machines provide an ideal setting. Such arrangements offer children numerous chances to engage in language activities such as greeting friends, asking questions, making suggestions and functioning successfully in a group. Language learning possibilities are significantly increased if the areas also include materials to make labels, posters, announcements and lists, as well as fiction and non-fiction texts related to the theme in question.

When working with young children, it is useful to have a variety of interesting and colourful objects at hand. Holiday travel and outings provide an opportunity to acquire a range of attractive and unusual items;

these may be shells and starfish from the seaside, or local costumes and toys from foreign countries. Such treasures offer stimuli for conversation and enquiry, and lead to students bringing items into class and making their own collections.

The events of school and family life enable teachers to create opportunities for grounded oral language. Such happenings as host country festivals or a piece of family news offer concrete possibilities for oral and practical activities that are close to children's interests. To carry out this sort of approach to maximum effect, the arrangement of the classroom needs to allow for the flexible grouping of children. Permanent fixtures, which impose a rigid seating pattern, offer far fewer possibilities for varied groupings. The provision of an array of art and construction materials is necessary for this type of approach, and facilities for drama, cookery and other practical activities are also valuable.

A similar need to provide a stimulating language environment holds good for older children. Second language students progress more rapidly in the learning of useful language if they are presented with real examples of language in use. The materials themselves differ for this age group, but should be designed to provide similar opportunities for purposeful language activity. Useful materials include posters, magazine cuttings, sports photographs, computer printouts and advanced construction materials, as well as a variety of books and printed matter. For all age groups, the provision of computers, CD-ROMs, and effective age-appropriate software, is of benefit.

Creating a positive social ambience

The social ambience of a classroom is equally important in promoting the most effective environment for language learning. In a classroom, which contains second language students, it is helpful to establish certain patterns of behaviour among the other children. The class as a whole needs to be tolerant of language mistakes and to make allowances for language learners. Class discussions, for instance, need careful management to ensure that second language children are given the time they need to formulate their oral contributions.

It is important that second language students are not regarded as language invalids. It is an effective strategy to arrange occasions when they can display in a natural fashion their command over their own language. For example, visits from a class of older children for the purpose of reading their own or published stories to a class of young children is a practice in some schools. These visits bring pleasure to second language children if an older child who speaks the same language reads a story written in that language in front of the whole class. It is an even more powerful teaching and learning strategy if the book is well illustrated and both children can explain the story to the rest of the class in English. The library or literacy centre provides another venue for further displays of second language children's ease and competence in their own language. (See pp. 252–7, The library or media centre, for fuller accounts of such strategies.)

An aim of teachers in international schools is to create the sort of open, positive and understanding classroom that includes all children in the mainstream. It is not helpful to second language children if they are singled out and made to feel different because of their lack of English. The integration of second language students is aided if, from the first, they are included in all the tasks and clearing-up duties of the class.

The notion that constructive talk is allowed in a classroom will be new for some second language students. Initially, these children often misread the situation and may imagine that the talk between neighbours is social conversation. The teacher needs to lay down clear ground rules about what sort of talk is acceptable, by modelling appropriate behaviour. Group talk concerned with achieving a co-operative solution is valuable, so too are constructive suggestions from another student.

The seating placement of second language students needs to be approached with care. There are both advantages and disadvantages in seating together children who speak the same language. If children sit together, they may benefit from being able to negotiate meaning in English through their own language. However, this benefit may be offset if the children create their own world and remain outside the mainstream of class life. Frequently too, one of the children is less confident than the other. In that case, the confident child tends to act as the spokesperson in English for both children. Naturally, parents and teacher are concerned to change this situation without depriving both children of a supportive friendship. An effective strategy is to seat such children separately for part of the day but occasionally to allow them time together in other groupings.

The First Days — Easing a Child's Entry

The teacher's role

A friendly face and positive body language carry the message that the new student is welcome. The reception, on the first meeting, of new second language children and their parents, sets the tone for their relationship with the teacher and the school. If parents feel assured that their child is in kindly and competent hands, the adjustment process for both parents and children is likely to be less painful.

During the early days, the child is introduced to the basic pattern of life in the class, information that will certainly need to be reinforced on later occasions. This is also the time to acquaint the new child with the students who will offer special support during the first weeks. It is unwise, however, to single out the child for too much overpowering attention; in many cultures children are not accustomed to an over-familiar relationship with teachers.

Classroom support — providing a 'buddy'

It is the practice in some schools to assign an English-speaking 'buddy' for each new second language child. The buddy acts as the new student's social guide and is responsible for ensuring that the child gets to class on time, knows where to go for lunch and is watched over during outdoor play. Among older children, this can be a successful strategy, providing, of course, that the buddy has volunteered to play this role.

Among younger children it is probably more suitable if the responsibility for helping the new second language child is shared among two or three students carefully monitored by the teacher. It is helpful during the early days in school, if one of these students speaks the same language as the new child.

Establishing routines

Routines and regular patterns in the school day provide all children with a feeling of security. For second language children, it is even more helpful to establish procedures and routines that are consistent. It gives a sense of knowing what is expected if, for instance, every day at recess time, they take their snack from their lockers, line up quietly and go out of school the same way. It is as helpful for older children to know that the day's lesson schedule and homework are always written in the same place on the blackboard. Storing classroom supplies, students' work and printed resources such as dictionaries, consistently in the same places also gives a feeling of control and security.

There is an important point to be made here relating to new second language learners in a classroom. It is a helpful strategy if the teacher consciously uses the same phrases and vocabulary in association with regular activities. The repetitive use of language related to concrete circumstances supplies second language children with effective access to meaning.

Textbox 4.1 Effective communication with new second language children — a checklist

- Speak clearly and slowly, but don't distort punctuation, e.g. continue to use I'm, he's, etc., rather than I am or he is.
- Do not speak more loudly than is natural.
- Use short simple sentences.
- Rephrase your sentence if the student does not understand the first time.
- Emphasise the nouns and verbs, which carry the main meaning.
- Repeat useful phrases often, e.g. raise your hand, start at the top of the page, time to clear up, etc.
- Use gestures to get your meaning across.
- Find time to address second language students directly.
- Give students time to understand a question, to think out the answer and to formulate the reply in English.
- Use consistent phraseology and vocabulary in the first weeks.
- Use concrete objects to illustrate your meaning.
- Use drawings.
- Put up a seating plan of the class with photographs and names.

With older students especially:

- Display a poster with basic sentences on it, e.g. May I go to the toilet? How do you spell...?
- Always start with a clean board rather than clearing a small space; if you write in the middle of a jumble of words it is difficult for students to pick out the message.
- Write clearly on the board or overhead projector; some students are used to reading only print, other are used to cursive handwriting.
- Give second language children enough time to copy off the board.
- Do not give homework that necessitates an advanced understanding of written English; neither parents nor students may be able to cope.
- Do not expect second language students to take the initiative in moving on to the next task; they tend to wait for the teacher to direct them.
- Do not overpraise or single out beginners; they may find this embarrassing.
- Rephrase other children's questions and answers in simpler English if necessary.

Early Language Learning

Survival English

Survival English is the language that non-English-speaking students need to acquire rapidly in order to cope practically and socially in school. First, they need to be able to ask for the toilet. Next, they need to acquire essential school vocabulary, followed by the ability to give information about themselves and to ask simple questions. From this base children acquire general social language through play, informal class times and co-operative work in the classroom.

The teacher contributes to the rapid acquisition of this type of language by consistently using the same structures and vocabulary in association with happenings in the school day. The students should be encouraged to move round the classroom to point to what they need. For older children a labelled plan of the school building is helpful. Second language children in the classroom and playground are surrounded by real examples of language in use and pressing reasons for learning to communicate. Many students quickly become adept at using appropriate classroom and social English. It is common to hear after a very few days new students using short English phrases to greet friends or to establish turn taking in a game.

It is easy to confuse this type of early spoken fluency with a real grasp of spoken and written structure. Teachers themselves need to bear this in mind when making their initial assessments of second language children. It is wise to keep parents informed about the normal development of second language learning for children in immersion situations. It is important that they understand the difference between this early super-ficial fluency and the advanced skills needed for success in the main-stream academic programme. It reduces the pressure on children and teachers if parents have a realistic understanding of the timescale involved in becoming a balanced bilingual.

Comprehensible input

Comprehensible input is the level of language, which is just beyond what students can produce themselves. It is generally held that children learn best if they are addressed at a comprehensible level about subjects that relate to their own interests. This is what happens between children and adults during the learning of the first language. Children tune-out conversation about matters that are not of interest to them and contain too many language items which are unfamiliar.

A similar process occurs with beginning learners of a second language if they are placed in an unmoderated language environment. Learners at this stage, for instance, gain little from watching standard television programmes or from listening to radio broadcasts. The level of language is so far beyond their own functioning that they are prevented from gaining meaning. All language learners will recognise the feeling of being overwhelmed by a flow of unknown words. On the other hand, they can make sense of language that relates to a familiar topic, contains a high number of known words and relatively few unfamiliar words, and is couched in short phrases with clear pronunciation.

Most teachers of second language children soon become expert in gauging the level of language which is comprehensible to a student. Well-tuned input at the correct level will enable the student to gain the meaning of unfamiliar words from the context of known language. Such strategies as repeating important phrases and emphasising key words are useful. Speaking clearly and slowly is also appropriate providing that this does not distort the natural intonation of the sentence. The process of communication is aided if the teacher illustrates the overall meaning by using concrete objects and gesture.

Creating a risk-taking environment

Children learn a new language best in an environment where they feel able to test out new patterns of spoken and written language without fear of ridicule or over-correction. Thus, teachers can help their students to learn most effectively by creating a **risk-taking** classroom.

Such a classroom is created by a combination of the right sort of social atmosphere and the teaching strategies chosen by the teacher. It is the aim of the latest language teaching methodology to construct opportunities for children to test out their use of language in a situation where there is a real need to communicate. It is ideal if second language children are involved in practical tasks together with other children in a context where simple communication is low risk and natural. Learners in this situation unconsciously test out the effectiveness of their contribution. Depending on whether their first attempts appear to have the desired effect, they change or expand their later efforts.

Second language students engage in this trial and error approach if the classroom is a positive environment where all students are encouraged to make suggestions and contributions, knowing that the teacher values their input.

One factor which affects the students' confidence and trust in the teacher is the over-use of correction. It might seem natural and helpful to point out mistakes of grammar, pronunciation and vocabulary. However, this is not what happens when very young children learn their first language. Providing the meaning is clear, adults do not correct the surface detail of their speech. In most homes, children are rewarded by the effectiveness of their communication. They move on to try out new patterns of speech. If every tiny slip is corrected, children may not feel able to engage in the trial and error process which is at the heart of acquiring a language.

Thus, in the early days of language learning the teacher's most useful contribution is to provide children with a wide range of opportunities to practise their English. They should confine their interventions to rephrasing incomprehensible speech. Later, as children become more confident speakers it may be appropriate to point out quietly how their meaning could be better understood. This remains an area where teachers need to act with sensitivity. Some children are more able to accept and act on suggestions; others feel cast down and discouraged from making further efforts.

Differences in Learning and Cognitive Styles

Most teachers are familiar with the concept of differences in learning styles. Certainly, this is a topic which figures frequently in the programmes of conferences and in-service sessions. Educators now accept that students process information in different ways. These variations in processing affect children's approaches to learning. Individual students learn most effectively when they are offered instructional material in ways which allow them to use their preferred learning styles.

Differences in learning styles are categorised in a number of ways in the professional literature. A distinction is generally made between learners who use analytic or global cognitive approaches. Learning styles are further described as visual, audio, tactile, kinaesthetic, print-based and so on. Besides these processing differences, other factors may affect an individual's capacity for learning. These include environmental circumstances such as the type of chair, degree of warmth and level of light; others are time of day, attitudes to learning and individual emotional and psychological characteristics. Learning style inventories exist which give a broad indication of an individual student's preferred learning style. Thus, a student may be described as being largely a convergent or divergent thinker or having a creative learning style.

In practice teachers generally respond to the presence of different learning styles by using a variety of teaching approaches. In presenting a new topic, they search for visual, audio and tactile material to supplement the printed page and the teacher's voice. The range of follow-up activities may include drama and role-play, artistic and craft elements, the creation of raps and songs as well as the customary writing and reading activities. Teachers offer children a further range of learning opportunities by varying the groupings within the classroom. Thus, children have the experience of working independently, with a partner or in small collaborative groups. If an individual child needs further help in grasping a concept many teachers build on their knowledge of her or his preferred learning style by reteaching the material using the most effective means of access for that child.

Second language children, however, present teachers with further challenges. The social norms of their culture and the methods of teaching and learning current in their home schools bring additional elements to the equation. These cultural expectations frequently seem to override individual learning style preferences. Experienced teachers in international schools quite soon become familiar with the apparent preferred modes of learning to be found among different groups of second language children within the school. Children from highly structured, teacher-centred systems are happier with a directed, sequential, writing-based approach. They rarely volunteer questions and seldom indicate if they need further help in understanding new material. Other cultures in which children are the focus of adult attention may produce learners who require individual explanation and encouragement from the teacher in order to settle to work.

This variety in learning experiences and styles can be testing for teachers. Common sense, however, dictates that teachers should view the presence of learning style differences as one of a number of factors on which to base instructional decisions. The use of a range of teaching strategies and the provision of varied learning opportunities should encompass the differences of most of the children. Nevertheless, in the early days of the school year, teachers should watch to see that new second language students are able to relate to the learning environment of the classroom. Occasionally new children have difficulty in making sense of the learning and teaching modes in international schools. It is a wise strategy, for instance, on occasion to give children from highly structured school environments the sort of sequenced, repetitive writing tasks with which they are familiar. These students can be introduced to a wider range of instructional approaches when they have made the initial adjustments.

A further point needs to be mentioned relating to second language students and preferred modes of learning. It sometimes becomes clear that individual children make better progress in learning English through interaction with one or other aspect of the language. Some children learn more rapidly through access to spoken English. They gain most through the opportunity to interact in conversation. With other students, it is apparent that they learn better from first seeing new language in a written form. These children progress more rapidly through practice in reading and writing. Others benefit more from the interaction between spoken and written language. This is an area where liaison between the classroom and ESL teacher can enable these preferences to be used to good effect.

Creating a Classroom That Reflects Cultural Diversity

One of the challenges for teachers in international schools is to create a classroom environment that acknowledges the diverse student population in a meaningful way. Most teachers wish to move beyond the practice of celebrating national festivals and recognising United Nations Day. They search for means to incorporate the cultural traditions and experiences of all the students in every aspect of classroom activity.

The visual appearance of the classroom can provide a concrete expression of the students' diverse backgrounds. Wall displays and exhibitions of children's work give teachers opportunities to make references to the history, geography and artistic heritage of students' cultures. Artefacts, photographs, and published material from sources other than Western publishing houses make connections in a concrete manner with the experiences of all the students.

The choice of books and other reading material in a classroom is central to providing a diverse experience. Myths, folk tales and children's stories from other cultures, in translation, provide a basis. Non-fiction texts such as dictionaries, encyclopaedias and guide books related to field trips provide support for older second language students' content work in English.

There is a place in the classrooms of younger children, for well-illustrated mother tongue fiction. The presence of such books affirms the existence of other languages and cultures, and gives students from those cultures a feeling of self-respect and pride. All the class can derive meaning from the illustrations, and the texts provide a basis for talk about how different cultures express meaning in writing.

The curriculum itself offers opportunities to draw on a variety of sources for materials and subject matter. It is usual for international school teachers to supplement textbooks by creating their own materials that incorporate a wide frame of reference. Social studies and science are two areas that offer opportunities for including illustrations, models and text from a variety of countries. (Parents of second language children are usually willing to help the teacher in finding appropriate and stimulating examples of illustrative material.)

Textbox 4.2 Drama as a means of celebrating diversity

A later textbox in Chapter 8 (see p. 196) describes a drama production in terms of its use for promoting language learning. Drama also offers opportunities for involving all students in a shared project, and, depending on the manner of production and choice of play, offers a unique opportunity to celebrate diversity in an international school.

First, teachers need to set aside traditional approaches to producing school plays. The classic formula of casting a word-based dramatic piece with the most articulate and talented student actors achieves only limited ends. Effective drama activities in international schools involve all the students and are constructed round flexible themes relating to many cultures. Such themes can be expressed through drama in a variety of ways. These include mime, dance, music, song, humour, acrobatics and special effects as well as speech. Many second language children have special skills in these areas.

Appropriate material exists which narrates the lives of mythical figures, tells global myths or encompasses environmental themes. All these subjects offer teachers the possibility of involving children in exciting movement, singing, dance and percussion activities. As described in the later textbox, some schools write their own broad outlines and create their own settings, costumes and props. The resulting benefits to all the children, but especially to second language children, take a number of forms. For some second language children, taking part in a drama production is the first time they feel completely at home in an international school. For others, the shared talk and focused activity enable them to make great strides forward in their learning of English. With others, the benefit may arise from an opportunity to shine before their classmates when they display an unsuspected expertise, perhaps related to their cultural traditions.

Some exciting and moving moments occur when second language children triumph in such productions. Hitherto quiet children find confidence in taking on another role and speak powerfully and clearly before a large audience. Demure Japanese girls surprise their peers with their expertise in playing the violin. Boys, who have shown their frustration in class at being unable to communicate in English, prove to be wonderful acrobats or players of percussion instruments. Teachers, parents and students from all parts of the international community participate in the preparation, management, clearing-up and final celebrations. Second language children who take part in positive experiences of this sort invariably emerge with enhanced confidence and self-respect.

The study of a social studies theme such as 'living in communities' might include a selection of books and media from a range of viewpoints, and involve artefacts and examples from all the students' countries. Such themes offer the opportunity for second language children to bring in relevant pictures, photos and objects that relate to their own experience.

Mathematics, science and environmental studies also offer possibilities for using a wider range of examples and illustrations than generally appear in published textbooks in English. Problem solving exercises and experiments can be designed to include diverse material and data. CD-ROM material and the Internet provide further means of deriving classroom material from a wide range of sources. The Internet has the advantage of providing access to material created at source by the tourist boards and other bodies of the countries themselves. This is a powerful means of bringing authentic material from other cultures into the classroom.

Art, music, sport and drama offer opportunities for incorporating a range of activities from diverse sources into the programme. Areas of artistic excellence in certain cultures, such as paper folding or mask making, can be readily integrated into many subject areas, as can the songs and instruments of students' countries. Parents may be expert in one of these creative fields, and willing to demonstrate their skill. Sport and physical activity need not be confined to the conventional team games and typical school pursuits. Classes in the martial arts and various types of dance offer children a range of new opportunities and demonstrate that other traditions are valued and respected in the school. Drama provides an opportunity for all these strands to be brought together in a stimulating and rewarding manner.

Language Topics

Transfer from the first language

Transfer is one term used to describe the impact of the student's first language on speech and writing in the second language. Transfer potentially affects such aspects of language as syntax (the structure of a language), vocabulary, spelling, pronunciation and intonation.

Teachers in international schools become familiar with the patterns of transfer of the major language groups in the school. The same mistakes and adaptations tend to recur in the spoken and written English of speakers of the same first language. They become adept at understanding what students are trying to say and write, and are able to explain to children the reasons for some of the persistent errors in their spoken and written English.

During the learning phase, the incidences of transfer that are likely to cause most frustration to students relate to pronunciation and intonation. Students may produce spoken English that is incomprehensible to their friends and teachers, not because of structural or vocabulary errors, but because pronunciation and intonation are far from native speaker norms.

Fortunately, very young learners are in a strong position regarding their eventual competence in these areas. As was mentioned on p. 47, young children learning a second language in positive circumstances are likely to acquire native-speaker proficiency in pronunciation and intonation.

Transfer is a normal feature of language learning. As students' general competence increases, so the frequency of errors due to transfer tends to decrease.

Intonation patterns

The term **intonation** is used by linguists to describe the tune of a language. Intonation conveys a good deal of information to the listener. It indicates the speaker's mood, it marks emphasis and it announces that the speaker is asking a question, exclaiming, being sarcastic and so on. Each language has typical tunes and linguists show intonation patterns by drawing directional lines above groups of words in a piece of speech. After a time in an international school, many teachers become expert at recognising intonation patterns from other languages in the spoken English of second language students.

Because intonation carries so much of the meaning in spoken English, it is important that second language students quickly learn the tunes of English. Children who find this difficult are often disappointed that their efforts to communicate, even when they use correct forms, are not understood. Teachers should take care that they themselves do not distort the typical patterns of spoken English by speaking in an artificial manner to second language children. The classic means for giving children practice in intonation are songs, rhymes and repetitive stories. Another effective method is to provide students with opportunities for meaningful conversation with first language speakers, about topics of real interest.

Appropriate language for different uses

Native speakers of a language make conscious and unconscious adjustments to the way they use English in different situations. One example is the formal phraseology that most young people use with someone who is obviously senior in status and age. They instinctively omit slang and bad language and unconsciously employ certain language features that express their respect for the other person. The same variation can be seen in forms of writing. A holiday postcard is written in a different style from a job application.

It is a typical feature of language learning that students inadvertently use inappropriate language. Very young children may not yet have reached the stage of development in their first language when they instinctively moderate their language to take account of circumstances. With older students, their use of inappropriate language generally arises from their lack of knowledge of English forms rather than from being unaware. It is a fact that many second language students come from cultures where differences of age and status are more generally acknowledged than in English-speaking countries. Students from these backgrounds will have instinctively learnt to vary their language appropriately. In some languages, Japanese, for example, profound differences in syntax and vocabulary indicate the degree of respect owed by the speaker to the person being addressed.

While they are learners, it is quite common for students to use the informal English of the playground in the formal setting of the classroom, or to sound over-familiar in their greetings to senior figures in the school. One means of influencing this behaviour is tactfully to rephrase the student's speech in a more appropriate form. However, in the case of both young and older children, teachers will find that the use of appropriate forms goes hand-in-hand with an overall development of language competence.

Varieties of English

The term **variety of English** describes, for example, the use of English in areas such as Singapore, the Caribbean, the Indian sub-continent and Africa, where English is used, partly or wholly, as a second common language for purposes of administration, business and daily life. (Things are changing: Many countries are moving towards replacing this use of English by another, indigenous official language.) In many cases, local languages and creoles continue to flourish alongside a distinct variety of English. A language variety develops its own characteristics as well as preserving certain structures, vocabulary and idiom from earlier stages in its development.

These varieties of English are now established as varieties in their own right. Such varieties include Indian English, Caribbean English and Singaporean English. They are a legitimate part of a student's language repertoire, and teachers who are speakers of other forms of English need to be sensitive in how they comment on differences of usage. They need to be especially careful during parent/teacher conferences not to imply that these varieties are inferior.

Eventually these speakers of a variety of English, like other students in international schools, tend to adopt the social English of the school while maintaining the use of their own variety at home. Writing in English presents fewer difficulties of this sort. Teachers can assume that parents are happy for their children to learn to read and write the English of the school.

After the First Few Weeks

Phases in language acquisition

Alongside factors that relate to a child's personal history, there exist typical phases in acquiring a language which may affect many students. A major cause of worry and misunderstanding to both teachers and parents is a lengthy continuation of the **silent period**. Many language learners need time before they are prepared to speak in the new language, however, with some children, this silent period may last for weeks or months. Occasionally students may not speak in English for most of a school year.

Naturally, parents are both frightened and frustrated when this happens. They feel guilt at having moved the child into a new language environment, and worry that she or he may be permanently damaged psychologically or lose out in the educational process. In the case of a prolonged silent phase, it is wise for new teachers to talk to a counsellor or to an experienced colleague, who will, no doubt, have seen this pattern of behaviour before. A joint session with the counsellor and the parents to discuss the child's history, to decide on useful strategies and to give reassurance, may also be helpful. It is important for both teachers and parents to try to remain relaxed with the child and not to make the lack of speech an issue.

Language learning progresses by fits and starts. Children may make rapid progress in the early stages and then, for no apparent reason, appear to stand still for a time. This phase is known as a **language plateau**, and may be connected with a build-up of fatigue, or with the need for a period of consolidation in the new language. There are many variations in speed of learning a new language.

Several weeks of little or no progress are common in the period before a major school holiday when children are tiring. Students become discouraged and parents worry that their children will lose touch with English during the holiday and fall back further. Frequently the reverse is true. During a holiday children appear to go through a process of internal consolidation with regard to their English. They return to school refreshed and after a few days of adjustment are able to move forward. The speed of acquisition then accelerates until the next period of consolidation and refreshment is needed.

What the teacher needs to know is how and when to intervene if there appears to be a long period of little progress. The lack of progress may be due to one of the recognised causes as suggested in the paragraphs above. The teacher would be wise to consider other possibilities, however, such as health factors, hearing problems, an extreme teaching and learning style mismatch or, perhaps, the presence of a specific learning difficulty. (See below, pp. 86–9.)

Patterns of behaviour

New second language students can act in surprising ways in the classroom. It may be helpful to know that these negative behaviour patterns are generally short-lived, and tend to disappear as students adjust to the new circumstances and become involved in the full life of the class.

For many children, their frustration and isolation result in a 'short fuse'. Times of physical contact with other students, such as lining-up or sitting closely, may erupt into pushing and kicking. Extrovert children, finding it impossible to sit still and listen quietly, will fiddle with pencils or disturb their neighbours. Wise teachers plan ways of avoiding the opportunities for this type of disruptive behaviour. It is possible, for instance, to give such students an assignment or practical task to carry out during times when the level of language is too advanced. This is an occasion when work at the computer may give the child a sensation of control and achievement. It is also a helpful strategy, in the case of restless early learners, to change the activity quite frequently so that a build-up of tension does not occur.

Other children, of a more introverted temperament, may become withdrawn and adopt the role of onlooker to an extreme extent. It is typical of this type of child that they keep their stationery items very near, often arranging them with great care in a certain order on their desks. They interact very little with other students. They withdraw into a smaller world where there is some possibility of control. The teacher needs to be sensitive in these cases, perhaps introducing the presence of another quiet child and involving both students in a practical task. Clear and consistent classroom routines are essential for this type of student, since they provide a framework to the school day that enables the student to relax and to gain confidence.

There are as many different sorts of behaviour in this situation as there are children. Certain students, for example, talk rapidly in their own language both to the teacher and their classmates, although it is obvious that they are not understood. Other children react by becoming sullen and rude. Such anti-social behaviour, unfortunately, has the sad effect of separating the student further from normal social contact, and of lengthening the time it takes to build friendships. There are yet other children who shout out or yell in class in their own language or English, in order, it seems, to try to break through the communication barrier.

In talking to parents about the behaviour of their children, teachers need to tread very carefully. It is likely that troubled behaviour is the result of the child's reaction to the new language and the new school. It is unkind to worry parents unduly about something that will probably pass, by showing extreme concern at an early stage. It is necessary, however, to monitor the development of the child's behaviour carefully.

If the extreme behaviour continues for a lengthy period, action must be taken to find out the cause. Meetings with the parents and counsellor may reveal a long-term problem or a short-term family difficulty that might account for the child's extreme response to the new circumstances. (Interpretation should be arranged if lack of English prevents real communication.) Experienced counsellors are familiar with this type of adjustment phenomenon and will have helpful advice for parents and teacher. It is useful to consult with the student's other teachers. This allows the classroom teacher to gain a more balanced view of the student's behaviour in a variety of situations. Classroom teachers are often surprised and relieved to hear that a child behaves differently in the ESL classroom or in subjects such as music, art or PE where he or she can take part more fully.

Patterns of fatigue

New second language children tend to become tired. This is partly the normal fatigue of any child adjusting to a new set of circumstances and partly due to the stress of being isolated in a foreign language environment. Most travellers have experienced something similar. Fatigue sets in and the ability to cope with unfamiliar circumstances is reduced.

There is a pattern to be seen in this cycle of fatigue, which it is helpful for teachers to recognise and to make allowances for. With younger children, the end of the school day is frequently a time of irritability particularly if they have a long bus ride. For all children, in the early days at a new school, the weekend comes as a much-needed two days away from the barrage of new experiences. A similar pattern occurs in the lead up to a holiday. Before mid-term breaks and major holidays, many second language children are existing on a low energy plane with a consequent loss in receptive capacity.

Students with special needs

Some new second language students arrive in school with a file describing previously diagnosed special needs. Their parents are generally eager to discuss their child's history and to share their concerns with the classroom teacher. In other cases of suspected specific learning difficulty, this documentation is not available.

Occasionally parents choose not to provide the new school with a full history of their child's educational experiences. They hope that their child can make a fresh start, free from the labels of 'difficult student' or 'special needs child'. Teachers who suspect the presence of specific learning difficulties may have a challenging task in persuading parents that action needs to be taken in their child's interest. This is a further case when an existing good relationship with parents allows teachers to talk openly to parents about sensitive areas.

In the case of struggling students from certain school systems in, for example, Africa, the Indian sub-continent and East Asia, the child's school record is unlikely to contain references to special needs. It is not customary in most schools in these systems to offer testing facilities or an adapted programme. The large numbers of children in a class and the teaching methods used in these systems do not, perhaps, allow the individual learning profiles of each child to be assessed. Failure in class tends to be ascribed to lack of hard work. This involves parents and students in loss of face and usually leads to unwillingness on their part to disclose a previous lack of progress to the new teacher.

Early indications of the presence of potential difficulties in a second language student who writes in Roman script are similar to those in first language speakers of English. Lack of focus, reluctance to settle to work, unformed handwriting and obvious spelling difficulties from an early stage are pointers. With new students who use other scripts or writing systems, these indications may not be available. In the case of young L2 children, a significant discrepancy between the level of a child's oral language and her or his progress in learning to read is a pointer to potential difficulties. Running records of a child's reading, even at a very early stage in a child's development, may indicate an area that needs special attention. It is vital, however, that teachers of second language students take into account the nature of some children's response to the new environment. It is possible that certain types of persistent behaviour are the result of continuing problems of adjustment.

The testing of second language children with suspected learning difficulties presents problems. Tests may not be available in the child's first language, and there may be no speaker of the child's language in the school to administer the tests if they are available. (In some cities, large expatriate groups offer testing services in their own languages.) Tests in English may contain cultural bias that limits their validity when used with

Textbox 4.3 Special needs students in an international school classroom

Suspected learning difficulties in second language learners present a challenge to classroom teachers in international schools. The variations in educational, linguistic and family histories combine to make that child's experience unique. This variation complicates the process of arriving at the assessment of a second language child. Besides the obvious factor that testing may be hindered by lack of English, it is seldom clear to what extent progress is affected by difficulties associated with learning a new language and with problems of adjustment at home and at school. Often, it is a combination of circumstances that affect a child's capacity to learn in the new environment.

Whatever the causes in the case of a particular child, teachers in international schools invariably cite their inability to meet the needs of second language children with learning difficulties, as the factor that causes the greatest stress in their professional lives. If children also exhibit behavioural disturbances then teachers are placed under a great strain in answering the needs of these children within the classroom. The expectations of families who send their children to international schools are high and it is teachers who experience the pressure of satisfying these expectations. It falls to them to cater for needy children while delivering a challenging programme to a diverse class.

Early diagnosis and adequate professional support are vital elements in catering for second language children with special needs. At the present time, however, there seem few consistent guidelines based on sound evidence to guide teachers and special needs professionals in making an early diagnosis of learning difficulties among mobile second language students with a minimal level of English. The range of variables is so great. Factors such as emotional and educational disruption caused by frequent moves, the pattern of previous language exposure and the introduction of English mean that a wholly satisfactory diagnosis is rarely achieved. Professionals working in international schools would welcome expert guidance in arriving at a better understanding of this challenging issue.

second language children. For practical reasons, testing is usually delayed until the child speaks sufficient English to participate.

In all cases, the classroom teacher and other professionals should consult with the parents. The student should be observed in a variety of classroom situations in order to collect evidence of her or his learning behaviour. Consultation between the parents and all the teachers who work with a student should continue on a regular basis in order to monitor the child's development and, eventually, to provide a consistent programme of support both in and out of the classroom.

Cases where second language students make only slow or erratic progress in learning English present a further assessment challenge to classroom teachers. Reading, writing and spelling are the areas that customarily cause difficulty. When factors such as hearing limitations, inappropriate teaching strategies and specific learning difficulties have been taken into account, a student may remain a slow and ineffective learner. In these instances, it is possible that less temporary difficulties are the basis of the student's failure to flourish. Working in their first language and in a stable location, students are frequently able to compensate effectively for slight learning difficulties. The move to the new school and the new language places a strain on the child and results in the accentuation of slight difficulties. The need to learn a second language and the disruption of a move are likely also to have a significant effect on some children (for example, with certain personality traits, and less than average language aptitude). Arriving at the reasons behind a second language student's learning difficulties is a recurring challenge to teachers in international schools.

The able second language student

The presence of able second language students, used to performing well in their home schools, calls for awareness from teachers. The circumstance of being placed in a language environment where they cannot succeed as they did previously, may be a cause of frustration and anxiety. Students in the upper grades of the elementary school experience these feelings of frustration to a greater extent. Their peers in the mainstream programme move on regardless of their own struggles with English. Able second language children feel that they are continually falling further behind in the race to catch up.

A further potential cause of a marked drop in self-esteem is the issue of grading or marking. Most schools have a policy of deferring the formal grading of new second language students' work until it can be assessed on similar criteria to competent English speakers. There is, however, a period when able second language children are likely to gain lower grades than they were accustomed to receive in their home systems. They, and their parents, frequently have difficulty in coming to terms with this circumstance.

These feelings are accentuated in some subject areas. Students from East Asia, for instance, generally arrive in an international school with a high degree of competence in mathematics. They find the computational exercises in an international school to be within their grasp. They quickly become aware, however, that problems couched in words are beyond their reach until their English is more advanced. For practical reasons schools who customarily group students by ability for mathematics frequently place second language students in classes designed for less strong students. Able second language mathematicians quickly perceive that their peers are less able than themselves and suffer varying degrees of frustration and shame.

This outcome can be remedied if the system is flexible enough to allow students to move into a more appropriate group once they have gained confidence and some skill in coping with the language of mathematics. The most effective policy of all is to offer language support in mathematics for beginning second language students, either in a separate class or on a small group basis.

In the academic subjects of the curriculum, that involve a high use of language, able students may experience a similar feeling of frustration. Ideally teachers cater for second language students' needs by using appropriate teaching strategies and adapted materials. Nevertheless, some able students are acutely aware of these concessions to their lack of English. They fret continually until they are able to do the same work as competent English speakers.

Summary

The physical and emotional environment of the classroom has a positive contribution to make to second language children's language learning. During the first weeks of school second language students must acquire survival English. This process is fostered by the consistent use of English structures and vocabulary to describe the routine procedures of the school day. Children's language learning is further promoted by providing an adequate input of comprehensible language and by creating a risk-taking classroom.

Further features contribute to second language children's integration and success in language learning. These include an awareness of individual learning style differences and the creation of a classroom where the diverse cultural and educational experiences of all the students are incorporated meaningfully into the instructional programme.

A knowledge of such language features as transfer, intonation, appropriate language usage and the varieties of English helps teachers to make sense of what they observe and to make sound instructional decisions for their second language students.

As children move through the first weeks and months in the new school, certain features related to their language learning may emerge. These include an extended silent period, erratic classroom behaviour, fatigue, the suspected presence of learning difficulty and significant frustration in able second language students.

Chapter 5
Day-to-Day Life in the Classroom — Management Issues

Introduction

The aim of this chapter is to help teachers to make better provision for second language students in the management of classroom life. The emphasis in discussing each topic is on the special aspects that relate to second language children.

The material falls broadly into two categories. The first includes areas where teachers need to be proactive in explaining school policy and classroom practice to second language students and their parents. Second language families new to international education arrive with expectations concerning school life current in their own cultures. In many cases, these expectations differ from practice in international schools. Teachers are able to build a sounder relationship with such families if they are aware of areas where they need to inform and explain. Sections relating to topics of this type include homework, grading policy, discipline and gender issues.

Other sections relate to the social, emotional and physical needs of second language students. It is hoped that teachers will benefit from an understanding of these factors and vary their classroom management decisions accordingly. Examples of such topics include free play, friendships, health matters and absence.

Placement of Students

Admissions offices and school administrators in international schools are frequently faced with a challenging task in deciding the appropriate year level and class for a new student. The difficulty arises out of the differences among school systems around the world and the variety of new children's previous educational experiences. The differences are accentuated in the case of second language students. At the beginning of the school year in September, new children frequently constitute up to a third of the class in an international school. Much of the teacher's time in the early days of the school year is related to settling these children and gaining an understanding of their previous educational experiences. Their presence also has a considerable impact on the teacher's choice of instructional strategies. Knowledge of what is involved in placing both former and new students in a class may help teachers to make more informed choices about classroom practice.

The policy in effective international schools is to place new second language children in the year level appropriate to their chronological age. This generally holds good regardless of the length of their previous educational experience or their proficiency in English. The social integration of children is felt to be of prime importance in achieving both academic success and happiness in school. There may be legitimate exceptions to this rule. Second language children whose entry into education was deferred for some reason, or who have experienced extreme dislocation in their schooling, may reasonably be placed in a class for children a little younger than themselves. This placement is held to be in their best interests since it allows them more time to make up missed aspects of the programme and to learn English. However, the child's physical size and level of emotional maturity need to be taken into account. These factors may make such a placement unsuitable.

A child's entry may be complicated by the challenge of placing a new student in a way that satisfies both school and parents. Misunderstandings arise when the naming systems used for classes in the new school and the child's former school do not coincide. Some national school systems, for instance, number their classes from an earlier starting point, with the result that children coming into an international school are placed in a class with the same name as the year they have just completed. The result may be that parents assume their children have been placed in a lower class. Even after explanatory meetings, these parents need continual reassurance from the classroom teacher that their children are not being held back

Second language children, whose home school systems do not start their school year in September, present another placement challenge. In Japan and Korea, for instance, the school year runs from April to March. Schools in the Southern Hemisphere, such as those in Papua New Guinea or Australia, start their school year in January. It follows, therefore, that international schools are sometimes faced in September with the need to find an appropriate placement for children who have already completed part of a school year. The outcome is rarely wholly satisfactory.

For second language students, it is usually the best option to place students in the year level that they have partially completed. Many parents welcome these few extra months at the same level. They recognise that it gives their children a chance to make progress in English without falling back too far in the mainstream programme. Other parents, frequently from countries with highly competitive examination systems, feel differently. They look ahead to their children's return to the home system when they must rejoin peers who will already have completed six months of a higher year level. Depending on the option that is chosen, the parents of these students watch carefully to ensure that their children's education is not held back by the placement.

Issues of placement become areas of concern to parents whose educational expectations lead them to assume that the programme at a year level is laid down and unalterable. The school needs to assure anxious parents that the teaching methodology and instructional programme in an international school take into account the varied educational histories of each student. Parents are rarely persuaded that this is the case unless they see concrete evidence that this is so. Teachers need to demonstrate by their assessment and instructional practices that they are varying the programme in ways that take account of each child's needs. Practical examples of variations in assignments and grouping strategies are valuable in persuading parents that their child is well placed.

A further placement factor has implications for teachers. Parents of new second language students quite frequently ask for their children to be placed in classes with friends of the same nationality who already attend the school. (Other parents request that their children be placed separately from children who speak their language.) The presence in a classroom of several children who speak the same language may cause difficulties to both teacher and students. There is a danger that the children who share a language will remain together as a group. This limits their integration and their access to English. It is generally preferable that each class at a year level contains a balanced group of children, taking into account languages, friendships, level of ability, and numbers of former and new students.

Student Names in International Schools

The names of second language students can be a potential cause of confusion for teachers as well as an area of interest. It is not unusual, for instance, for the same student's names to appear with different spellings and in different forms on school documents. Variations of this type usually arise because the spellings represent transliterations into Roman script from other writing systems, such as Arabic, Hebrew, Hindi or Japanese.

The composition of names also varies in different parts of the world. In countries in East Asia, such as China, Japan and Korea, the family name is written first and the child's personal name last. In many cases, the child has a short westernised name, which is used for most purposes, while the personal name is reserved for close family members or for use in national contexts.

It takes only a short time for teachers to become used to the naming systems among the nationality groups that comprise the student body of a school. Where there is a doubt about the correct form of a student's name, teachers should talk to the students themselves, or to the parents. They should find out how the name is customarily spelt in Roman script and how it is pronounced. It is not uncommon to hear student's names consistently mispronounced for the whole time they spend in a school. Students are reluctant in the early days to correct adults, and, later, feel awkward about pointing out the mistake.

Transport

All new students feel a degree of anxiety about getting to and from school. For second language students there is the added fear of being lost or forgotten without the means to make themselves understood in any language.

It is vital that on the first day of school, the teacher, the student and parents agree about how the child is to get home. Often during the first weeks, families stay in temporary accommodation. Teachers must be prepared for travel arrangements to change when the family moves to its permanent home. The school should keep on file telephone numbers and addresses for both office and home in case of difficulties. Teachers should also be aware that newly arrived parents sometimes lose their way to the new school or underestimate the time of the journey.

If new children are to take the bus without the company of older siblings, it is essential for teachers to see the child on to the bus and to make sure that the driver understands where the child is to be dropped off. Likewise, there should be no misunderstandings about the pick-up points. It is a traumatic experience for the student, parents and teacher if a child is stranded or appears to be lost. It should be made clear to parents that changes in travel arrangements should be communicated by means of a signed note. Parents who are not used to school bus systems frequently fail to understand the complexities of keeping track of children during the process.

Free Play

Times of free play in the playground and classroom may present difficulties to second language children. Socially confident children make contact with other students who speak their language or join in a game or activity with a wider group. This provides a natural structure for social interaction, which in turn leads to rapid language learning and the making of friends.

Less outgoing and confident second language students may become isolated during times of free play. It is common to see new non-speakers of English on the fringe of playground activity. Happily, it is the norm in many international schools for established children to include new children in play. In some schools, a 'buddy' or other support system tides children over the first difficult days (see p. 73). On occasion, it is helpful if teachers themselves initiate a playground activity to include isolated students.

In most cases, it is only a matter of time before new students become involved to the degree that suits them. It should be recognised that some children need times away from the need to speak English. There are, however, always certain children, both first and second language, who remain detached from mainstream play, and teachers need to monitor this circumstance carefully and intervene where appropriate.

Snacks and Lunchtime

Food and eating are areas where cultural differences may be quite marked. In most international schools, this is not an occasion for difficulty. Children accept without question that different students prefer different food. Problems arise if children are expected to eat something strange or in a manner that is foreign to them. Thus, teachers need to ensure that snacks brought into the class to be shared are generally recognisable and acceptable to all the students. They should not assume, either, that meals associated with festivals will be enjoyed by every child.

At lunchtime, most schools ensure that there is a choice of meal or that the option exists to bring food from home. Food provision becomes critical during residential field trips. Before such trips, it is vital that teachers make themselves aware of any religious or health requirements related to food.

Student Supplies

An area of concern for new parents and students is the provision of stationery and other school supplies. Teachers in international schools are unlikely to show anger or impatience about a lack of equipment. Both parents and students, however, are anxious until they know how to obtain what is necessary.

It is wise for the school and individual teachers to be specific about what they require. New students and parents will not have a common understanding of what is meant by, for example, 'a large notebook' or 'gym shoes'. (Notebooks are called by many names in international schools — jotters, exercise books, cahiers, files, folders etc. Gym shoes may be called trainers, tennis shoes, plimsols or pumps.) It should be made clear before the start of school, how parents are to obtain any uniform items such as PE clothing. The aim is to minimise the likelihood of anxiety and uncertainty for both students and parents.

Homework

Second language students come from national school systems where homework expectations may be different from an international school's published policy or the teacher's experience. Scandinavian children, for instance, have little homework at the elementary stage, while Japanese and Indian children are used to considerable quantities. Teachers should explain the school's homework policy to parents and students at the earliest opportunity, and make clear the expectations concerning second language students.

When setting homework for these students, it is wise to observe certain ground rules. Homework assignments that require students to tackle an unfamiliar topic present the child (and the parents) with too great a challenge. It is not appropriate to set work that involves extensive reading, too much new vocabulary, or the advanced language skills of problem solving.

Ideal homework for new second language students involves relatively simple repetitive tasks based on language and vocabulary that is familiar. The assignment itself should be clearly stated in writing and broken down into manageable parts. As the student's English improves, so the teacher can modify the content of homework accordingly.

Teachers should make clear to parents the length of time they expect second language children to spend on their homework. Both parents and students may feel that homework must be finished regardless of how long it takes. Some parents and students may feel anxious if an assignment is not completed; highly motivated students may feel a sense of failure.

Teachers should lay down guidelines relating to parental help with homework. This issue is involved with cultural expectations. Parents from countries such as Korea and Japan feel that it is their role to help with homework. Other parents leave the child to carry out assignments unaided. Teachers should make clear their expectations in speech and in writing. There are homework assignments where parental help is

Textbox 5.1 Homework expectations in South Korea

During my visit to South Korea, the topic of homework occurred frequently in conversations with adults and children about the Korean education system. Korean parents view educational success as the chief means of ensuring that their children have a successful and stable life. The need for stability and security is an important feature of Korean life and perhaps explains the unquestioning dedication to achieving economic growth and prosperity. The sense of insecurity exists because most adults over the age of 40 have a story to tell of privations and sacrifices made during the Korean War of the 1950s. These memories are kept alive by the ever-present threat of further aggression on the part of their neighbour, North Korea. The hard lives that many South Korean adults have endured until quite recently may explain their acceptance of the need for their children to study for long hours. They hope that the hours of study will be rewarded, eventually, by acceptance into the best universities and the possibility of well-paid and secure employment.

A short extract from a handbook entitled, 'Living in Korea', published by The American Chamber of Commerce in Korea, gives an account of Korean mothers' devotion to their children's academic success. These stories were repeated to me several times during conversations with Korean parents:

'Each parent deeply wants a university education for her or his children. Six years of elementary school lead to three years each of middle and high school. The school day is followed by long hours of homework to enable students to pass the rigorous university entrance examinations. So many hours of study are required that a Korean saying sums it up: Any high school student who sleeps five hours each night will never go to college; but if he averages only four, his chances are good. There are many families where the senior high school student's Mom will lie down on the senior's bed so that the student is not tempted to sleep before the appropriate time.'

The Korean press frequently runs stories relating to the issue of homework, particularly concerning elementary school students, where there is some perception that the long hours may be counter-productive. While in Seoul, I read in an English-language newspaper that the Korean Ministry of Education had mandated one 'bag-free' day each month for elementary school students. This 'bag-free' day would ensure that on at least one day a month, Korean children would be free from homework. However, life for young Korean students remains hard. I have frequently been told by yawning Korean children in my own classes that they have been studying until one or two in the morning. What is remarkable is the stoic acceptance and good humour that these students generally show. They are as committed as their parents to the idea that educational success offers a path to a secure and prosperous future.

valuable, and others where teachers will wish to find out what the child can do independently.

It is useful to establish some means of communication, where parents and teachers can comment on matters relating to homework. Many schools use a daily journal for this purpose. Such a journal allows parents to comment if homework seems too heavy or too light, or if the student is struggling with the content of the assignments. Teachers in turn can use the journal to make special requests and to respond to parents' comments. This journal is also a useful vehicle for writing short notes concerning the student's needs or for giving general information about classroom happenings.

Grading or Marking Policy

Teachers should explain the school's grading or marking policy to both students and parents at the first opportunity. (The term **grading** is used in American-style international schools to describe how an assignment, test or examination is rated; the term **marking** is used in many other schools. Both terms are also used to describe the process of picking out and correcting individual errors.) It is wise to give accurate information in both speech and writing concerning the school's expectations for second language students in this area. Grading is an issue that causes concern to both parents and students and it is in a teacher's best interests to remove any uncertainty about the school's practice.

Many schools put aside formal grading or marking for second language children until it is useful and appropriate. Teachers need to communicate the reasons for this decision. Parents and students may have expectations about correction and grading that differ from practice in most international schools. It is customary in some education systems, in Japan and Korea, for example, for the wrong answers to be given a check or tick mark. The right answers are circled in red. This relates particularly to mathematics. It is clearly necessary for teachers to explain the practice which prevails in international schools.

Other differences in expectation may cause confusion and even suspicion about a teacher's competence. It is the custom in many school systems for every mistake in a piece of work to be corrected. If this is left undone, parents may feel that the teacher is slack and that work is not being properly assessed. Teachers need to explain, for instance, that they may frequently limit their correction on a piece of work to a single type of language error. The work is then used for later explanations related to this item of language. (See pp. 103–4 for a fuller discussion of this area.)

Grading can be introduced gradually as the English language competence of second language students increases. In some areas, such as mathematics computation, it is reasonable to introduce grades at an earlier stage. It is helpful to explain to parents and students how the grade is calculated. In most international schools, a proportion of the grade is based on effort, with the rest being given for achievement. Many schools give quite high grades to average students in order to reflect effort and progress rather than actual achievement. It is vital for the school to explain this humanitarian rationale to parents, so that misunderstandings about a child's true capabilities do not arise. (See p. 23 for further discussion concerning differences in educational expectations.)

Discipline

Few school systems in the world outside the English-speaking countries have the same approach to discipline as is found in international schools. Children from the school systems of continental Europe, the Middle East, Asia and Africa are generally accustomed to a structured, rule-based approach to discipline. (Israel, due to its unique history, is an exception to general remarks about education systems in the Middle East.) Students and teachers understand what is expected of them and the sanctions for breaking the rules are laid down.

Students from these systems, accustomed to relatively severe sanctions, and perhaps, corporal punishment, may find the relaxed and friendly atmosphere of international schools difficult to comprehend. They are likely to be used to a more structured and hierarchical relationship between teachers, older students and young students. They will be unfamiliar with the notion of consideration for others as the basis for regulating behaviour. The acceptance of talk and movement within the classroom may be strange. They are unlikely to perceive the boundaries of courtesy and respect that underpin the informal and friendly relationship with teachers. New children may be surprised when a student receives only a verbal rebuke for late homework. (See pp. 25–7 for further discussion on students' expectations.)

Other children may find the environment of a large international school overwhelming. Parents and students from certain education systems, such as Scandinavia, may feel that the children's day is too structured. Schools in these systems tend to allow children a good deal of time to play and to make choices about what work they do in school. These parents and students may feel that teachers in international schools have expectations regarding work habits and behaviour that are unreasonably demanding.

It is important that teachers establish ground rules from the beginning

Textbox 5.2 Not stupid, but soft! — 6th graders' views on discipline in international schools

A class of second language boys aged between 11 and 12 years were eager to participate when I asked for their views on how they perceived discipline in an international school. The make-up of the group was typical of a pull-out ESL class — it comprised four Japanese, two Koreans and one student each from Chile, Morocco, Portugal and Turkey. The fact that the class consisted entirely of boys was unusual but probably led to a more open expression of opinion than if girls had been present.

All the boys in the class had been used to mainstream classes of 30 or more students. Classes of 22 students are usual for students of their age in international schools. The Korean boys had been used to classes of 50 or 60 students during their time in school, with ten classes at a grade level.

All the students saw the smaller classes as being a big factor in the social and organisational differences they found. In general, they felt that the informal relationship with the teacher derived from the intimacy allowed by the small class sizes and by the different arrangement of the desks in a classroom. All the boys had been used to sitting in rows of desks facing the teacher at the front of the room and only the Chilean and Portuguese boys were used to any sort of informal and friendly relationship with the teacher. The Korean boys had viewed their teachers as distant figures employed to deliver the set programme and with great power over their future prospects. The Japanese quartet described a somewhat different situation, one which agreed with my own perceptions during my visits to the local Japanese school in Brussels and to schools in Japan. Japanese children in school are expected to concentrate and to study hard, but the relationship with their teacher did not seem to me to be unduly distant or threatening. There is a lot of laughter and the usual sorts of jostling and play in the corridors.

The Turkish boy's experience in his previous school was the most different. He had been in a class of 40 boys and the discipline had been based, as I understood it, on a system of threats and corporal punishment. Children who failed to give work in on time were beaten after the second offence. The Korean boys, too, accepted corporal punishment as a natural way of controlling large numbers of students.

Their view of the disciplinary code in the new school was interesting. They all agreed that when they first came there had appeared to be no system of keeping order at all. However, each of them had been so taken up with the struggle to survive in the new language environment that they felt they had made little real contact with other students for some weeks. When they emerged from the initial state of shock, they began to realise that they were expected to keep themselves on task and that certain expectations with regard to other students were in place. They all felt that students were polite to each other and that there was no bullying of the overt physical sort. When students were late to class, failed to deliver homework on time or were unpleasant to other children, the teacher took them on one side and talked to them. All the boys felt that more

Textbox 5.2 (*cont.*)

laughter, horseplay and talking in class were allowed in the international school than in their previous schools. Some of them would have preferred a more orderly approach in classrooms. When I asked whether they thought we were stupid to imagine that behaviour between students can be based on a consideration for others, one of the boys replied: 'No, not stupid, but soft.'

of the school year so that expectations concerning discipline are clearly understood. These rules should be easily explained and enforced, as well as being transparently fair. They should exemplify the school's philosophy concerning respect for others. If the school has a system of sanctions in place, they should be made clear also. A framework of this type makes new children feel more secure. They know how other children are expected to behave and what they must do themselves in order to fit in.

Some teachers find that class meetings supply a useful forum for arriving at a mutual understanding of acceptable behaviour. For obvious reasons, an oral interchange of this sort is not an effective way of communicating with second language children in the early stages of learning English. These students may feel shy about speaking out in a group and lack the language to discuss abstract concepts. It is likely that teachers will have to talk directly to second language speakers in any discussion of this type.

Teachers should, however, retain the freedom to treat individual cases where second language children are involved in disorderly behaviour with flexibility and tact. New second language children who behave in unconventional ways are frequently exhibiting symptoms of stress. This is often the case when punching and kicking are involved. If it is necessary to be severe, teachers should always talk to students away from other children and show understanding and a degree of sympathy when explaining that the behaviour is unacceptable. It is important to insist on orderly behaviour, however, in order to confirm the existence of a basic structure and for other children's peace of mind.

Dress

Dress is an area where difference is an issue for second language children at the upper year levels of elementary schools. Among all pre-adolescent children there is liable to be an element of competition about clothing and any variation from the dress of the mainstream group may result in teasing and even exclusion. Despite the generally tolerant climate that exists in international schools dress can be the cause of pain to second language children. The difficulty is acute for children who desire to be part of the mainstream. Certain children rapidly adapt their clothing so that their dress conforms to the accepted norm of the school. Other children continue to wear their usual school wear, often more formal than is customary in many international schools, and occasionally their national dress. These children have made the conscious or unconscious decision to make friends with one or two children only, often second language speakers like themselves.

Muslim girls who are accustomed to covering their hair are to be found in many schools. Unlike many national schools, this is not generally a sensitive issue in international schools. Usually the school is situated in a location where other conservative Muslim families send their children to school. In these circumstances, the wearing of a head covering is considered unremarkable. In other schools, conservative Muslim girls generally group together and lead their own social life. They are accepting of their family traditions, and other children are generally respectful of their beliefs and customs.

Further occasions when second language children may be made to feel awkward are at times when a particular style of dress is customarily worn. The mainstream social group of the class has ready access to knowledge about what is expected at graduations, at musical presentations or at parties. Teachers should make explicit, verbally and in writing, what is the appropriate dress for a special occasion. Most parents are sensitive to this issue and prefer their children to be dressed similarly to their classmates.

Friendships

In writing about problems of adjustment among second language students, it is possible to give the impression that the process is invariably painful. Each person who experiences changes of location and language suffers times of frustrations and even misery. Fortunately, there are circumstances which alter the balance and turn the new experience into a manageable challenge. Making a friend or joining a wider friendship group is a key factor of this sort.

Among second language children, making friends seems to mark a watershed in the process of adjustment. The fact of being open to friendship signifies with some children an acceptance of the situation in which they have been placed. The presence of an ally diminishes the feelings of isolation and gives second language students a certain social standing in the eyes of their peers. It is remarkable how children who do not share each other's languages are able to bridge the verbal divide.

Generally, friendships of this type lead to the rapid acquisition of survival English.

Cases of friendship between children who speak the same language occasionally cause anxiety to their parents. They are worried that the friendship may become exclusive and limit each child's progress in English. This is a circumstance that can be managed, however. Teachers can ensure that children have a wide exposure to English by varying the grouping arrangements in the classroom. Children are free to develop friendships with whom they choose during unstructured classroom times and play.

Health

Children who move to a new school in a new location tend to suffer more illness than previously. This may be due to the fatigue and stress of adjustment, or perhaps to new strains of microbes and a different climate. For whatever reason, some second language children are absent often, which has the effect of limiting their learning and of slowing down their social integration. Undoubtedly for some children the move from a warm dry climate to a cold and damp one, for instance, may trigger bouts of asthma or persistent colds and sore throats. Similarly, a polluted atmosphere or the need to live constantly in air-conditioning may change the pattern of a child's health. (See pp. 109–10, Absences.)

There are other symptoms, however, such as recurring stomach problems and headaches, which may stem from the child's insecurity and unease. Quite possibly, the parents may wish to talk about specific causes, and teachers should always listen with care and take action if necessary. However, it is sometimes the case that the parents themselves are involved in the cycle of cause and symptom. The spouse at home is lonely and anxious, and the children's state of mind and health assumes an overwhelming importance. New teachers may want to consult a school counsellor or an experienced colleague if they sense that continual absences are not due to specific illness.

Assessment and Evaluation

The topic of evaluation and assessment is closely linked with grading and written reports (See elsewhere in this chapter, particularly pp. 98–9 and pp. 106–8). Among second language families, there is a variety of expectations about how achievement is measured. Many second language students are used to taking timed tests and examinations in their home school systems. These examinations are given grades or marks based on the number of errors, and the results are posted or read out to the class in ranked order. Other students of the same age will never have taken a formal test or examination.

The parents of students in the first group will need reassurance that the lack of examinations and ranking does not imply carelessness about standards. Teachers need, therefore, to explain the school's rationale on assessment and evaluation at the first opportunity, whether that is at an open evening or parent-teacher conference. It may be wise to meet parents before these events are held. It is wise to be proactive in order to avoid possible difficulties later.

Teachers can calm anxious parents' fears by explaining how they monitor a child's progress. They should give concrete examples of their assessment practices and demonstrate how they record their observations. They should show how knowledge of a student's needs, related to the demands of the curriculum, drives future decisions about instruction. They should detail assessment practices that relate to second language students' status as language learners — that the teacher may choose to concentrate on content alone in marking children's work rather than on correcting every mistake of English, or that on other occasions they may prefer to select only language errors for correction and comment. Finally they should explain the grading system to parents, where appropriate, and indicate the extent to which effort and achievement are recognised in the final total.

Teachers may find that several conversations on this topic are needed before parents come to trust their judgement. Parents who do not recognise the methods of measurement used in their children's school naturally need explanation and concrete evidence before they are convinced that the school is committed to high standards. (See p. 23 for further comments related to this area.)

Second Language Students and Standardised Tests

Many international schools give sets of standardised tests to their students. Generally, this is to reassure parents of first language children that the international school is maintaining similar standards to those in their home country. (Standardised tests are series of objective tests normed on specific populations of students, frequently in one state or national system.) The chosen battery of tests tends to reflect the origin of the majority English-speaking group in the school. Schools commonly use for testing purposes, among others, the Iowa Tests of Basic Skills or assessment tasks related to the key stages of the English National Curriculum. In some schools these tests are given to all students. In others, parents are given the option of deciding whether their children should take them or not. Parents of second language students frequently come to the classroom or ESL teacher to ask for their advice.

In order to inform parents adequately it is vital that teachers (or the testing co-ordinator) take time to explain the rationale for these tests and how the results should be evaluated. Research shows (Collier, 1989) that it may take between five and seven years of learning English before second language students perform on standardised tests at the same level as first language children. It is likely that second language students will not achieve high scores for reasons that need to be explained in advance to parents and students.

Among these reasons is the likely presence of cultural bias in tests which derive from a single English-speaking source. Such tests tend to include references to situations which are familiar to children from English-speaking countries, but which are outside the experience of some second language children. There are frequent allusions to seaside holidays and visits to restaurants, two activities that may seldom figure in the lives of second language children. The method of indicating the answers is also likely to be unfamiliar. Tests, such as the IOWAs, require students to pick out one in a row of small oval-shaped disc to represent their choice of answer. For many children this extra symbolic step takes up time and adds a degree of confusion.

Second language children are also disadvantaged in the parts of the tests that require students to search for answers in short paragraphs made up of two or three sentences. Second language students gain meaning from written texts through a wide range of contextual clues that are absent in an isolated paragraph of this sort. They often perform below their own and the school's expectations in language tests. In mathematics tests involving computation alone, the difficulty is much less, and it may make good sense for second language children to take only these parts of the test battery.

It is essential to forewarn parents about the possibility of low scores, and to prevent students from seeing the scores unless it is appropriate. Teachers additionally need to assure second language parents that their child's move into the next year level is not dependent on the results of these tests. Parents from some school systems may assume that their children will be held back if they do not take the tests, or if they achieve only low scores.

The usefulness of standardised tests is an area for debate. Many administrators and teachers feel that standardised tests are of limited use in guiding instructional decisions, since they give little information regarding a student's ability to perform meaningful tasks in English. Scores from tests such as these reflect only a student's strengths and weaknesses in carrying out the tasks required by the tests. There exist other, less widely used standardised tests, such as the ERB (Educational Records Bureau) test, published by Educational Testing Service in the United States. This test measures students' ability to write an extended piece of English. A list of criteria sets out the expectations against which the test is scored. Tests of this type supply information about second language students' abilities that is more useful to teachers than the widely used batteries of standardised tests.

Parent Conferences and Written Reports

It is in the interests of the school and teachers, as well as of students and parents, that good communication is maintained between them. International schools customarily employ a range of methods to keep in contact with parents about all aspects of their children's lives in school. Reporting on children's academic and social development is given in writing and at scheduled conferences with parents. It is also the custom in international schools for parents to be able to arrange informal conferences with teachers at any time in the school year.

When talking and writing to second language parents, teachers should take care to make their meaning very clear. They should adopt a simple and jargon-free vocabulary and avoid complicated constructions. In the case of conversations with second language parents, teachers should be prepared to re-phrase their remarks so that the message is clearly understood.

At the first scheduled meeting with parents, teachers should explain the content and style of the programme and the school's policies in key areas such as grading, homework and assessment. This is an occasion for the teacher to inform parents of matters relating specifically to second language students. Such topics include the deferment of grades, the need for good communication between parents and teachers about homework, and a realistic timetable for reaching the desirable level of competence in English. It is good practice for teachers to supply a clearly worded written version of this information.

As mentioned in the sections above, the assessment practices found in international schools are unfamiliar to some second language parents. They are used to grades, examinations and class-rankings as means of measuring students' progress. Such parents will have their anxieties calmed if they are assured that teachers are effectively monitoring the progress of their child. Examples of children's work, its assessment and the consequent instructional decisions will make this task of explanation easier.

Other parents may feel that high expectations and the quantity of homework place their children under pressure. Teachers should show interest in these views and respond accordingly if the parents' remarks seem justified.

Several issues occur often in conversations with parents of second language children. The length of time in the ESL programme and the learning of a third language are areas of concern. These are topics where both classroom and ESL teachers need to be certain of giving identical opinions. It is helpful to underline the distinction between quickly acquired social fluency and the advanced skills needed for success in the academic programme. It is wise to be realistic about the length of time that most children need to achieve the necessary level of competence. Teachers should, however, assure parents that children are moved out of the ESL programme immediately they are ready to do so.

Placement of children in ability groups for such subjects as mathematics is a frequent cause of parental concern. Careful explanation is required when able children are placed in lower groups than their ability would normally warrant, because of their limited English. It should be a policy of the school that children in this position are moved to a more advanced group as soon as their level of English makes it appropriate. If, at any time, a child's placement is to be changed it is advisable to consult with parents and students beforehand in order to explain the rationale behind the move.

Teachers in international schools, tend in conversations with parents, to talk positively about a child and to emphasise achievements rather than dwell on limitations. It is vital, however, even if language presents a barrier, to make it clear to parents if there are actual or potential problems concerning their child. Most parents prefer to receive a concerned and courteous warning rather than to be faced later with a major difficulty about which they have heard nothing. It is always better to speak to parents face-to-face before they receive written reports about areas of difficulty.

Finally, it must be said, that interviews with second language parents may be challenging for teachers. It may be difficult to find a common language in which to communicate. Sometimes parents can understand English but are less confident about speaking. Under these circumstances, it is common for the teacher to be required to talk alone for most of the session. If communication is difficult it may be valuable to use an interpreter. (The appropriate embassy or company may be able to supply this type of help.) It may be possible for older siblings who speak good

English to assume this role. Sometimes both teacher and parents can converse more effectively in the host country language.

Other aspects may make parent and teacher meetings stressful. Parents' own problems of adjustment together with anxiety about their children's welfare in an unfamiliar school system sometimes lead to questions and opinions being expressed in a hostile manner. The roles of the parents themselves may have changed in the new location. It is common for the working partner to be the parent who can communicate effectively in English. This occurs most frequently in families from cultures where the mother's role is chiefly within the home. Consequently, the father carries out the communication at a conference while the mother sits in silence. In this situation, there tend to be anxious exchanges between mother and father in their own language as the mother tries to express her concerns. The body language of onlooking parents may indicate their frustration at being excluded from the possibility of real communication. Teachers in turn feel a sense of frustration at their inability to cross the language barrier.

All efforts to communicate are valuable. New second language parents feel a particular need to see that their children are spending their days with a kindly and encouraging teacher as well as making good academic progress. Sometimes it will become apparent that parents themselves are finding the adjustment process difficult. It is worthwhile, not only as professionals, but also as human beings, to take the time to listen and to share these experiences.

Social Occasions

Social occasions inside and outside the classroom are areas of potential difficulty for second language families. Such occasions are parent coffee mornings, festival days, end-of-term parties and fund-raising events. It would be easy to assume that these occasions offer untroubled opportunities for parents and children to get to know one another better in a relaxed atmosphere. In fact, the unstructured nature of informal social events may prove to be more problematic than the secure framework of the school day.

Asking second language parents to contribute food for class celebrations or snack-time may be a cause of uncertainty and concern for the families involved. Teachers should offer suggestions about what parents might bring since children are liable to refuse to eat anything unfamiliar. It is embarrassing to teacher, parents and children if such a contribution is rejected.

Textbox 5.3 Parties and pencil cases:

Social relations in a classroom have a great impact on the happiness of children. Difficulties in social matters have the potential to cause unease and even pain to all children and particularly to new second language students.

A sensitive issue is the holding of birthday parties. In anticipation of hurt feelings, most classroom teachers make it clear to parents that publicly issued invitations should include all the children. For some second language children, however, birthday parties present a social minefield; many cultures do not attach the importance to the celebration of birthdays that is normal in English-speaking countries. Parents and children may therefore be unacquainted with the expectations associated with these events.

It is likely, for instance, that when some second language children receive an invitation they fail to respond. Their parents may deliver them early or late and without an appropriate gift. They may not wear the party clothing which is expected among the children in that school. For some sensitive children, these failures to conform cause distress and a sense of isolation. Other social events customary among students in international schools similarly affect children who are unused to them. Sleepovers, shared meals, and visits to restaurants place some children in situations where they do not know what to expect. It is not the custom among many parents of second language children to arrange a programme of after-school activities and social visits.

It is interesting to observe the ways in which second language children cope with the perceived differences in social life. Some embrace the mainstream culture of the class in every detail. They cajole their parents into buying the latest fashion in pencil cases and classroom knick-knacks. They gradually replace their usual school clothing with similar items to those worn by the influential social group in the class. They learn what is expected in celebrating a birthday. Other children retain a strong aura of their own culture. They continue to wear their accustomed school clothing and remain within their cultural group outside school. In the face of these differences it is remarkable how most children in international schools achieve an acceptable degree of social integration. Teachers are largely responsible for creating the sort of tolerant, accepting social climate that allows this to happen.

Absences

In international schools, there is more absence from school among students from all backgrounds than would be considered normal in a national school. It is useful for teachers to understand the pattern of this non-attendance among second language students and the reasons for it.

Children beginning a new school year in international schools frequently arrive several days after the opening of school. Second language children often leave school one or two days early before a holiday break. They arrive at school several days late after a break. There tend to be high levels of absence on Mondays and Fridays when families take long weekends to go travelling or to visit relatives, as well as occasional absences for longer periods.

Absence from school does not imply that parents do not take their children's schooling seriously. Parents of new students may have no choice over travel arrangements to the new location. Other types of absence are taken for reasons which parents feel are justified. Among these reasons are the advantageous fare structures offered by airlines to travellers in less busy seasons. Opportunities for children to travel to interesting places, attendance at religious festivals and visits from relations are further reasons for planned absences. Longer periods of absence in home countries may be due to the illness of grandparents and other family members, or the necessity for children to spend some time in the home school system in order to keep in touch. (Certain school systems require students to sit and pass regular examinations in order to be allowed to move on to the next year level.)

Teachers sometimes feel a sense of frustration at this inconsistent attendance. They are legitimately concerned that unnecessary absence may slow down a child's acquisition of English and delay his or her ability to engage with the mainstream programme. A further cause for concern is the negative impact that irregular attendance is likely to have on the child's social integration.

Teachers in international schools learn to adopt a pragmatic attitude to this issue. The opportunity to spend time with visiting grandparents or cousins arguably contributes more to a child's well-being in a foreign posting than is lost by one or two days away from school. The same is true of time spent in travelling to new places with well-informed parents. Flexibility on the issue of absence is sometimes a teacher's most appropriate response. They should, however, constantly monitor and observe children who are frequently absent in case there are deep-seated factors behind the absence such as social unhappiness, academic difficulties, or possibly, school phobia. Teachers should intervene if they notice that a child is being placed at a disadvantage at school because of avoidable absence. Then it is reasonable to talk to parents and to point out the undesirable effects of inconsistent attendance. This message needs to be given tactfully. Communication on this topic will be more effective if a relationship of trust and goodwill already exists between parents and teacher.

Extra-curricular Activities

Extra-curricular activities such as after-school sport, drama clubs and craft and computer classes provide excellent means for both language learning and social integration. Such activities are generally of a practical, hands-on nature and provide the concrete circumstances that enable language learning to take place most successfully. They have the added advantage of allowing second language students to shine in areas such as sport or music, where English language competence is not necessary.

Extra-curricular activities are not the norm in many cultures, however, and some second language parents may view them as a diversion from homework, or as unnecessary. Transport may also prove a problem with sessions that take place after school. It is desirable, however, that the school makes it possible for all children to have access to extra-curricular activities. To overcome any difficulties, many international schools schedule a regular time once a week during the school day when clubs and activities take place. Other international schools offer a programme of sport, drama and other activities at the weekends, together with supervision and transport. In many cases, these weekend programmes involve the participation of parents. International schools, as mentioned in Chapter 1, frequently provide facilities for social and recreational activity among the local expatriate population.

Residential Field Trips

Residential field trips are a notable feature of many international schools. Children at the elementary school age are taken away for one or two days, or for as much as a week, in the company of teachers, to extend their knowledge of an historic area, to carry out a field study connected with science or to engage in a sport. These trips are usually the highlights of a child's time in an international school and remain a vivid memory.

Residential field trips may be times of stress for second language children due to homesickness, fatigue and even hunger. Teachers should monitor the behaviour of second language children and take time to speak to them in English at a comprehensible level. They should be especially aware of health, dietary and social issues, where they may need to intervene on the second language student's behalf.

During the time leading-up to a residential trip, many second language students experience a build-up of tension. This arises from a general feeling of apprehension, but also for specific reasons. International schools are generally careful to communicate fully about events such as residential field trips. They give out information in written form and commonly hold open meetings so that parents can ask questions. It may still be the case, after this process, that some second language parents and their children are uncertain about essential details of the arrangements. Teachers should be especially sensitive to the possibility of unease caused by such a lack of knowledge. It may be appropriate to arrange for an interpreter to clarify any issues of concern. It is essential that parents and students understand passport and visa stipulations, clothing and money needs, the envisaged pattern of the trip, sleeping and meal arrangements and provision in case of illness.

It is vital, also, for the school to gather information about individual dietary requirements and health issues. There needs to be a clearly understood system for informing parents about the safe progress of the trip. Nevertheless, despite everyone's best efforts, residential field trips are a potential time of stress. It is usually better if such trips are kept for the latter part of the school year so that friendships have been established and progress made in English. (See pp. 237–40.)

Textbox 5.4 Friendships and fatigue on field trips

My experience as a chaperone on extended field trips to Florence with 11- and 12-year-old children has left me with vivid impressions of the impact of such trips on second language students. Florence is a city that offers a variety of extraordinary experiences. Besides offering a living example of a renaissance city, it offers today's children the experience of exploring a city, in relative safety, on foot for several days. Even second language children in the early stages of learning English seem to gain from both the social and academic aspects of the visit. Each 6th grade graduation speech cites the Florence trip as the climax of the school year. Most second language students, however, experience occasional times of intense stress on even the most successful trips. This stress is related to living in close contact with their classmates in an English-speaking environment for 24 hours a day.

For all children the fact of leaving the known structure of home and school life may be a source of difficulty. For second language children the degree to which they are stepping into the unknown is greater. They worry in advance about sleeping arrangements, the kind of food they will be required to eat and whether they will be able to cope in English. However much teachers try to reassure them, they and their parents experience some degree of apprehension.

On the trip itself, two factors make significant contributions to second language children's enjoyment of the experience. One is the avoidance of overwhelming fatigue and the other is the presence of close friends. In the case of fatigue, it is essential for teachers to take a broad view of field trips. One church or museum left unseen will not alter students' lives. It is far more important to give children opportunities to shop, play and just hang out. In this way they can take time out from the barrage of new experiences and avoid becoming overtired. With a little imagination, teachers can give students unique and

Textbox 5.4 (*cont.*)

memorable experiences while achieving this end. In Florence, for example, we allow children time to kick a ball round the Piazza Santa Croce as Florentine children have done for centuries, and arrange carefully managed sorties into the Straw Market to buy souvenirs and presents.

The friendship factor is not so easy to manage. Travelling down in the train overnight, sharing a room and walking round the city are exciting and manageable experiences for second language students if these things happen in the company of a friend to whom they can talk. For lone speakers of a language, though, they may be overwhelming.

Teachers need to make arrangements that support second language students without allowing them to remain solely in the company of compatriots. In my experience, night-time is the critical period. At this times, second language children need to be able to share the experiences of the day, and to sleep in the company of someone they can converse with easily. For these reasons, second language students should share a room with a real friend. Children can be grouped in different ways during the day so that they have access to a wider group of students and to more English. With these arrangements in place, it remains essential for teachers to watch out for second language children at all times. Sometimes conversation in comprehensible English with an adult can prevent a small upset turning into a major problem.

Gender Issues

In a culturally diverse environment such as an international school, gender issues need to be handled with care. In a national school system, there is often a general understanding of what is the norm for the relations between boys and girls and men and women. The majority view in that society usually prevails. In some countries the rights of boys and girls are established and underpinned by equal rights legislation.

In an international school, teachers need to be sensitive in talking to parents and children about matters of behaviour and school life that challenge the traditional values of their culture and religion. Parents who opt to place their children in international schools are, presumably, prepared for some differences of custom. Teachers need to employ tact at all times, however. It is essential to avoid causing difficulties within a student's family or to appear to speak slightingly of other cultural norms.

It is helpful to divide issues concerning gender into two groups: those where it seems reasonable for both boys and girls to adapt to the culture of the school, and those where an element of choice should be offered to the families concerned.

The issue of classroom behaviour falls in the first group. There exists well-established evidence to show that boys tend to take up more teacher time than girls. In an international school, this tendency may be marked among boys from certain cultures who are accustomed to occupying the prime position in the family. The teacher, in this case, will need to establish firm ground rules and routines to ensure that girls receive an equal amount of attention.

It is the assumption in some cultures that boys and girls should conduct themselves differently. Boys are expected to ask and answer questions, to take a leading role, and to be more rowdy and physical in their play. Girls, on the other hand, are expected to take a somewhat more passive role, to sit in relative silence, and to move with grace and modesty. The teacher's task is to encourage all children to gain the most from their experience in school by tactfully encouraging boys to modify their behaviour and girls, where necessary, to be more outgoing.

Most international schools feel it reasonable for girls and boys to be taught by men or women. In some cultures, in observant Muslim countries for example, young children and adolescent girls are not taught by men, and women rarely teach boys above the age of seven. Neither are older boys and girls taught together. It is remarkable, however, to what extent children adapt to living in two worlds simultaneously. In school, girls and boys mix together, and girls relate in an educationally productive way to male teachers. In the home setting, children fall naturally into the role that is usual in their culture.

There are other issues concerned with gender and culture, where it is appropriate to offer an element of choice to parents. In most national schools where sex-education classes are included in the programme, prior permission for their children's attendance is required. This is the invariable practice in international schools. It is essential that teachers take adequate time to explain the content of the lessons to second language parents and whether boys and girls are taught together. There are certain cultures where such classes would cause unease, and even a degree of alienation. It is wise to emphasise that these classes are optional.

Physical education is a further area where cultural norms may be offended. In certain cultures, even very young boys and girls do not change clothes together in the same room. Neither is it customary for older boys and girls to take part together in PE and swimming classes. International schools in regions where these views hold sway, or whose student populations includes children from these backgrounds, invariably arrange separate changing rooms for all boys and girls, and separate PE and swimming lessons.

Finally, residential class trips need to be handled with sensitivity, as they involve a closer proximity with the other sex than is normal in some cultures. Towards the end of elementary school some girls may be withdrawn from involvement in residential field trips. The children concerned rarely show resentment and their peers tend to follow the teacher's lead in accepting the circumstance without comment.

Festivals

Festivals have traditionally been celebrated in elementary schools in most national education systems. They provide colour and excitement and a sense of identity, as well as giving a pattern to the school year. In international schools, the celebration of festivals offers further benefits in providing one way of acknowledging the diverse cultures within a school. Schools miss a valuable opportunity if they confine their celebrations to western festivals such as St. Valentine's Day and Hallowe'en.

Most international schools, therefore, recognise and celebrate festivals from a wider range of traditions. Divali and appropriate festivals from the Jewish calendar may be celebrated. UN Day is frequently observed by the wearing of national dress, performances of songs and dances and the sampling of national cuisines. The festivals of the host country are a further rich source for diverse celebrations. Celebrating local festivals brings the added advantage of providing contact in a meaningful and lively way with the host country culture and language.

Tourist and National web sites on the Internet provide useful material to augment and underpin the celebration of festivals. Children from the countries concerned can be charged with researching and downloading materials that give an accurate view of costumes, dances, songs and cuisine. This material can be used to create authentic celebrations and to give a sense of pride and ownership to the students concerned. A further site on the Internet offers the possibility of extending and enhancing the usual approach to festivals found in schools. Under the name, *Kidlink's Kidproj Multi-Cultural Calendar*, this Website gathers input from children all round the world about events, festivals, and celebrations that are part of their culture. (Website addresses (URLs) are to be found in Appendix B.) The contributions are written in English and derive from countries in all regions of the world.

Current thinking in international schools, however, requires teachers to be clear about their reasons for giving undue amounts of time to this type of celebration. Festivals, with their associated national costume parades and food tastings, may too easily be seen as the sole answer to the acknowledgment of cultural diversity in international schools. Most schools are now concerned to reflect the cultures of their students in ways that are better integrated into the daily life of the classroom. (See pp. 79–81 for a wider discussion of this area.)

Summary

The presence of second language students in a classroom requires teachers to be proactive in managing certain areas of classroom life. Second language students and their parents have a range of expectations about what is the norm in classroom practice. Teachers and students benefit if differences in practice and policy are clearly explained at an early stage to both parents and students. School policy relating to discipline, homework, grading and assessment practices falls into this category.

An awareness of aspects of school life which impact on second language students in special ways enables teachers to provide an appropriate level of support to students and parents. Social life in the classroom and playground, the making of friends and the reasons for absences and disturbances in health are typical areas where new second language children's experiences may differ significantly from children already established in the school.

Change and impact of new circumstances are potentially stressful features of second language children's lives. Knowledgeable and sensitive teachers can contribute significantly to reducing that stress.

Chapter 6
Day-to-Day Life in the Classroom —
Strategies that Support Second
Language Students

Introduction

The responsibility for the well-being and progress of second language students rests chiefly with the classroom teacher. Experienced teachers recognise that second language learners require language support in all areas of school life. This can be achieved by consistently employing an effective set of strategies.

The first two sections of this chapter suggest general strategies to support second language children in the formal and informal aspects of classroom life. The consistent use of these strategies allows second language students to participate in both the recreational and academic areas of the programme. (Later chapters deal with strategies and modifications in specific subject areas.) The third section of this chapter discusses the issues involved in assessing second language students in the mainstream classroom.

The content of the first two sections is divided into two parts. The first relates to young second language children and the second to older students. Within each section, the material is further divided into strategies for use in whole class situations or with large groups, and strategies for use with small groups or individual children. In this and the following pedagogic chapters the short form, L1, is used in place of the phrase, first language, and L2 is used in place of the phrase, second language.

Effective Strategies for General Use With Young Second Language Children in the Mainstream Classroom

Broad approaches

Teachers of young children are well placed to incorporate L2 learners into the instructional mainstream of the class. Features such as themed play areas, learning centres, predictable and repetitive illustrated stories, show-and-tell sessions, songs and puppetry, together with small group activity, are effective contexts for young children to acquire oral language and early literacy skills. The participatory and hands-on nature of activity in these classrooms allows L2 children access to the content of the programme. The integrated approaches that are a feature of educating young children likewise supply positive circumstances for second language acquisition.

Experienced teachers supplement these basic elements with strategies designed to support L2 students emotionally and socially as well as to achieve specific language learning outcomes.

The needs of new second language students in the classroom

All young children need support and care during their first days in a new classroom. Teachers of this age group have a range of strategies at their disposal for ensuring that new students are guided through the school day until they become familiar with the routine. Young L2 students, however, bring with them a further range of factors that make this settling-in process potentially more challenging. Their command of English is limited. As a result of the move, they are likely to have left behind friends and significant family members such as grandparents. They may be starting school for the first time or their previous experience of school may have been different.

Young children who are complete non-speakers of English require consistent support. The teacher needs to guide the child at every point of the school day and explain in similar phrases on each occasion what is about to happen next. Consistency and routine supply young L2 children with a sense of security and control. The repeated use of the same words and phrases, related to regular procedures is helpful, so is an unaltered placement of furniture and an organised system of storage for classroom supplies, for example, pencils, colouring equipment, glue and scissors.

Other children arrive with a seemingly greater competence in English. Teachers should be aware, however, that these superficially fluent children may also experience language difficulties. The teacher's variety of spoken English may be unfamiliar to them. Young speakers of Singaporean or Indian English, for example, may find it difficult to gain meaning from speakers of American, British or Australian English. They may have difficulty in associating their known vocabulary with the unfamiliar objects they see in the classroom. Classroom topics in the new school may bear no relationship to their former experiences.

Activities associated with the seasons and the weather, for example, may be sources of bewilderment to new L2 children. Not only do the seasons and climate vary in different parts of the world, but the terminology varies also. Autumn activities such as collecting fallen leaves and picking corn or apples that are customary in the Northern Hemisphere, for instance, are likely to be unfamiliar to children from regions with different seasonal patterns and vegetation. Teachers will need to introduce all second language children, both fluent speakers of English and beginning speakers, to new concepts and new items of vocabulary for them to make sense of this topic.

Lack of familiarity with the detail of typical themes in standard use in young children's classrooms is usual. Sets of farm animals and many books in English include only animals from temperate climates. Many of these animals will be strange to young L2 children who come from different regions. Even quite competent English speakers will not know their names, and feel diminished and perhaps ashamed. These topic areas need to be introduced carefully to new young L2 children. It is a helpful practice to check that books, artefacts and sets of models in international school classrooms relate to life in many parts of the world. Holiday trips, international fairs and kind second language parents are useful resources in gathering a variety of objects and resources.

Teachers of new young L2 children need to be aware that students' previous experiences of school may differ widely from what they find in their new school. Most students, even the very young, in Africa, the Indian sub-continent and parts of East Asia, will have spent their school days sitting at a desk in classes of forty or more children, listening to the teacher and copying off the board. All their experiences will have varied in detail. How children ask to go to the toilet varies from school to school. It is vital that teachers guide children in asking and finding the toilet facilities. It is vital for their peace of mind and comfort.

Teachers need to ensure that new L2 children are given the support that enables them to make sense of the school day. If they do not speak English, they need to be escorted physically from place to place and they need to be shown what is expected of them. Teachers need to maintain this support over a lengthy period and to watch for occasions when a slight change to the school day leaves L2 students confused and miserable. Very young children cannot be expected to make independent decisions in the face of altered circumstances. Beginning speakers of English are unlikely to have the language in place to ask for help.

Teachers cannot depend, for example, on the spoken word to tell children of changes in their travel arrangements. They must ensure that someone waits with a child who is to be met by her or his mother rather than go home on the school bus. Teachers of young children are, of course, accustomed to this caring role. Young L2 students will, however, need the care to continue for much of the school year and into higher age levels.

It is also necessary to give this type of guidance to young L2 learners in the curriculum areas. Teachers are unwise to make assumptions about how L2 students have previously carried out their learning. They need to show by example what is required during each activity. (Chapter 7, and Chapters 9 to 11, in this handbook, offer detailed strategies related to the curriculum areas.)

Young L2 students need direction and explanation with concrete examples in all cases, and this degree of care needs to continue until the child appears to understand the system and feels able to be independent. Even at this stage there will be times, perhaps on days when the child is tired or is about to be ill, when an adult needs to resume this close supervisory role.

Ensuring comprehensible input

The provision of language at or just above the L2 child's level of comprehension relating to near-at-hand concrete events is essential for language learning to take place. Teachers and aides need to find the time to talk face-to-face with children in language that takes into account their existing level of comprehension. This is especially important when explaining to L2 students what is to happen next and what they are expected to do. L2 children, unless they are very competent in understanding spoken English, are unlikely to gain that sort of information from a general announcement. With young learners, much of the general conversation and teacher talk in a classroom is above their level of comprehension.

The provision of comprehensible language is one of the chief uses of specific ESL support for young children. ESL teachers generally work with small groups of children either in the classroom or as part of a pull-out programme. In this situation, they are able to provide comprehensible input about near-at-hand, familiar topics, backed up by practical activity and story-telling. This caretaker language allows young children the maximum access to new vocabulary and structures. Classroom teachers will gain support that is even more effective for their L2 children if they include the ESL teacher in the planning of their general class programme.

Vocabulary building strategies

Today's effective classrooms offer exposure to areas of vocabulary in high use in the daily life of a young child, frequently in association with early mathematics and literacy activities. Valuable vocabulary occurs in an unforced way during work with such topics as numbers and counting, colours, shapes, school, animals and transport. Play and guided tasks with other children in learning centres provide further opportunities for meaningful practice in vocabulary areas such as the home, shopping, and the family.

This exposure is reinforced by the reading aloud, shared reading and guided reading of thematically linked children's literature and by related individual and small-group activities. (See Chapter 7, for a full discussion of these reading strategies.) The more concrete the activity, the better it is for the purposes of language learning. Modelling in plasticene and clay, cooking, block building, collecting and sorting offer opportunities for the repeated use of topic words in context.

Learning spoken structures

Teachers can contribute to L2 children's grasp of spoken structures by constructing opportunities for directed activity and play with other children. In these circumstances, a child in a small group is likely to be involved in talk with other children at an appropriate level of language about matters, which engage her or his attention and call for active communication. Block-building, shared construction activities, playing at the water or sand table are rich opportunities for this type of interaction.

The place of literature in fostering language learning

Strategies for use with young L2 learners in the area of literacy teaching, are described in greater detail in Chapter 7. Access to well-illustrated, attractively presented children's literature, both fiction and non-fiction, in big book as well as in standard format, offers the possibility of enriching a young child's language throughout the school day.

The use of literature to introduce, explore and expand on all forms of class talk and activity supplies the repetition of vocabulary and structure which consolidates language learning. High quality illustrations provide visual clues to back up oral and written language. Topics such as school celebrations, family news, news about pets, as well as the content areas and social themes appropriate to young children supply effective opportunities for the introduction of stories, poems and non-fiction texts. Talk of all sorts related to thematically linked fiction and non-fiction texts is valuable.

Incorporating music and chants into themed learning

Music and rhythm are a standard feature of most young children's classrooms. Songs and chants offer good opportunities for practising intonation and speech patterns. The impact on children's language learning, however, is increased if the content of the musical offerings

Textbox 6.1 Language learning through play

Both free and guided play offers effective arenas for language learning. I observed a successful example of the contribution that guided play can make to language learning while visiting a school in Bangkok. The children had access to all sorts of objects and written materials to be found in airports and on planes. These included luggage, an aircraft chair, tickets, boarding cards, in-flight magazines and construction materials for creating an airport or plane. The suitcases were old and battered and the chair about to collapse, but that seemed not to diminish the children's pleasure and enthusiasm in any way.

Clearly a teacher had been involved initially, but later the children had taken the project to their hearts and had constructed replica computers (even though real ones were available), conveyor belts, trays of airline food, etc. and had organised the space into check-out and passport control areas, and the plane itself. When I arrived I was seized by the two six-year-old girls playing in the area at that time, and instantly became a passenger to be processed through their system. The home language of one child was Thai and the other was a speaker of Mandarin.

I was struck by how apt the choice of theme had been on someone's part. Air travel and airports are a way of life to children in international schools. Both children in this instance had experienced and observed a mass of detail concerning air travel, and used with ease and understanding such phrases as: 'What airline do you want to travel on?', 'We are now selling duty-free goods,' and 'We are expecting turbulence, please fasten your safety belts.'

Materials had been made available for children to construct and write their own tickets, passports and menus. I noticed from the tickets lying about that previous users of the play space had made tickets by dividing paper into the usual boxes, but that some children had used scribble writing and others developmental or approximated spelling in filling in the spaces. The two children I observed were ready to take risks in trying out new spoken forms and in putting pencil to paper. They were also totally engaged and involved in solving problems co-operatively.

Several similar themes would lend themselves to this sort of activity and with which many of our students are familiar. These might include life in a hotel, a visit to a restaurant or organising a birthday party. Perhaps a cautionary footnote should be added here. Some L2 parents (and many L1 parents), may initially feel uneasy about this type of activity. They may find it difficult to see how play is a useful way of spending time in school. Teachers should be ready to explain very clearly the purpose and value of guided play, and what is its value to young children.

relates to other happenings in class life. The usefulness is increased if children have shared in the creation of the lyrics and witnessed them being written down on a large song sheet. Used in this way, the words of songs associated with stories, festivals and family happenings offer a confirmation of the use of vocabulary and structures already familiar to the child in other contexts. Music, song and rhythm are made especially enjoyable and useful for young L2 children if examples from their own culture are included in the everyday activities of the class. L2 parents are sometimes willing to come into the classroom to share songs and music with the children.

Shared tasks

Involving young L2 children immediately in classroom tasks is useful for two reasons. Firstly, the children are brought into the heart of class life, and viewed from the first as full members of the social group. Secondly, practical tasks such as clearing-up, washing paint brushes and stacking things neatly, offer precisely the opportunities where language learning takes place best. Talk associated with these tasks is predictable, repetitive, associated with near-at-hand physical circumstances and takes place in a constructive atmosphere.

The role of parents

Involving L2 parents in the learning of their children is the best means of ensuring that children receive support in all aspects of school life. Inviting parents into the classroom is also a means of overcoming any lack of knowledge or unease about unfamiliar aspects of an international school. The positive outcomes arising from the involvement of L2 parents in school and classroom support activities have been discussed more fully in Chapter 2.

Placing value on the home culture and learning

New L2 learners in an international school bring knowledge of their own language and culture. This involves an understanding of the mode of family life customary in their culture, and their social customs and festivals. It is important that the value of this knowledge and experience is acknowledged and built upon.

In the classroom, the teacher can build on prior experience in a number of ways. Children should be encouraged to write and draw from their own knowledge about life outside school, and class talk should incorporate references and examples from the cultures of all the children in the class. Parents should be encouraged to contribute in class with stories, music and practical activities, which reflect their cultural heritage.

The best way for teachers to ensure that children feel their culture is valued is to make themselves knowledgeable about the countries, cultures and, if possible, the linguistic backgrounds of their students. Children will enjoy sharing their personal stories with teachers if they sense a genuine interest and eagerness to hear and understand.

Strategies for individuals or small groups

Individual listening centres

Use listening centres that allow children to listen on tape to age-appropriate stories with matching books, songs and chants. If possible find retellings of stories that are already familiar from commercial videos. Many young L2 children, particularly those from East Asia, have extensive video libraries.

Games

Reinforce vocabulary areas by involving children in games such as animal dominoes, simple board games and Lotto. Teachers can make their own pairs of cards related to vocabulary areas in high use, which can be used to play card matching or memory games. The players should speak different languages so that they are required to talk in English. It is also advisable that the games should not be too competitive.

Creating written signs, titles, and instructions

Set up writing centres with selections of paper, card, markers and large pencils. Encourage children to label their drawings, write signs on model shops and give titles to displays. Incorporate these activities into shop and house areas in the classroom. Ask children to write short instructions relating to the use of classroom areas, (for example, please clear up when you have finished, wash your paintbrushes, always put the lids on felt-tipped markers).

Home-made books

Children love small things. Encourage children to make and staple together small books. The text can be written in scribble writing and illustrated, or can be used for labelled drawings. This is an effective strategy for L2 learners used to scripts that run from right to left or down the page, especially if the form of the books encourages left to right usage. Encourage them to set out the books as in English.

Laminated activity sheets from published books

Overcome the habits of a lifetime and break up a copy of one of the children's favourite stories. Those used during times of shared reading will have the maximum effect. Laminate each page of the book and design activities that require children to look carefully at the illustrations and associated text. The most useful books for this purpose are those containing detailed illustrations or repetitive text using vocabulary in high use such as colours, numbers and shapes. Activities can include asking children to draw all the blue things, all the things made up of squares, all the animals, and so on. Ask them to expand the illustrations. This can be done by getting children to draw the inside of a house only seen from the outside in the picture or by showing what the characters wear when they go to the beach or to school. Ask them to carry out age-appropriate labelling and writing tasks based on the story.

Picture sequencing

Ask L2 children to place in the correct sequence pictures describing a familiar story or activity. Carried out in pairs this involves students in the need to talk together.

The use of the computer

Early literacy programs such as *Wiggleworks*, published by Scholastic, Inc., and other effective programs on disk and on CD-ROM designed for young children, allow L2 students to engage in profitable language learning activities. The use of technology provides variety for young L2 students and offers them a sense of control over their own learning that may be lacking in other parts of the programme. (Chapter 7, p. 138 and Chapter 11, p. 242 offer a variety of suggestions for individual and small group use of the computer.)

Effective Strategies for General Use With Older Second Language Children in the Mainstream Classroom

Broad strategies

Let students know what is planned

Announce clearly the aims of a lesson and what activities are planned. Let L2 learners know what use of language they should look out for. Let them know how they will be helped to master that particular skill. In turn, give L2 students time to express their concerns about language areas that are unfamiliar or need practice.

List instructions step-by-step

When giving instructions, allow L2 students time to understand each step before moving on to the next. It is difficult to take in a list of directions given without pauses. Give written instructions as well as verbal directions in the case of complicated assignments.

Develop and maintain routines

Be consistent in classroom procedures. Routines will help L2 students anticipate what is going to happen without having to rely solely on language cues. This applies to such areas as how instructions are given, ways students are expected to set out work and what is expected from students in completing different types of assignments.

Present information in varied ways

Use a variety of media and methods to present information. This includes information about events in the school day or upcoming field trips. Use visuals, graphs, charts and maps. Invite visitors with expertise or a point of view to talk to students. Use authentic materials such as tourist brochures and magazine cuttings. This reduces the necessity of relying solely on oral language and gives the information a context from which the student can derive meaning. Offer a range of written resource materials — fiction and encyclopaedias, as well as textbooks. Use the Internet to find original source material, perhaps in the students' own languages. Giving information in a number of ways offers the best chance of addressing students' preferred learning styles.

Check constantly that students have understood

Ask questions; give spoken and visual reviews; ask for re-tellings; encourage the sort of classroom environment where students can admit to not understanding.

Adjust the level of English where appropriate

Use a simple mode of speech; talk only about important points rather than give too many details; emphasise key words. Rephrase information if it is apparent that L2 children have not understood the first time. Repeat in simpler English the answers that other students supply to oral questions.

Teach study skills explicitly

Give step-by-step instructions about such areas as gaining information from texts, creating a piece of writing and writing-up reports. Do not assume that students have carried out similar tasks before. If they have, they will benefit in any case from firm guidelines in English. (Detailed suggestions for teaching second language students the language skills required in the specific subject areas of language arts and social studies and science are given in Chapters 7, 8 and 10.)

Asking questions

Ask factual questions first, including some with yes/no answers. Later move on to questions that require students to make deductions and inferences. Leave questions that require the expression of abstract and conceptual thinking until the students' English is of a high enough level. Concentrate on the content of students' answers. Avoid undermining children's confidence or being diverted by superficial language mistakes. What matters is whether students have understood the key points of the information.

Use paired and group activities

Placing students in pairs or small groups enables students at varying levels of English to contribute to a project. It also diminishes student anxiety. For grouping to be effective as a teaching and learning strategy, it is essential that each student has a task, which they must accomplish. Tasks include acting as recorder, materials collector, illustrator and collator. (Detailed suggestions related to instructional groups are included in the following chapters under subject area headings.) Working in pairs is always appropriate at the experimental phase of a science project. Working in a group to solve a mathematics problem is valuable for two reasons: it allows students to experience the language used by proficient speakers of English in solving problems and it gives them access to the mathematics content involved in reaching the solution.

Use peer tutoring where appropriate

The student doing the tutoring learns to explain and clarify concepts. Tutored students have the benefit of focused one-to-one time in a non-threatening context. However, a word of warning is appropriate. Do not overdo this strategy, and do vary the personnel. Parents of student tutors sometimes need convincing that this strategy is to the benefit of their children.

When introducing a new topic try to incorporate students' own experience

It is a standard strategy when beginning a new topic to find out what students already know. It is a valuable additional step to encourage L2 students to offer contributions based on their own experiences in their own culture and geographical location. Teachers need to direct conversations carefully so that L2 speakers have a chance to marshal their thoughts, and give children notice of a new topic so that they can bring in relevant artefacts and pictures.

Involve students in hands-on and active strategies

Remember that beginning and intermediate students can participate and show understanding in all subject areas by means other than writing. These include hands-on science experiments and projects, the construction of mathematics models, role-play, dramatic retellings, and model and relief map construction. The student is further supported if these activities are carried out in a co-operative group setting.

Plan lessons around questionnaires or interviews

These are excellent strategies for use with students at various levels of language competence. Involve groups of children in designing appropriate questions round the computer, and allow students to ask questions in pairs if necessary. Make clear the framework for reporting the answers. Allow students to record the answers on a cassette recorder so that they can discuss the meaning more fully later. Consider asking for answers in the form of a graph or checklist for beginner or early intermediate L2 students. The question and answer format is an accessible way for L2 students to gain the information needed when constructing an oral presentation or carrying out a written assignment. Ask them to write a biography of a friend, or family member, based on a question and answer session, or arrange for them to interview a knowledgeable adult about an area of social studies, science or art. Information gained in this way gives L2 students a framework around which to create the final piece of work.

Design lessons that involve musical or jazz chant activities

Such activities teach English pronunciation and intonation patterns as well as reinforcing concepts and facts. Creating raps or chants about topics such as the rain forest or historical and mythological figures involves children talking together about the use of language. Good published materials also exist.

Incorporate information technology into all aspects of classroom life

Many L2 students have a confident and risk-taking approach to the use of electronic technology. This adventurous spirit is valuable when transferred to working in English on the computer. Teachers of this type of student should build on their expertise to aid them in accessing subject area content in English. The Internet and CD-ROM materials offer students language learning practice while extending their understanding of academic content. (Chapter 11, p. 242, gives suggestions for the use of electronic technology as a resource for language learners.)

Involve students in monitoring their own learning

Ask L2 students to talk or write about their language learning. Ask them to list their strengths and weaknesses. Ask how they feel they learn best. Teach them to become more aware of when they need help. Students who feel responsible for their own learning become more motivated to learn and more effective as learners. A rewarding use of this strategy is for teacher and student to sit down together after a period of work on an extended project in order to reflect on the process and to evaluate the outcomes. This sort of reflective discussion enables teacher and student to agree on the successes and limitations of the piece of work and to note where a change in approach might lead to more effective results.

Strategies for individuals or small groups

Simple substitution exercises for beginning learners of English

Ask children to create a variety of simple sentences by substituting new vocabulary in a pattern sentence. The new words can be derived from labelled illustrations associated with classroom content topics.

Regular daily diary

Model example sentences using the simple past tense. Read extracts from a published diary at an appropriate language level. Read out an example of your own diary writing. It is an effective strategy for teacher and students to correspond via a two-way diary. The content can be varied according to the level of English competence of the student. Thus, early subject matter might include simple descriptions of daily events at home and in school. At a later stage, it is appropriate to incorporate thoughts and feelings. Eventually, comments about books and reading, and about how the student views her or his progress in school may be included.

Ask students to make a drawing or other visual representation of information heard or read

Give the student a pre-created visual organiser to fill in. Such an organiser could supply headings for key vocabulary, proper names or places, or require students to list key events in sequence.

Have the student build a bilingual dictionary

On an on-going basis ask students to create their own dictionary in an attractive and sturdy notebook. Students can illustrate words with drawings or cut out illustrations. Magazines, shopping catalogues and tourist brochures are a valuable resource.

Laminated sheets from published texts

Break down fiction and non-fiction texts and laminate individual sheets. Use these sheets for guided expansion work on class topics. Choose sheets with good quality illustrations and photographs that give a context and help convey the meaning of text. The use of single sheets rather than a lengthy chapter or whole book avoids students from being overwhelmed by the quantity of information.

Incorporate the computer into the life of the class

Use not only the word processing application, but also programs on CD-ROM. Make extensive use of the Internet. Give small groups of children tasks to solve together round the computer. Some L2 children are highly motivated to engage in work at the computer because of their mastery and enjoyment of the technology. This enjoyment motivates some L2 children to read challenging materials and to take risks in their writing. (Further uses of the computer are included in Chapters 7 to 10, and specifically in Chapter 11, p. 242.)

Assessing and Evaluating Second Language Children in the Mainstream Classroom

Introduction

The topics of assessment and evaluation, grading policy, written reports and standardised tests have previously been addressed under those headings in Chapter 5. There the emphasis was placed on the need to make full explanations to parents of L2 students concerning practice in international schools. Teachers, however, need to take further account of the presence of L2 learners in their choice of assessment and evaluation procedures.

International schools vary in the assessment practices they use. This variety largely reflects the state of flux to be found in the national school systems in English-speaking countries. Some international schools continue to rely on end of unit tests in textbooks for assessment information and others largely on examinations. Many schools have adopted, wholly or partly, a range of assessment practices which relate to current thinking. These include anecdotal evidence, checklists of student behaviours in subject areas, the use of running records in the assessment of reading, portfolio collections of children's work and tests of actual student performance in the classroom. It is common to find schools whose assessment practices include elements of each type of approach.

This variety of approach lends itself quite well to the assessment of

Textbox 6.2 A checklist of approaches that support second language students

---

Giving Instructions
- Reword instructions.
- Repeat instructions.
- Call attention to a vital piece of information: 'Listen now because I want you to remember this.'
- Write instructions on the board.
- Ensure that students have written down homework instructions.
- Write homework assignments in the same place on the board.
- Erase unnecessary material from the board so that current information is presented clearly.
- When handing out assignments, give L2 children only one new assignment at a time. L2 students tend to feel overwhelmed when faced with several assignments at the same time.

Presenting Material
- Do not expect teacher talk alone to carry information adequately.
- Avoid the use of idiom or slang in presenting material.
- Show real objects.
- Use gestures.
- Introduce a topic with visual materials: photos, maps, graphs and puppets.
- Use visuals rather than print.
- Use a well-illustrated story to introduce a theme.
- Use a filmstrip with the sound off. Supply the commentary at an appropriate level.
- Use many devices to give information: blackboard, whiteboard, overheads, student-made posters or charts and collages.

Making material more accessible to the student
- Use short sentences.
- Provide vocabulary lists — talk about new words.
- Break down the material into manageable parts.
- Supply visuals with word problems.
- Give students time to read silently before being asked to read aloud or to respond orally.
- Teach learning strategies explicitly.
- Allow students to work with an English-speaking partner.

Students Recording Information
- Give students long enough to copy from the board or overhead.
- Understand that they may not be able to read cursive script.
- Write legibly.
- Do not expect competence in note taking.

Textbox 6.2 (*cont.*)

- Leave note taking until English is well established.
- Supply your own visual or simplified word-based summaries.
- Help students keep an organised notebook.
- Allow time to finish an assignment.

Be Explicit

- Verbalise your actions: 'Now I'm going to.....'
- Always articulate what you expect students to do.
- Tell students what they will need for the next activity, lesson or day: Notebooks, files, textbook, ruler and writing supplies.
- Model the task you want students to carry out, either orally or in writing.

Interaction with students

- Where possible, ask students to talk about what they are doing.
- Provide additional time for students to respond to questions.
- Do not overcorrect pronunciation or surface mistakes of language. It is the meaning that is important.
- Try, on occasion, to address students individually in comprehensible language.
- Give praise where it is due.
- Do not single out students with an embarrassing level of praise.
- Be sure to invite students to join groups and to carry out general classroom tasks. They rarely volunteer.
- Recognise that you will have to direct students about their next move. They will not, in the early days, take independent learning decisions.

Marking/Grading

- Do not leave students' work unmarked from a misplaced unwillingness to pick out errors; students do not understand if teachers leave their work untouched.
- Do not mark every error.
- Indicate which type of error you are marking.

Making L2 Students Feel at Ease

- Do not place students under too much pressure.
- Do not underestimate L2 students — their only problem is that they cannot speak English.
- Allow students to remain quiet on occasion.
- Have some meaningful peaceful tasks available for the times when students need to switch off.
- Recognise when the student has opted out. Give encouragement and support when necessary.
- Smile and look interested. Never sigh, raise your eyes to heaven or groan! You are responsible for the positive atmosphere in your classroom.

---

diverse classes. With mobile second language learners, however, a number of additional features are significant and need to be considered.

The initial assessment of second language students

With new L2 students, as with L1 students, the teacher's aim is to build up a picture of the student's capacity in the subject areas of the curriculum, and to construct an instructional programme that allows students to move on in their learning. This is a major task for teachers in international schools. The difficulty lies in the fact that many new L2 students speak little or no English. Despite this hurdle, international schools are committed to providing mobile students with a continuous experience of learning. It is not a viable option to place a student's learning of subject material 'on hold' during the time it takes her or him to acquire English. This would not be a positive strategy in relation to students' learning in any case. It is now generally recognised that the subject areas themselves offer L2 students a powerful means of acquiring useful English.

Teachers have a range of possibilities at hand to enable them to assess L2 students' previous experiences in education. They should consult the notes from the students' former school and talk to parents where their level of English allows. If feasible, they should talk to students themselves in English or their own language. They should measure, fully, children's performance wherever possible, for example, in the purely computational areas of mathematics. The aim is to ensure that expectations of L2 students' functioning should be based, not on their level of English, but on an understanding of their previous experiences and capacity.

It is not a useful strategy, for instance, in schools where students are divided into ability groups for mathematics, to place L2 students invariably in the lower groups. Students from East Asia and elsewhere, come from school systems with strong mathematics programmes. For these students the strength of their mathematics knowledge underpins their acquisition of the English needed in that subject. Their knowledge of the likely form and outcomes of mathematics problems strengthens their ability to draw meaning from the English in which they are couched. A good degree of prior knowledge has the same effect in science and geography, two curriculum areas that may be presented visually and which tend to be less language-based.

Early assessment of the reading level of students, particularly in the case of young children, is a vital component in constructing a programme of instruction that takes account of the existing knowledge of an individual student. The means are available to assess even students with little English. These means include assessment instruments that measure children's letter recognition and their understandings about print concepts. Running records of children's reading offer an evidential basis for assessing children's ability to process a text. (Running records chart the growth of children's ability to use meaning, syntax and visual cues to solve the meaning of an unfamiliar word.) Armed with this type of assessment information about a child's reading development, teachers are enabled to give immediately useful instruction and to report effectively and precisely to parents. (See Chapter 7, p. 138, for a fuller discussion of assessment.)

In the case of new L2 children at the higher levels in elementary schools who are complete non-speakers of English, lists of reading in the students' own languages and the actual books themselves, may supply valuable indications of their level of reading. Such lists also give insights into a student's interests. This is useful information since it can guide future recommendations to that student about reading in English. Looking through students' previous notebooks, even if the assignments are written in an incomprehensible language, also gives valuable information. Teachers can gauge the quality and quantity of a student's writing, and gain an impression of the sorts of topics that have been part of a student's previous programme. Pointers to areas of difficulty may also be revealed in handwriting, the quantity of work achieved in each assignment, how the work is set out on the page and the number of marked errors.

Assessing a student's competence in English

The most useful assessments of L2 students' competence in English are based on their ability to function in the mainstream programme. Assessment practices based on tests of language proficiency in isolated areas such as vocabulary and grammar have only limited value in predicting how children will perform in the classroom. Assessment that is based on how students perform when carrying out authentic language tasks allows teachers to plan an instructional programme that addresses their real language needs. Such assessment opportunities occur when students are asked to answer questions relating to books read in class in which they are required to make inferences or to select from text. Examples of this type of question include asking students to pick out the pivotal scenes in a narrative, or where they are required to write their own descriptions of a character, giving examples to illustrate their points. Comparing a student's ability to write a straightforward retelling of a narrative with the same student's performance in completing a task that requires higher-order thinking, gives teachers useful insights into the level at which L2 students can perform cognitively demanding tasks.

Further useful assessment opportunities include occasions such as group activity and conferences between teacher and student as well as structured assignments. Methods of recording students' achievements also include anecdotal records and checklists of identifiable language behaviours. With young children, running records are effective methods of assessing children's on-going progress in reading. An effective means of evaluating progress in the area of writing and students' response to reading is to keep samples of students' writing in the same format carried out at intervals during the school year. Portfolios of young students' writing skills should also include examples of how students perform on word tests and assessments of vocabulary knowledge.

Portfolios of significant pieces of work in other areas are also useful. These can include copies of social studies and science assignments, work on tape, reading journals, spelling tests involving subject-related vocabulary and language work related to mathematics. The overall intent of such assessment is to measure a student's increasing ability to function in the mainstream programme.

Sharing assessment information with the ESL specialist

The ESL teacher's role is to offer English language support to L2 students related to the specific language requirements of the mainstream classroom. A continuous exchange of assessment information between the classroom and ESL teacher allows both to offer the most effective support. ESL teachers can then target their teaching, whether in a pull-out programme or through mainstream classroom support, to the precise areas where L2 students need help. (See Chapter 3, pp. 53–6, for a fuller discussion on this topic.)

Assessing second language children in the subject areas

Teachers of L2 learners are faced with the need to evaluate L2 students' understanding of subject area material. Productive assessment procedures not only describe students' grasp of the material but also give information to teachers about the effectiveness of their programme modifications.

It is essential that teachers test L2 learners in ways that reflect the manner in which they are instructed. It undermines students' confidence and provides few useful results to give L2 learners tests designed for L1 students or competent L2 users of English. An effective policy is to employ modified assessment techniques. These may entail restricting the assessment of beginning students' progress to informal means such as observation and dialogue.

Further techniques can be used when the level of students' English allows. These include asking students to carry out closed and open cloze tests (filling in gaps in a passage either from a list of words or with words of their own choosing), filling in graphs and charts and completing visual organisers. Sorting and ordering illustrations or single words into meaningful patterns or constructing flow charts are other useful strategies. Providing each student's contribution is monitored carefully, it is also appropriate for children to carry out these activities in pairs. The chief objective is not to ensure that the task is completed in a certain manner, but that teachers arrive at an understanding of what children have learnt.

Reporting the progress of L2 students to parents

Assessment of older students at the upper levels of an elementary school generally includes the grading or marking of regular classroom or homework assignments. These grades or marks are officially recorded and written reports to parents partially relate to the level of achievement expressed by these grades. Few international schools base their final reports solely on grades. Most schools do not formally grade the work of L2 students until their level of English allows them to carry out the same assignments as competent users of English in the class. As was mentioned in Chapter 5, pp. 98–9, where grading or marking systems are used, teachers should make clear to parents and students how the grade is calculated. Many teachers give L2 children a high proportion of marks for effort. This occasionally leads to misunderstandings about a child's real level of competence.

Summary

Teachers need a flexible approach to the initial assessment of new L2 students. Effective evaluation and assessment practices for the continuing assessment of L2 students give valuable information in a number of areas. Such practices give evidence of a student's ability to function in English in mainstream classes and demonstrate the student's understanding of content area material. They indicate to teachers the types of strategies and programme modifications that work most effectively with their L2 students. They inform specialist ESL teachers of specific language areas where L2 students need support. Most importantly, effective evaluation and assessment provides teachers with the evidence on which to base a tailored instructional programme that takes account of the needs of each child.

A broadly based array of procedures is effective in providing this evidence. The use of systematic assessment approaches such as the taking of running records of young children's reading gives evidentially-based knowledge on which to build in planning instruction. Informal methods of assessment such as anecdotal observations and dialogue may be appropriate for use with older beginning learners of English. Students at a later stage can be assessed using authentic classroom activities. Written reports to parents should not rely solely on grades. Written remarks are a more appropriate means of reporting on beginning and intermediate students' progress.

Teaching Language Arts to Young Second Language Students in Mainstream Classrooms

Introduction

The aim of this chapter is to alert teachers of young second language students to areas in the teaching of language arts where these children need special consideration. For this aim to be fulfilled it is necessary to say something about the nature of language arts teaching in international schools.

Teachers in most international schools teach young children to read, write and talk using methods current in New Zealand, Australia and much of North America. The interrelated nature of all literacy activities is a feature that underpins this approach. The emphasis is on equipping children with the strategies that enable them to become independent readers and writers. In the teaching of reading, students are given a variety of experiences involving text. It is a feature of this type of programme that the children hear and read only whole stories and meaningful pieces of language. Effective programmes involve books carefully selected by level, which are used to teach a strategic approach to reading.

In the teaching of writing, books and other texts are a starting point of focused writing. Children are also encouraged to write out of their own experience. In most international schools the process approach to writing is in use. This involves children in pre-writing activities, composing drafts, reflecting, editing and producing a finished piece.

The teaching of language arts to young children in international schools is not uniform, however. Some schools use published courses to teach reading and writing and many use reading series. In a few cases, methods dating back many years have remained in use. The on-going assessment of young children's reading and writing is another area where a variety of practice can be observed. The mobile nature of the administrative and teaching staff in an international school frequently leads to wholesale changes or fine-tuning of the language arts programme. Teachers in international schools learn to be flexible.

Most of the content of this chapter is grouped under the headings used to describe generally recognised strategies in the teaching of reading and writing to young children. Many or all of these elements are found in most international schools today. Short descriptions of these pedagogic approaches emphasise the features that are effective in teaching second language students. Specific points relating to second language children's participation follow each description. Further sections, and textboxes, address other issues relating to young second language students and the teaching of language arts. The first section is concerned with the teaching of reading and the following one with the teaching of writing, although they tend to overlap and interconnect.

Reading

The relationship between oral competence and ease in reading

In international schools young children are surrounded and exposed to print from their first days in school. They immediately become involved in literacy activities. These include listening to stories and having access to writing materials in play areas and learning centres. This exposure is beneficial for young L2 students, since one aspect of language reinforces another. Many young L2 learners, indeed, can be seen to consolidate their grasp of spoken structure during the early phases of learning to read.

A sound grasp of oral English, however, is an advantage in learning to read and write. Effective early teaching of reading aims to give children the strategic skills to process text. Two of the main strategies that enable children to become effective processors are meaning and structure. Young native speakers of English approach early reading with the ability to derive meaning from context and this understanding aids them in predicting the meaning of an unfamiliar word. Likewise, their innate knowledge of the structure of English gives young first language speakers of English important cues in predicting the structure of a sentence. Young L2 students, and beginning L2 learners especially, benefit greatly from a sound grasp of spoken English. A rich foundation in oral English supports their progress in acquiring all the skills of language.

Reading aloud to the whole class

Reading aloud to the whole class is a regular practice in young children's classrooms in international schools. It is a basic strategy in teaching children about the nature of books and in promoting enjoyment of all that books have to offer. Reading aloud gives children opportunities to hear stories and non-fiction texts that are beyond their present reading level. It allows teachers to introduce reading material on all subjects and in a variety of genres. Children acquire valuable insights into the construction of a story, the forms of literary language and how books work. It is a time of pleasure when children and teachers can read and talk together.

For young L2 children, who speak little or no English, this usually positive experience may induce a sense of frustration and lead in turn to disruptive behaviour or to passive withdrawal. There are several features in reading to the whole class which may lead to this outcome. A group of 20 or so students is too large for an individual child to feel personally addressed. The language used in introducing, reading and discussing the book may be above an L2 student's level of English. This leads to students feeling little sense of connection with what is going on around them and becoming disengaged from the process.

If teachers have assistance in the classroom, beginning L2 students may be better employed away from the reading circle in the early days. The time can be spent in playing a language game or in sharing a book that is comprehensible to the child. The value of this one-to-one time is that talk can be targeted at or near the child's level of English. When L2 children sit in the circle, they should be seated near the teacher so that they can be included on a more personal basis in the activity of the group. The use of classroom objects, family photos and holiday souvenirs, together with puppets, and other means of bringing the story to life, are all valuable. Strategies that make reading with the whole class more accessible to L2 children are suggested under the heading, Shared reading, below.

Using rhymes and songs to teach early reading

Rhymes and songs are not only an enjoyable means of reinforcing second language students' language learning; they are also a valuable potential means of giving very young children an understanding of the use of text to express meaning. Teachers will find appropriate material for this purpose among traditional and modern children's songs and rhymes or they can create their own with the students' help using content and vocabulary from classroom themes. Pocket charts are a useful method of displaying the lines of text, and allow children to be involved in inserting individual words. Pocket charts also have the advantage of enabling teachers to replace words with pictures if the text is too difficult, and to point out and move around words that resemble each other or have final syllables that rhyme. A valuable aspect of using the text of songs and rhymes is the possibility of incorporating body movement to enhance and reflect the meaning. Thus, young children can be taught to mime, move and play percussion instruments in ways that reflect the content of the songs or rhymes. This type of activity gives enjoyable and communal reinforcement to the idea that words convey meaning.

Shared reading

Shared reading is the second major strategy that leads to children becoming independent readers. The teacher reads with the class using a pointer to guide the students through the text. Shared reading gives early readers valuable support in reading longer pieces of writing. It gives children information about the layout of a page, the relationship of text to illustration and how stories are constructed. Where useful, teachers engage children in noticing significant letter patterns and word facts.

Providing a context

Whether the writing to be shared is a story, a poem or an informational piece, it is valuable to supply L2 students with a context for the reading. Setting the scene in this way enables L2 students to make connections with previous experiences, and to transfer this knowledge to the English they hear from the teacher and see on the page. It is helpful if the piece of writing relates to a theme that has been part of an extended study in the classroom. Published materials such as the **Sunshine Science** series, entitled *Investigating Our World*, offer useful resources. This series, developed in New Zealand, provides Big Books and smaller texts at varying levels that tie in with standard science themes in young children's classrooms. Meeting the same words that they have heard and seen previously, not only reinforces students' understanding, but also builds up a sense of confidence and faith in their own ability to make sense of the written language. (The full details of books and publishers mentioned in this chapter are given in Appendix A: Resources for Teachers.)

Providing a context or setting the scene can take many forms. Real objects, photos, items from home or around the classroom, puppets, flannel and magnet board activities, and teachers' drawings are all effective. These can be used to introduce the story, to alert the children to the key points, or, if useful, to give an outline of the story.

Choice of books

Teachers should choose books for shared reading that they think will interest and delight children. Other criteria are important factors in the choice. The structure of the text has a major contribution to make in allowing young children to access meaning.

All children's grasp of meaning and written structure is aided, during the early stages of learning to read, if the text is repetitive and predictable, and if only one word or phrase changes from page to page. Books containing rhyme and a strong rhythm are also valuable. They make the text easy to memorise as well as offering practice to L2 students in English intonation. Books which incorporate familiar early vocabulary themes such as colours, animals and family words in a simple repetitive or cumulative format are opportunities for L2 children to gain fluency in reading and to acquire confidence. Texts in Big Book format that contain these elements are especially useful, and those published by **Sundance Publishers** and **Scholastic Big Books,** among others, have the added advantage of offering stories that include a range of settings and cultural references. Books which tell stories known to most children are also valuable since L2 children can use their prior knowledge of the story in their home language to support their understanding of the text.

Shared reading is a time when teachers in international schools can introduce books that tell traditional stories, or stories with a modern setting, from different regions of the world. Catalogues such as those of the **African Books Collective Ltd**, offer a specialised collection of children's literature from Africa translated from the African languages or written in English, while **SOMA** and **Kane/Miller Book Publishers** offer lists of books for young children from all over the world translated into English. Informational books related to an on-going science or social studies theme that contain photographs and illustrations from many countries are also a useful resource in an international school classroom. (See the **Sunshine Science** series mentioned above and the two **Steck-Vaughn** series, *Postcards From* and *Where We Live*.) There are further effective uses for books of this type, both for reading aloud and in shared reading sessions. Many international schools recognise the National Days of the countries represented among the student body. It is a pleasant practice to read from a book that relates to a country on its National Day. The reading material can be either a piece of fiction set in the country concerned or book that supplies information and illustrations. A similar range of books also offers the means to bring to life for other children in a class, the countries from which individual students come.

The use of illustration and text layout to enhance the meaning of the text

All children, but especially L2 learners, gain benefit from using illustrations as clues to the meaning of the text. It is a key strategy for early readers and has important implications for teachers in choosing books for both shared and guided reading. (See Guided reading, pp. 145–51.) At the start of the year it is helpful to work with books where the illustrations supply the meaning of the story and the text is limited to a few words alongside the illustrations. The much-loved *Rosie's Walk* by Patricia Hutchins is a story typical of this type. (*Rosie's Walk* is also helpful for introducing and reinforcing the use of prepositions. An enjoyable and effective extension strategy is for the teacher and class to create a fresh text with different animals, following a similar format, during shared and interactive writing sessions.)

As children's processing skills develop, the balance changes, and the text takes its place as the prime conveyor of meaning. At this stage, the role of the illustrations is to support the text by reinforcing and underpinning the narrative. Appropriate books are those where a limited number of lines of text tell a story that is described visually by an accompanying illustration. Fairy stories designed for young children often fall into this category. Pages where the text and illustrations are mingled or where illustrations are used sparsely are for use with advanced readers. Teachers should not forget wordless books as a means of developing vocabulary and speculative language in L2 students. Books such as Tana Hoban's *Look, Look, Look!*, with its original and creative photographs, offer many opportunities for using colour words, adjectives and prepositions.

Teachers should offer children a variety of experiences with illustration since many children have strong preferences. Some children respond to clear, simply drawn illustrations with firm outlines and bold colours. Other children enjoy the deceptively simple and witty type of line-drawing that is used, for example, to illustrate the Greenlandic author, Ole Hertz' series about a fisherman named Tobias originally written in Danish. Many children are attracted and engaged by imaginative and original artwork. Among the books that offer beautiful illustrations are those published by houses specialising in English translations of traditional tales and modern stories from non-English-speaking cultures. The tellings in English of Japanese traditional and modern stories published by **Heian International Inc.**, fall into this category. Other children, however, relate more readily to photographs and obtain more support in their reading from pictures of familiar places, objects and people. The series of little books, for example, published by **Shortland Publications Ltd** of Auckland, New Zealand, offer children accessible content on early vocabulary topics illustrated by charming and uncluttered photographs.

The layout of the print on the page is also a significant factor in guiding the choice of reading material for shared and guided reading. L2 students benefit from working with text where the layout of the print offers maximum support. For early readers single lines of text should be clearly printed in large writing surrounded by white space rather than contained within an illustration. As children progress, they are able to accommodate a more varied layout. It remains helpful, however, if teachers choose text where new sentences and phrases are placed in each case on new lines. Teachers with L2 students whose home language scripts are written from right to left or from top to bottom of the page, should lay particular emphasis on the directionality of the print through the book and where each sentence starts.

Books where the layout of the text gives clues to the meaning are helpful to all children and especially to young L2 learners. This is why some books, such as *Brown Bear, Brown Bear, What Do You See?* by Bill Martin, Jr., illustrated with torn collage work by Eric Carle, remain popular with children and effective in teaching them to read. The vocabulary is related to two familiar areas, colours and animals. The illustrations are graphic and engaging, and pictorial clues on the right-hand page help children to predict the answers given on the following left-hand page. Helpful too are books where repeated structures, with only one changed word, appear in the same place on the page, next to illustrations which give a clue concerning the meaning of the new word.

Managing class discussion to include L2 students

Class discussions are a valuable element in teaching children the use of focused oral language. Teachers need all their skill in managing such discussions. Young children often have difficulty in listening to their peers and show their impatience by jumping up and down or by insistently raising their hands. Confident and articulate children tend to take a greater share of the talk time than timid and less articulate students. Certain rules need to be understood, and in place, and teachers should remind children when they infringe them. Teachers need to employ further specific strategies to allow L2 students to play their part in the discussions that are an integral part of the shared reading and shared and interactive writing approaches.

For discussions about words, books and reading to be successful for L2 children, the atmosphere needs to be calm, focused and respectful. Contributions which involve children in thinking on a number of different levels as happens when they try to solve the meaning of unfamiliar words require time and space. L2 children, especially, need to feel free from the pressure to speak immediately. In those circumstances, many children refuse to speak at all.

It is helpful if teachers construct questions for beginning L2 children that require only a 'yes' or 'no' answer or even a nod or shake of the head. Early questions should contain frequent repetitions of phrases from the shared book and be phrased in simple language. Open-ended questions and the use of complex phrasing and unfamiliar vocabulary words are rarely appropriate in the early months. However, L2 children vary like all other children and some students love to be asked questions and show confidence and daring in trying to formulate answers. This is particularly true if a confident child is read a familiar story, and, for once, feels sure of her or his ground.

One final remark should made about L2 children in group discussions. Some L2 children are unused to being asked to make comments or to contribute their thoughts about work in class. These children may have come from home school systems where even very young students sit in rows of desks facing the teacher. The teaching methodology in this type of classroom may involve a good deal of copying from the board and rote learning. Such L2 students need to be encouraged on an individual basis or in small groups to express their thoughts.

Guided reading

The guided reading phase is an essential part of teaching reading to young students. Guided reading is the phase in which the children are taught strategic skills that enable them to process text. The ability to use meaning, syntax and visual cues to solve the meaning of unfamiliar words is essential if children are to become independent readers.

The teacher works with a small group of children on the same book. Two features are critical in carrying out guided reading successfully. The first is the need to vary the make-up of the group in response to children's reading development. Teachers needs to employ a systematic assessment approach to keep track of each child's reading development. Taking running records and noting children's reading behaviours on checklists are possible means. This assessment information is used as a guide to inform the creation of groups of children at approximately the same stage of reading independence and fluency. The groups should be assessed every few weeks or so to take account of children's changed needs.

The second key component of an effective guided reading programme is the provision of meticulously levelled sets of books. The material may comprise individual pieces of children's literature, be drawn from collections such as the **Sunshine** or **Ready to Read** series, or, even, from among stories in published literature collections. It is a basic tenet that all the books should be interesting to children and be appropriately laid out and attractively illustrated. The careful categorising of books allows children to work with new texts that contain only one or two new reading puzzles to solve. The teacher's skill is required in selecting texts for groups of children at an appropriate level of difficulty. If books are too hard they do not allow children to use their existing processing skills to solve the meaning of unfamiliar words.

The ultimate aim of guided reading is for each child to become an independent reader. This is achieved by teaching each child to utilise independently a number of strategies. These strategies enable children to use their own processing power on the text in order to decode unfamiliar words and to gain meaning from them in the given context.

For L2 students, a guided reading phase is an essential component in learning to read. (The used of graded reading series in some schools serves something like the same purpose.) Some young L1 students, especially those who come from homes where books and reading are valued, may make the leap to independent reading by being read to, and sharing in the reading of books with the whole class, as in shared reading. This is unlikely to be the case with L2 students. Most L2 children need more time to learn letters and to carry out alphabet activities, more listening to stories, more shared reading time, more one-to-one talk about books and more time in the guided reading phase. They benefit also from more time spent in early writing activities, particularly those that reinforce the content, structures and vocabulary found in their reading books. As was mentioned in the first paragraph of this chapter, (The relationship between oral competence and ease in reading), L2 students with a firm grasp of basic spoken structure approach the process of learning to read in English with an in-built advantage. Some key considerations relating to L2 students in guided reading groups are listed below.

Grouping

- The ability to move from group to group is vital to L2 students' confidence and sense of self-esteem. If groups in a classroom are static, L2 students tend to remain in the lower groups.
- Small groups allow L2 children to read in a social context and with the support of other children. The optimum size for a group, around six children, allows the teacher to give each child individual help.
- According to the content of the book, and the teacher's knowledge of the children in the group, the introduction can take a variety of forms. A short discussion, or an opening sentence linking the book with existing knowledge, may be adequate. Teachers may feel that longer introductions involving the discussion of vocabulary items related to the topic of the book may be appropriate in the case of L2 students. (However, if there are many unfamiliar words then the book's level of difficulty is too high to be useful for the guided reading phase.)
- The teacher only intervenes when necessary. The role of the teacher

is to observe each child at work, to answer queries or requests for help, or to intervene if progress is halting or laboured.

L2 learners and reading strategies

- L1 children's knowledge of how the spoken language works allows them to check whether their reading makes sense. Young L2 learners are unlikely to have this inner knowledge of the syntactic patterns of the language. Most L2 students learn to read before their oral language is fully established. They therefore have a lesser knowledge of what sounds right or makes sense syntactically. In order to promote this inner understanding, teachers need to supply L2 students with numerous opportunities to practise basic oral and written structures in meaningful contexts.

- Transition texts, those that include short sentences in written oral language, are effective with beginning L2 students since they relate to the language skill that is usually most developed in young L2 students. Books such as those in the **PM Starters One** series, published by **Rigby**, are a useful resource. These little books provide a single line of text couched in written oral language that relates to a photograph on the opposite page. They are attractive to children because each book deals with a familiar child-oriented topic that relates to the lives of most students in international schools.

- L1 children use meaning (or semantics as it is sometimes termed) as a powerful strategy in testing whether what they read is making sense. They gain this meaning from their prior knowledge about the subject of the book and from their existing vocabulary. An effective introduction allows L2 students increased access to the use of meaning in processing unfamiliar words or structures in the text. The aim is to enable the child to answer the internal question, 'Does this make sense?'

- Books about a topic that is familiar from their home language reading, or that tell a story previously seen on film or television, motivate L2 children and support them in trying to make sense of text. A prior acquaintance with the story through their home language also allows children to predict with more certainty what may come next in a text and to associate vocabulary in their own language with unfamiliar English words.

Visual cues — the relationship between sounds and what is written on the page

- A further major cue used by young readers in trying to solve the meaning of an unfamiliar word in continuous text is the use of visual information related to the letters and form of the word. Visual cues are involved when children relate visual information to sounds. Even a limited knowledge of letter sounds and the number of letters needed to write down words of different lengths, allows children to check, and if necessary, self-correct their reading after a second glance. Effective readers combine information from several sources, visual, semantic and syntactic, when they process a text.

- Learning the relationship between sounds and graphic symbols is useful for L2 students because they may have less access to the cues of meaning and syntax than L1 children. Teaching children to sound out words slowly is a useful strategy. This practice breaks down words into phonemes. (Phonemes are the smallest sounds that a word can be divided into, e.g. sh-i-p, M-o-n-d-ay.) By sounding out the words slowly children are thus given time to build and act on the knowledge of how individual phonemes are customarily written down in English. With this knowledge, they can check that their reading of word makes sense visually.

- L2 children benefit from carrying out many activities involving the sounds and names of alphabet letters. Children's own names and the names of the children in the class supply a ready route to constantly used letters. Alphabet charts using consistent script and drawings are helpful. Teachers should make sure that the drawings are of objects familiar to L2 students. The reading and making of their own ABC books in various formats is enjoyable, and reinforces the process of memorising the sounds and related symbols.

- L2 students need to be specifically taught how to sound out unfamiliar words. They need to be taught to look at the first letters, the last letters, and then at the intervening consonants.

- They need to learn, through practice in sorting and listing words, to identify clusters of letters that habitually stand together, and how they are pronounced in individual words. These words should be provided with some sort of context.

- Stopping to sound out words isolates words from their context and tends to reduce the effectiveness of meaning and syntactic cues. It is essential that a text for guided reading contains only a limited number of new words.

- It is possible that L2 children may succeed in sounding out the word and still have no understanding of its meaning.

- During shared reading with the whole class, and during guided reading with an individual, it is helpful for teachers to point out connections and relationships between words. Teaching children to identify, for example, the root word in 'playtime' and 'playground' gives children help in decoding and establishing the likely meaning.

Teaching children to understand the text

- Some L2 students become fluent decoders of simple text. However, they may have little understanding of what they are reading or how to carry out extension work on the text. Teachers need to give these L2 students practical demonstrations of how to draw inferences from text or from illustrations. They should ask such questions as: How can you tell what the weather is like in the picture? Are the people who live in this house rich or poor? You've read lots of fairy stories, do you think the Giant is really going to eat Jack?
- Extension work related to the content of guided reading books can be used to reinforce children's comprehension of the text and to carry out activities associated with new facts about words. These activities can be carried out in groups, in pairs, or individually. They can be part of the work of literature groups or they can be set up in a learning centre. Such activities might include collaborative re-tellings in writing in various formats, creating a frieze showing the characters and happenings of the story, or creating a puppet show. L2 children benefit especially from being able to hear the same story repeatedly via a listening centre

Assessment

- Guided reading time can be used by teachers to make anecdotal assessment notes, to fill in checklists of reading behaviours and to take running records of children's reading. The use of a systematic means of recording what children actually do and say when they are reading allows teachers to arrive at an exact understanding of the strategies children are using to process an unfamiliar word. This knowledge is used to make book selections that move children on in their learning most effectively and to guide teachers' work with individual children.
- In the case of young L2 students who are failing to make steady progress in reading, teachers should take note of instances where there is a significant discrepancy in the level of the child's oral language and her or his progress in reading. It is often not easy to establish the precise cause of an L2 child's minimal progress. Teachers should, however, call in specialist help at an early stage, rather than allow an L2 child to develop feelings of low morale and loss of confidence.

Textbox 7.1 The use of published language arts courses and graded reading schemes

Some international schools choose to depend for their early literacy teaching on published language arts courses and graded reading schemes. We are not talking here of the basal textbooks that were common in American-based international schools some ten years ago. Modern language arts series published by American publishing houses provide an array of materials, including sets of small themed books, computer software and teachers' manuals. The methodology and terminology reflect current thinking in the teaching of language arts. Not surprisingly, some schools prefer the consistency and coverage offered by courses such as these.

I have seen such courses in use in a number of international schools and they have certain advantages in some contexts. The most effective use was in a bilingual school, in the Middle East, where the majority of teachers were highly competent bilinguals (most were, in fact, Arabic, English and French trilinguals). The published course, in this instance, had moved teachers on from a narrow approach to the teaching of language arts in which children read only limited reading selections and filled in worksheets. The presence of a course based on current thinking gave these teachers the confidence to use methods and materials which they had not experienced at first hand, and allowed them to give the students a wide experience of all forms of reading and writing in English. In general, the limitation of these courses is not that the material is too limited, but rather that it is overwhelming in quantity. Such a wealth of reading matter has a tendency to overwhelm children (and teachers) and to diminish their sense of ownership of their own reading and writing. Since, also, such courses are written chiefly with first language populations in view, the instructions and captions tend to be expressed in language at too high a level for young L2 learners.

Modern reading schemes are in much wider use in international schools, where they provide the core thrust of many reading programmes. Schemes, such the **Sunshine Series**, and **The Oxford Reading Tree**, provide complete stories, at many reading levels, individually bound in small books. In some series, the characters recur in most of the books, and poetry and short plays may be included in the collection. Nearly all teachers supplement the use of these readers with further reading to the whole class and with shared reading sessions. In general, L2 children enjoy the sense of moving through a series of books. They gain a sense of their own progress. The disadvantages of such an approach remain, however. Some children experience the feeling of being left behind by their more successful peers; others, used to the security of the reading scheme, have difficulty in making the leap to authentic material.

In view of the mobility of the children, the changes in class sizes and the movement among teachers in international schools, many administrators opt for the security of this type of reading programme. Many teachers, also, welcome the framework that these schemes provide. One important point remains to be made. The nature of the reading material is a key element in

Textbox 7.1 (*cont.*)

---

teaching children to read. The essential feature, however, is the teachers' input. Young learners need to acquire the independent strategies that will enable them to process what they read. Teachers have a choice in what materials they use to achieve that end.

Independent reading

Children are asked to read independently at all stages in the early literacy programme. Beginning L2 students can start with wordless story books and books with single words and matching illustrations. Books on subjects such as colour, animals, the home, the family and transport provide reinforcement of vocabulary together with pictures of known objects.

Many teachers of young children plan a regular independent reading time each day. Children are encouraged to carry out one of a number of reading activities appropriate to their reading level. These include, for very early readers, reading little book copies of the big books used during shared reading, following a story while listening to a tape in a listening centre and reading stories created and published by the whole class in shared writing times. L2 students can benefit from all these activities provided that the level of text is appropriate.

Most class libraries contain books on a variety of subjects and a range of genres. These books can be placed on shelves or in boxes to be made available to children for independent reading. Children are guided in making an informed selection if books are grouped together by author, by illustrator, by genre or by subject. Many teachers borrow extensively from the main school library to create a collection relating to a class theme or topic.

Another important collection comprises further copies of books used in guided reading time. These books are either kept together by level or grouped according to theme. To guide the children in making appropriate and manageable choices these books are colour-coded with sticky tape according to reading level. Most children like to read and re-read favourite books. L2 children's confidence in their ability as readers is increased if they have access to familiar books at a level that they know they can read with ease.

Writing

The reading, writing and speaking connection

In today's classrooms for young children their experience of language is likely to be multi-faceted and classroom activities rarely require children to practise one language skill in isolation. This integrated approach offers an effective environment for supporting young L2 students in their literacy learning. Their experience of English in one area interconnects with another and underpins their language learning as a whole. This approach is especially evident in the relationship between reading and writing and many of the writing strategies given below involve children in reading. Constructive and focused talking and listening are also integral to every activity.

Teaching Roman script and the layout of text in English

Many young children entering international schools speak languages that are written down in ways other than in Roman script. Some countries use different alphabets (e.g. Cyrillic for Russian and Hangul for Korean), or place the main emphasis on recording consonants (e.g. Arabic and Hebrew), or syllables (e.g. Hindi). Japanese is written down using two parallel alphabets of 48 words written in different forms, and includes Chinese characters known as ideograms. Some languages are written from right to left across the page (Arabic and Hebrew) while Japanese is written from right to left and down the page in columns. In these last cases books in those languages start from what English-speakers would think of as the back. Teachers in international schools come to understand the nature of the directionality and scripts of their students' writing systems.

In practice, enabling children to make the move, where necessary, into Roman script and to change the direction of their writing is not the major hurdle that it might seem. L2 children who have learnt to read and write in any writing system start their literacy studies in English with significant advantages. They understand the relationship between sounds and graphic symbols, and they have gained the fine motor control involved in forming graphic symbols on the page. These children, unless a diagnosed or undiagnosed learning disability is present, generally make the move to Roman script quite smoothly. L2 Children who have not yet started their literacy studies, learn to read and write the Roman alphabet from the same starting point as children whose languages are written in Roman script.

Specific teaching is valuable in reinforcing the differences, in all cases. L2 children who are unused to Roman script may take longer to learn how to form the letters of the Roman alphabet. They may take time to perceive the differences between upper and lower case letters. They will need practice of all sorts. Work with various types of ABC books is a valuable way of giving this practice in an agreeable form. Children who must change their accustomed view of the directionality of writing also need specific help in making the change smoothly. Teachers can give this help by offering children chances to illustrate, use scribble writing, or to write conventionally, in formats that guide the direction of their work. This can be done by using teacher-created books, where the numbering or the graphic layout require children to fill in spaces through the book from left to right or from top to bottom. Concertina books, fan books and note pads have this effect. The computer is also a useful tool in accustoming children to write from left to right and to observe the return sweep to the beginning of the next line on the left-hand side of the page.

Shared Writing

Shared writing is a teaching approach that involves the teacher acting as scribe for a shared piece of writing composed by a group of children or the whole class. The teacher guides, makes suggestions and directs the creation of the piece of writing on large pieces of chart paper. The topic of the writing relates to a shared experience, an on-going classroom project or to a shared story. The writing can take various forms including recounting an experience in the first person plural, a retelling of a story in the third person, creating an invitation, or writing a letter. Children can be given photocopied versions of the final version to illustrate, to read during independent reading and to take home to read with parents. Children enjoy the process because of their intimate knowledge of the subject matter. All children gain an understanding of how a piece of writing is constructed: where to begin to write on the page, how to construct the first sentence, how to create a sequenced narrative, how to add detail and how to finish off.

L2 children gain in many ways from the shared writing experience. They not only learn to enjoy the process of writing without the sometimes painful process of thinking about words and writing them down, but they also gain knowledge about language in a way that is useful to them. They gain reinforcement of previously heard new vocabulary items; they hear children and teachers discuss the formation of simple narrative structures; they gain practice in the use of appropriate pronouns, link words and prepositions; they witness the reasoning behind the use of different tense forms.

The teacher's management of the discussion and of children's contributions makes a real difference to the value of the shared writing experience to L2 children. For such students to gain all the potential benefits it is essential that they are involved in composing the piece of writing and take ownership of the final product. As mentioned under the heading, Shared reading, p. 144, the teacher should have in place set routines and specific rules for use during whole class discussions.

Textbox 7.2 An enjoyable writing experience for young second language students

It is generally the case with most young L2 students that they require many opportunities to extend their experience and to practise their skills as they learn to read and write. It is common for their reading and writing competence to lag some way behind the level of their speaking and listening skills. Some children are aware of their slow progress and they become bored, frustrated and occasionally ashamed at their inability to perform in the same way as their L1 classmates.

In order to keep L2 students on task and to keep them interested and positive about reading and writing, there are many schemes and strategies that teachers can use to make reading and writing fun. One small group of L2 boys, all highly verbal, had reached a plateau in their reading and writing development. They regularly carried out a range of reading and writing activities, but were not yet fluent readers or writers. It seemed time to think up a novel approach to boost their morale and retain their interest.

The outcome was an extensive project involving a range of contextualised reading and writing opportunities that became an object of interest for the rest of the children who watched its progress day-by-day. The boys were all used to flying, and could talk fluently about their experiences using a wide range of associated vocabulary. The construction of an airport runway was begun in an open space outside the classroom, and the project was gradually extended to include the creation of hangars, a control tower and public buildings. The boys vied with each other to create the signs for each area, and soon examples of their writing appeared on most surfaces. Useful items arrived from home, including air tickets, baggage labels, menus, and so on. Each boy made his own passport with photo and personal description. A display area was created to lay out these items. Each boy made a plane painted with the livery and logo of his national airline. A monster jumbo jet was created in the colours of Sabena, the Belgian airline.

Finally the crunch came for the boys and it was time to write and illustrate a Big Book related to this topic. The boys discussed how they would approach the task. Eventually it was decided that they would narrate the experience of a passenger from the time he arrived at the airport to the time he arrived at his destination. The writing was achieved, interspersed by refreshing periods of play in the model airport, using a mixture of dictation and individual student writing. There were many arguments about who was going to illustrate key moments in the narrative such as taking off and having lunch on a tray. A group photograph was taken of the boys in front of their work and placed on the cover. Each boy wrote a brief note about his contribution to the project.

This book was read by each boy to the class using the illustrations as cues, and relying to some extent on memory. The class was properly appreciative and clearly viewed the project as a significant and prestigious achievement. The Big Book has since become one of the standard favourites for subsequent

Textbox 7.2 (*cont.*)

---

generations of second language children, providing the stimulus for discussion and extension activities. When I meet one of the boys in the corridor, (they are all fluent readers and writers now), they ask: 'Do you remember the airport we made?'

Interactive writing

The approaches given here under the heading, interactive writing, are sometimes included under the general heading of shared writing. The use of the two headings reminds teachers of a distinction in the nature of collaborative composing sessions with children. Interactive writing places the responsibility for composing and writing down a piece of text in the hands of the children. With the teacher's guidance, children create the precise wording of sentences, contribute suggestions about spelling and punctuation, and write the words down themselves. Certain materials and pieces of classroom equipment are valuable aids in enabling children to take a proactive part in contributing to the piece of writing. Picture dictionaries, pocket charts, sentence strips, flash cards and plastic alphabet letters provide the means for a trial and error approach to composition. Large-sized sheets of paper and wall charts at the children's eye level allow students to work on a large scale such as in producing a story map.

Interactive writing gives children opportunities to learn how words are constructed and how an extended text is created. It provides an arena for contextualised discussion about spelling patterns and vocabulary. It introduces the idea of writing for varying audiences.

The writing can take many forms. These include retellings of shared stories, narratives modelled on the pattern of familiar stories and accounts of shared events in classroom and school life. It might also take the form of a daily journal recounting the progress of nearby building works or of a major class project.

Some observations relating to L2 children's participation in interactive writing activities

- Interactive writing allows L2 children to gain experience in constructing a piece of writing in English in a supportive context.
- L2 children can see that creating a piece of writing is hard work for everyone.
- Interactive writing allows teachers to include even beginning L2 students in the collaborative effort by asking them to be the scribes

in writing short familiar words from early vocabulary topics. Such topics include colours, numbers, animals, and so on.

- L2 children who have little experience of creating an original piece of writing (they may be more used to copying) are able to observe the step-by-step process involved in writing.
- Interactive writing involves writing about subjects close to children's interests and experiences, an approach that is invaluable with L2 children. Contact with dynamic subject matter in the child's environment provides an effective stimulus for interactive writing. Children can be taken to view a building site on a regular basis, for example, and be introduced to the words for describing the various actions and features found on a site. They can then return to the classroom to write together about the progress of the work.
- Interactive writing enables L2 children to see that trial and error is a valuable strategy in creating a piece of writing.
- It allows teachers to show that a writer's first thoughts can be changed after reflection.
- L2 children are able to observe the layout and use of language involved in writing in different formats. These formats are modelled through authentic writing tasks — e.g. a journal entry, an invitation to a school event, a letter to grandparents.
- Interactive writing allows teachers to explain and model the uses of punctuation and capital letters in authentic contexts. This is especially helpful to L2 children who write in different scripts.
- Interactive writing allows teachers to model the use of a consistent strategic approach to spelling.
- It allows teachers to draw L2 children's attention to word families and differences in spelling words that sound the same.
- It allows teachers to introduce talk about the use of tenses, and their formation, in meaningful contexts.

Guided writing or writers' workshop

Guided writing (or writers' workshop) refers to the time given to children to create a piece of writing under the guidance of the teacher. The children may be asked to write in a variety of formats or from personal experience. They engage in pre-writing activities including discussion and the graphic representation of ideas involving webbing. The layout of different writing formats may be modelled via an authentic writing activity on the overhead projector or on chart paper.

Children create a first draft, concentrating their efforts on what they want to say. Teachers and children then talk together in small groups, or on a one-to-one basis, to discuss the writing and to talk about possible changes. Teachers take note of areas relating to layout, grammar, spelling and punctuation that would benefit from specific instruction. This instruction is given immediately to the individual child, or given later in a short lesson to the whole class or to a targeted small group of children. Appropriate changes are made to the first draft and the final version is copied out. Illustrations are added. Children then read their finished version to the whole class or it is made into a book and 'published'. Teachers take the opportunity during each stage to jot down notes or to make systematic observations relating to each child's writing behaviours. These are used to inform subsequent instructional decisions.

Issues that arise from the participation of L2 students in guided writing activities

- L2 children are likely to have difficulty for some time in supplying ideas in advance of their writing. At an early stage of language learning they can only talk about the here-and-now. The spoken structures needed for speculation and suggestion involve a level of English that is out of their reach.
- The pre-writing phase needs to take a different form with L2 students. The topic of the writing needs to be related to a familiar story or a content area studied in class. Teachers need to supply children with simple pattern structures that move the story along or describe the subject of an informational piece. Children need visual cues to explain the meaning of useful vocabulary words such as nouns and verbs. A sequence of pictures gives L2 children support in constructing their writing.
- Most L2 children will achieve only the drafting phase of the writing process. The effort needed for them to put pencil to paper is so great that it is frequently counter-productive to ask L2 children to spend time on producing a final version.
- Teachers can make good use of an L2 child's draft by using it to focus the child on a language item or a fact about spelling or punctuation. Depending on the child's language development, it is wise to give the child only one or two pieces of information at a time. Give the child meaningful further practice involving examples of the item in use.
- Teachers should be prepared for L2 children to produce very small amounts of writing for many months or even a year. If a teacher's records show little or no progress after such a period, it is wise to

seek professional help from a counsellor or special needs teacher. Experienced teachers know, however, how widely L2 children's writing development can vary.

- The parents of some L2 students may not understand the rationale behind the drafting phase of the writing process, with its concentration on content and fluency. In their culture it may be acceptable to produce only correct work. The notion of risk-taking, or a trial-and-error approach, may be unusual to families from school systems with large numbers of children in a class and a formal relationship between teacher and student. Such an approach is only feasible with relatively small classes and the possibility of an individual relationship with the teacher.

- Teachers should be ready to explain their system of correction to the parents of L2 children. The aim is not to shame the child by drawing attention to mistakes but rather to use the piece of writing to teach children strategies that lead them to a greater mastery. Most teachers make their corrections in small discreet handwriting above the word. Many teachers choose to focus their comments on only one or two language items. The rationale behind this approach to correction should be explained to parents at an early stage of the school year.

- Young L2 children from some school systems may be unprepared for structured literacy teaching at the time when it is a routine practice in international schools. They may come from school systems where they do not start learning to read and write until they are six or seven. In those circumstances, teachers must be prepared to take a child through all the pre-writing, and early writing activities, before expecting children to be able to participate in guided writing sessions.

Independent writing

The fundamental aim of any writing programme is for young students to become independent writers, prepared to write in a variety of ways and for different purposes and audiences. With L2 students, the child's personality plays a significant part in the move to independence in writing. Some children are prepared to write on their own from the earliest days, taking risks with setting down words and making creative use of the vocabulary and structures that they have acquired. Other children are reluctant to commit themselves to paper. They may be fearful of making mistakes or have difficulty in transferring their knowledge of the spoken language into writing. Thus, L2 children may take months before they start writing independently of the teacher. Some L2 children, still within the range of the norm, take more than a year before they are able to express their thoughts in writing.

The aim of independent writing time is to allow young students to create their own pieces of writing. The pieces can derive from the child's own experience or relate to an on-going social studies or science topic. The writing may take the form of extension activities related to books that have been read during shared or guided reading. These activities might include retellings where children write individually or where several children join together to recount different parts of a story and the creation of plays and poems. According to age, appropriate illustration is a legitimate and valuable part of independent writing.

Children are also writing independently when they create lists of instructions and write tickets and labels in themed play areas. Further opportunities are created when teachers set up a personal mailbox and correspond with each child on an on-going basis. Such strategies as providing boards for messages and school mail services also allow children to engage in independent writing in a low-risk, meaningful context. An array of writing materials and implements should be readily available to encourage children to write independently. These should include large-sized card, coloured paper, notebooks, and a selection of pens, pencils, markers and chalks.

Writing of this type can be carried out by individuals, in pairs, or in small collaborative groups. When working in a group, however, it is essential that each child have an independent writing task to carry out that will eventually combine to make a whole. Writing as a group is a difficult task for children to manage at any age. Students should be encouraged with all writing tasks to brainstorm initially, to draft their piece, consult with their peers, make changes and produce a finished version. The teacher intervenes when asked and offers help to struggling students. These writing times are valuable occasions for observing and assessing children's development in writing independently.

Teachers may find that they need to supply initial and continuing support to L2 children in order for them to write independently. It is a useful practice in the early months for the teacher to take down the child's dictated story or stream of thought in writing. This gives teachers time to talk to individual children about vocabulary, about the formation of words, about the construction of simple sentences and how to structure a piece of writing. Pocket charts or word and letter tiles are a concrete means of allowing children to create a short piece of writing. Encouragement and praise related to persistent effort are always valuable.

Using the computer to teach early literacy to young second language students

The presence of stand-alone computers in young children's classrooms, and the existence of mini-labs where networked computers are grouped together, allows teachers access to a range of learning opportunities for L2 students in relation to language arts. The opportunities can be divided into two groups: those related to general applications such as word-processing, and those arising from the use of specific software titles. The word-processing application allows L2 students to type words and short pieces of writing with the knowledge that they can alter their initial attempts with ease. It also offers, as was mentioned above, the opportunity for students who write in different scripts, and use writing systems with a right-to-left directionality, to observe and practise the use of Roman script and its left to right movement.

Effective software titles offer a range of possibilities in the teaching of language arts. The most valuable to teachers and students are those that combine genuine learning opportunities with features that are attractive and engaging for young children. A program that aims to fulfil both these criteria is *Bailey's Book House*, created by **Edmark**. This program, according to the disk cover, is designed to give children opportunities to learn the names of letters, recognise uppercase and lowercase letters, recognise rhyming words, sound out word beginnings and endings, learn and use common adjectives and prepositions, increase reading vocabulary, and print storybooks and cards.

Such extensive claims need careful evaluation on the part of teachers in order to establish the real value of such programs. In this connection, most teachers would say that the value of this, and similar software titles, lies in the opportunities they give to children to gain reinforcement in areas that are already familiar from work done in the classroom. The unique advantage of the computer is that it allows children to manage their own learning, at their own pace, in a supportive environment that offers positive feedback on achievement. It is this capacity to provide students with the means to learn independently that makes the computer such a positive resource for use with L2 children. So much of the time for new L2 children with limited spoken English is spent in a situation where they have little control over their learning.

Other titles from Edmark provide opportunities that are specifically suited to the needs of L2 children. *Thinkin' Things*, for example, offers L2 students at an early stage in their language learning, the possibility of engaging in higher-order thinking activities. This is achieved by the use of limited simple text combined with visual and sound cues. There exist numerous catalogues, (the **Edmark Catalog**, among them), that provide lists of selected titles for use with young children in all areas of learning. A word of caution should be inserted here, however. Computer software, like other media, is variable in quality. Teachers should only purchase new items after they have seen the software in use and understand the nature of the hardware that is needed to allow the program to function in its entirety and at an appropriate speed.

Finally, there exist interactive systems that are designed to introduce, illustrate and reinforce all aspects of early literacy learning. These include *Wiggleworks*, created by **Scholastic Inc.**, available on CD-ROM or floppy disk, which is an interactive system that also provides linked print material in the form of literature titles, teachers' manuals, etc. These teaching packages offer the advantages provided by other effective pieces of software and are useful for providing L2 students with the quantity of early literacy practice that they are likely to need. Even the manufacturers, however, are wary of making their claims too extensive. *Wiggleworks*, for instance, is advertised as being an 'extra pair of hands' for busy teachers, and this is a realistic assessment of its value. Administrators and teachers need to evaluate with care the expenditure of the large sums involved in acquiring this type of package.

The need to explain the rationale behind the acceptance of developmental spelling

The topic of spelling is often a cause for controversy. For many adults, correct spelling is the criterion by which a school's literacy programme is judged. Teachers in international schools should recognise that the practice of allowing young children to use developmental spelling is a potential source of misunderstanding and parental unease.

Developmental or invented or approximated spelling is regarded as a legitimate phase in young children's literacy development in today's classrooms. In the case of some L2 parents, however, teachers will need to explain fully and effectively the rationale behind allowing children to create their own spelling approximations. The unease, which some parents feel, derives from several possible sources. In many cultures, the memorisation and reproduction of an accepted body of knowledge are highly valued. Indeed this is the purpose for attending school. Correct spelling is part of the knowledge that children must acquire. Such parents are unaccustomed to the idea that children benefit from being able to write down their thoughts before they have a knowledge or understanding of conventional spelling. Many parents, too, value correctness of structure and spelling above original thought or fluency.

Parents from certain language backgrounds, including Chinese and Japanese, are used to writing systems that wholly or partly comprise characters or ideograms. Children learn to write by memorising and copying these ideograms. Japanese children learn around 2000 ideograms during their time at school, and authors and wordsmiths employ many more. A minute variation in the outline gives the ideogram a different meaning. This is unlike spelling in English where misspelt words still largely convey the appropriate meaning. Japanese parents need a careful and respectful explanation about the value of accepting developmental spelling in English. Teachers need to show the stages through which children's developmental spelling passes as it moves nearer to conventional forms. Above all, teachers need to declare and illustrate their commitment to helping children become correct conventional spellers.

L2 children and spelling

A helpful general strategy with L2 children is to consider the learning of vocabulary and the teaching of spelling as two parts of a whole. When new words are introduced in talk, during reading or as required in writing, this is the time to point out spelling connections with words already part of the student's repertoire. Discussion of new vocabulary leads to talk about word families, ways of writing down the sounds of English, the formation of plurals, verb endings, and so on. L2 children, in particular, benefit from being made aware of connections and similarities between new words and known words.

Involving L2 children in writing down words relating to class topics and themes can take several forms. Children can make their own picture dictionaries or use a publisher's aid such as the *Steck Vaughn Writing Dictionary* to check off and add to lists of words in alphabetical order. Other ways of collecting and listing words include making and displaying lists of word families and making large illustrations with labels. These listings should be used as a resource for authentic reading and writing activities associated with the topic. Many teachers make use of these topic-related groups of words to give children spelling tests. The difference between this type of test, and the old sort drawn from vocabulary lists in spelling books, is that children are constantly practising these words in their reading and writing. The spelling test is a further means of reinforcing children's acquaintance with the meaning and spelling of the words. The factor that supports L2 children's acquisition and spelling of new vocabulary is for them to experience new words in use via all four language skills.

Displaying young children's writing

How and when to display young students' work is an area of debate among educators in international schools where there are beginning writers of English at every level. Positive learning environments for young children give validity to a trial and error approach and to taking risks in learning to speak, read and write. Children benefit from knowing that they will not be reprimanded or penalised for making mistakes. By encouraging children to reflect on their work and make changes, children gain a better understanding of the process of creating effective writing. For young L2 children this is a significant factor in enabling them to make rapid and stress-free progress in their language learning.

Most administrators, however, prefer that work displayed in corridors, on classroom walls and in literary magazines, is free of error. They feel that to display work containing errors indicates to parents, and other visitors, that the school is careless of standards or has failed to notice the mistakes. Teachers are therefore faced with a dilemma: they wish to encourage the valuable practice of risk-taking with its resultant errors, but they must ensure that each child's piece is error-free when it is finished. L2 children, in particular, present teachers with this problem.

Some teachers find a way round the difficulty by displaying work at the draft stage with the errors marked on the page. A notice with the words, 'work in progress', signifies that the teacher is aware of the errors. Some teachers inform children that the final aim of all their writing is to produce a correct version, and intervene themselves (or involve parents) at the publishing stage to achieve an error-free copy. These are useful strategies. The most effective solution, however, is to ensure that parents are kept well informed about the school's approach to the teaching of writing. If parents understand the rationale underpinning each stage of the process, they are better able to place individual pieces of students' work in context.

Summary

L2 students benefit from many of the practices current in today's classrooms for young children. The integration of the four skills of language — listening, speaking, reading and writing, provides reinforcement for all aspects of language learning. The thematic approach to subject matter and classroom activity gives L2 children many opportunities to experience the same language items in authentic contexts.

The use of consistent strategies in teaching reading and writing, give children the means to become independent readers and writers. However, L2 students may have trouble in processing text and in creating a piece of writing due to their uncertain grasp of oral English. Access to the meaning of the context of an unfamiliar word, and an inner understanding of how language is constructed and how words work, aid children in acquiring essential reading and writing strategies. New young L2 students lack this innate knowledge and may take longer to become fluent and effective readers and writers. They need many opportunities to carry out stimulating reading and writing activities in authentic contexts at every phase of the literacy programme.

Teachers of L2 students need to explain fully to parents certain aspects of the practice in international schools that may be unfamiliar to them. Such areas include the acceptance of spelling approximations, methods of correction and the notion of drafting a piece of writing.

Chapter 8

Teaching Language Arts to Older Second Language Students in Mainstream Classrooms

Introduction

This chapter is concerned with the integration of older second language students into the language arts programmes of mainstream classrooms. Children of this age entering an international school are likely to be able to read and write in their own languages. Their competence in English is variable, however. Some children are complete non-speakers of English, others, because of previous English tuition, have progressed some way towards competence in speaking, listening, reading and writing. It is the task of teachers in international schools to provide a language arts programme that responds to the various language needs of second language students while providing a challenging learning experience for competent users of English. A further aspect of teaching language arts to second language students is the need for teachers to make connections with language needs in other curriculum areas. When teachers use consistent approaches in teaching reading, writing and speaking across the curriculum, they provide students with the optimum circumstances for gaining access to subject matter and for acquiring the language skills they need to flourish in those areas.

The language arts programmes in many international schools for older students at the elementary level are based on a literature-based integrated approach to the teaching of literacy and oracy. A variety of authentic literature is used in the teaching of reading, associated with extension activities that require students' responses in speech and in writing, and the performance of meaningful tasks. The process approach to writing is commonly used in many international schools. Thus, most students engage in pre-writing activities before moving through the stages of drafting, reflection, editing and publishing. In an integrated literature-based programme, the teaching of English usage, grammar, vocabulary and spelling is, in theory, related to authentic contexts and practised in

165

meaningful pieces of writing rather than through isolated exercises. Practice tends to vary in these areas, however. Administrators, teachers and parents, to varying degrees, tend to prefer a more sequenced and structured approach that takes a number of forms. In most schools, connections between talk, reading and writing underline an integrated approach to the mastery of language arts skills.

Programmes of this type offer an effective basis for work with second language children. The aim of this chapter is to indicate the areas where the presence of these students may require teachers to modify their teaching approaches and to vary the content of the programme. The first section of the chapter is concerned with reading, the second with writing and the third with teaching the spoken English necessary for academic purposes. In the classroom, however, these areas cross over and intercon- nect. Teachers will find that content from all three sections applies to the delivery of an integrated language arts programme.

Reading

Older children's acquisition of the skills of English — speaking and listening go hand-in-hand with reading and writing

The practice of allowing language learners to develop oral competence before moving on to reading and writing is not feasible for older L2 children entering the upper grades of an international school. The demands of the mainstream programme make it essential that students begin to learn to read and write at the same time as they strengthen their mastery of speaking and listening. In the case of older children, the outcome is generally positive — access at an early stage to reading and writing reinforces their acquisition of the oral skills of language.

Making the transition into the second language

L2 students who read in their own language generally make the transition quite smoothly, over time, to decoding the target language. Two groups of children may prove the exception to this pattern: Those who need to learn a new script or writing system, and those with mild or severe learning difficulties. It is a longer process to acquire the understanding of a written text that is required for full participation in the mainstream programme.

Older children have certain advantages in learning to read in a second language. Their wider experience of life and competence in their first language has a positive impact on their reading in English. Their understanding about the construction of a story allows them to predict the course of a narrative. Their prior knowledge helps them to make sense of settings and character types. Their knowledge of the vocabulary of their own language aids them in making intelligent guesses about the likely meaning of unfamiliar words. Experienced teachers maximise the use of this existing knowledge in older L2 students by their choice of reading material.

Teachers reading to students

The practice of reading aloud to the class is valuable for older students. For L2 students, in particular, reading aloud gives teachers the opportunity to introduce a range of material at a higher reading level than the L2 children can yet read with ease. Teachers should not limit their choice of reading to standard classroom material only. The aim is to stimulate, instruct and delight children and to lead them to make wider choices in their own reading.

The choice of possible reading material includes extracts and short pieces from fiction and non-fiction sources and from newspapers and magazines. These pieces can relate to a class study or to a theme in the news of potential interest to students. Appropriate selections can be used to introduce a new reading genre or writing format. Other material can be chosen from the favourite reading of the teacher or of one of the students. Occasionally it is valuable to use a piece of reading to introduce a discussion about a source of anxiety or stress in the classroom. Reading aloud is also an opportunity for teachers to introduce literature and non-fiction materials from backgrounds other than the English speaking countries. It is a useful practice to consult the parents of L2 students about writing in English that relates to their culture and geographical region.

Introducing a piece of fiction

It is standard practice to provide an introduction to a piece of fiction before students begin to read a book as part of the reading programme. For L2 students, however, an effective introduction is an essential requirement. Carefully chosen pre-reading activities allow L2 students to approach a new text equipped to gain meaning from what they read. The choice of reading material is also a significant factor in allowing L2 children access to authentic reading experiences at an early stage in their learning.

Introductory strategies

- Establish a context for the story. Bring in an object or piece of clothing that gives a lead-in to the narrative. Give a visual account

Textbox 8.1 Selecting reading material for an international school classroom

Selecting reading material for use with older children at the elementary level in an international school can be a challenging and time-consuming business. Most teachers are aware of the desirability of broadening their choice of fiction and non-fiction titles to include books that reflect the backgrounds and experiences of the students in their classes. Many teachers also wish to offer titles in English that relate in some way to the region in which the school is located. In many instances, tried and tested favourites that were appropriate for use in an English-speaking country seem inappropriate for use in classrooms that contain the diversity typical of most international schools. Books that have limited relevance include some that are described in their country of origin as suitable for use with multicultural groups of children, a description that might be thought to apply also to students in international schools. Such stories, designed to be read by groups of children in national school system, frequently recount the experiences of children from in-coming minorities as they come to terms with living in a new country. The tone of these books and the experiences they describe are subtly different from the experiences of children in international schools. One or two of such books provide insights that are valuable to all young readers; however, teachers in international schools will need to look further in order to offer relevant and meaningful reading experiences to their students.

Non-fiction titles perhaps provide an easier way of introducing a global perspective into the classroom providing that teachers move away from the standard offerings of educational publishers. Biographies of Martin Luther King and John F. Kennedy abound. It is possible, for instance, to find biographies of historical and contemporary figures written in English that offer a wider view of world history. Biographies of such subjects as Genghis Khan, Alexander the Great, Chiang Kai-Shek, Mikhail Gorbachev, Kwame Nkrumah and Golda Meir provide a useful resource when studying the history and culture of the region in which an international school is situated. Teachers should also have available, as a standard resource, non-fiction texts relating to countries and regions around the world and to the full range of natural habitats. Sport is another area where teachers should ensure that all the world's popular sports are represented in the class library rather than solely those played in the school.

Finding children's fiction of quality in English, with settings and characters from countries outside the English-speaking world is a more difficult matter. Many teachers prefer, for understandable reasons, to stay with classic pieces of children's fiction written by English-speaking authors or translated into English. This need not necessarily be a limiting choice. Some of these titles, such as *Robinson Crusoe* and *The Swiss Family Robinson*, allow teachers to introduce global themes and to carry out extension work that involves children in writing out of their own experience and knowledge. Translations of traditional stories, myths and legends from around the world offer further fruitful possibilities. (See Appendix A: Resources for Teachers, pp. 259–63, for

Textbox 8.1 (*cont.*)

---

a list of publishing houses that offer such translations.) Such texts lend themselves readily to dramatic activity, artwork and collaborative writing schemes.

Literature selections that relate to the location or region in which the school is placed have the potential to provide profound and enriching experiences to children in international schools. An outstanding example of a school that has made such a connection is the International School of Hiroshima. On the school's Internet Website, students all round the world are invited to read *Sadako and the Thousand Cranes* by Eleanor Coerr. This is a story of a young girl who dies from leukaemia following the dropping of the atomic bomb on Hiroshima. By sending a paper crane and a donation to The 1000 Crane Club, students can share in the building of an International Children's Peace Monument where the paper cranes are to be collected. A later page illustrates how the cranes are made. The Internet offers further useful opportunities for exchanges of information between teachers about titles and follow-up activities appropriate to international school students. Sites that offer possibilities for this type of exchange are mentioned in Chapter 11 — Electronic technology, and in Appendix B.

---

of the setting, via slides or photographs or projected pictures. Relate the story to another piece of fiction that is familiar to students. Music and rhyme are further means of establishing atmosphere, time and setting

- Consider giving the outline of the story in advance. This can be done by talking the students through the illustrations in the text, by story mapping and by webs and flow charts showing the action and the relationships between the characters.
- During the introductory discussion, draw out the key words that are central to the plot. A prior knowledge of these words allows L2 students to move through the narrative and to make informed guesses about unfamiliar words.
- Lists of vocabulary words with definitions are of limited use unless they are given a context related to the story. Schemes that make connections between words or illustrate their use are more effective. In the case of Robin Hood stories, for instance, an effective way to indicate the significance of the titles of noblemen and church dignitaries is to represent the hierarchies in a tree form.
- The use of filmed or taped television productions of well-known stories to give children an understanding of the plot is an option. However, many teachers prefer children to see such versions after they have read the book. Children relate strongly to the visual image and it is possible that seeing a story on film, or in cartoon form, may

limit the pleasure to be gained from reading the original version. It may be more acceptable and appropriate to use short extracts from filmed material as a means of establishing setting, period, tone and character.

- The reading of biography is a different circumstance. Introducing a biography with a montage of appropriate filmed material brings relevance and immediacy to reading someone's life story. Such material is not difficult to obtain in the case of typical subjects such as Martin Luther King, Nelson Mandela or Mother Theresa.

Choice of reading material

- Choose works of fiction with settings likely to be familiar to L2 students. This builds on what they know and allows them a route into an understanding of the text.
- The optimum choices for beginning and early intermediate students are retellings of stories familiar from film or television as well as from reading. Stories of folk heroes such as Robin Hood, and repetitive adventure stories with a strong narrative line, are useful. An ability to recognise the story line gives L2 students immediate access to the core of the story and motivates them to try to make sense of unfamiliar words or difficult passages.
- Consider using simplified tellings of the text being studied. Known as high interest, low reading level material, these versions contain tellings of well-known modern and classic stories in graded language. It is possible, for example, to find three or four different version of the Robin Hood story aimed at L2 learners at different levels of reading competence. The easiest stories are highly illustrated with a simple narrative that avoids detail or complex structure. As they progress in difficulty so the level of support from illustration diminishes and more complex structures and advanced vocabulary are introduced. By using these books it is possible for even beginning L2 students to join with the rest of the class in appropriately designed extension activities related to the story.

The complete beginner in reading lessons

It is fair to acknowledge the difficulty of occupying L2 beginners during home classroom reading lessons. Most teachers evolve over time a range of effective strategies for use with advancing L2 learners. With complete beginners, on the other hand, the most experienced teachers are stretched to the limit to involve such students meaningfully in the general work of the class.

Grouping children in various ways is an effective strategy. Groups may be made up of students of different levels of language competence or of students at the same level. Paired activities where the beginning student reads to a more competent L2 student or an L1 student are also useful. Detailed comments on grouping children for reading are included under the next heading, Literature study groups.

There are times, however, when the teacher wishes to work with the whole class at a level of language that is too far above an L2 student's competence to be comprehensible. This is a time when it is permissible and even useful to give L2 beginners a task that involves repetitive reading and writing exercises. Some teachers mistakenly feel a sense of guilt in these circumstances. Beginning students are easily fatigued; they live in a world where they have only a partial understanding of what goes on around them. In the early days, such students have little sense of control over their own destinies. It is a valid strategy to allow them time occasionally to work their way through repetitive, cumulative exercises involving simple reading and writing tasks. For many children, this gives a feeling of satisfaction and achievement, a feeling that is unlikely to be present in other areas of their lives at this time.

Such activity can be made more valuable if the exercises involve vocabulary and structures that relate to the student's social language or an on-going theme in the classroom. Simple reading and writing exercises that allow practice of language items previously heard in different contexts are a useful reinforcement for students at this level. This is an occasion when drill and review exercises on the computer are appropriate. Activity of this type only becomes harmful if used too frequently or when it prevents an L2 student on a consistent basis from participation in whole class experiences.

Literature study groups

Studying the same book, or books grouped round a theme or by the same author, in a small group, is a valuable strategy for use with classes that contain L2 children. Such groups allow the use of a range of books in the classroom differentiated by reading level. They allow L2 students to contribute at their own level in a supportive environment. The strategy of mixed ability grouping, whereby competent users of English are placed with beginning and intermediate L2 children, allows L2 students to experience a high level of English in meaningful use.

Children can be placed in literature study groups for all phases of reading activity. This includes the introductory phase on occasions when each group is reading from a different text. The teacher moves round the room talking to the children in each group, the aim being to introduce the book and to show how it fits in with the whole-class theme. The reading of the book itself can also be carried out partly or wholly as a group activity. Children can read independently chapter by chapter and then pause to discuss their views, or can read aloud to each other in pairs. Choral reading and the dramatic rendering of pieces of dialogue are further options. Finally, many extension and follow-up activities lend themselves to collaborative group work. The advantage to L2 students of this approach is that they are able to participate in whole class activities that would be beyond their reach to carry out independently. The following list of points relates to issues that classroom teachers should acknowledge and plan for in grouping classes of diverse children for literature study:

L2 children in literature study groups

- Collaborative activities can be planned to allow all children access to challenging learning opportunities.
- Students need to be taught how to contribute positively in a small group. Teachers should begin the year by demonstrating how to carry out a task co-operatively.
- Teachers can profitably group students in a class in different ways for different learning purposes. They should feel free to alter the personnel of a group if it does not function smoothly. It is important, however, to allow children time to settle into a pattern of working together.
- An essential feature of effective collaborative work is to ensure that each child contributes at an optimum level. This includes ensuring that able children are sufficiently challenged and that quiet L1 or L2 children are allowed time to make their contributions and to be involved in meaningful ways in carrying out the group task.
- To ensure that all children contribute in a collaborative activity, it is wise for teachers to assign specific tasks to each member. (Later in the year, group members may be able to share out the tasks appropriately among themselves.) Tasks can include acting as researcher, collator, scribe, illustrator or reporter.
- Asking the group to present their findings to the whole class is an effective strategy for keeping the children on task. (The inclusion of a graphic element in the activity gives the reporter a concrete support during the presentation phase.)
- Children can be asked to respond as individuals within the group as well as in a collaborative manner. Individual contributions can be

designed to unite in a whole. (See the paragraphs headed Co-operative writing possibilities on pp. 185–6.)

- Teachers can cater for the varying levels of language competence in a group by constructing a range of response activities. Practical as well as text-based tasks ensure that all students can participate. Practical tasks include making detailed drawings of a character or location in the story, creating a cartoon strip of one part of the action and designing and constructing a model or frieze illustrating all or one part of the story.

- Teachers need to structure the grid so that children make choices requiring a range of reading responses and language skills. Examples of reading responses include writing a physical description of a character, describing how a character's actions give insights into her or his personality, creating a board game that relates closely to the narrative and suggesting alternative outcomes to the story. Examples of language activities include work with parts of speech that figure prominently in the story such as adjectives or adverbs, the creation of further dialogue written and punctuated correctly, and exercises that require students to rewrite dialogue from the story as reported speech.

- A range of activities constructed in a grid format allows children to make choices according to their preferred learning styles. Examples of this range include dramatic role-play, art and craft activities, oral retellings, and finding information about the author or illustrator via one of the publishers' sites on the Internet.

- Teachers should be prepared to explain, and if necessary, defend, the use of co-operative groupings. Parents of both L1 and L2 students may not feel that such approaches comprise a rigorous course of study.

- Teachers need to make systematic observations of each child's contribution to a group project. They need to vary the criteria on which they base their grouping to ensure that all children are adequately challenged. They need to utilise a range of grouping strategies in their teaching rather than restrict themselves too narrowly to one approach. This range should include whole class teaching, independent work, as well as pair and small group activity.

Responding to a text — promoting higher-order thinking skills

Responding to a text through talk and in writing is an essential phase in studying a piece of fiction or non-fiction. Teachers are faced with a number of challenges in trying to involve beginning and early intermediate L2 students in meaningful ways in this aspect of literature study.

Whole class discussion of a text is standard practice in most classrooms. Bringing the whole class together makes reading a shared experience and allows ideas to be exchanged and understandings to be deepened. It provides an opportunity for teacher and students to make connections with other curriculum areas and to draw on previous reading and life experiences in interpreting the text.

Such conversations also allow the teacher to introduce questions and ideas that require students to engage in higher-order thinking. Bloom (1956) categorised thinking skills as low, middle and high. Higher-order skills involve analysis, evaluation and synthesis. In practical terms higher-order thinking skills are required when teachers ask students to compare and contrast the way different authors write about a topic, to trace cause and effect in a narrative, to provide alternative endings or to combine their knowledge from several sources. All the professional literature concerned with provision for L2 students in mainstream classrooms urges teachers to find ways of engaging these students in higher-order thinking. To fail in this is to limit such students' access to the full academic programme and to exclude them from achieving complete success in English-medium international schools.

Practically, teachers have to overcome several hurdles in order to engage L2 students in general conversation about books and in higher-order thinking. The management of focused discussion groups that contain L2 learners is itself a significant challenge. (Detailed suggestions for managing class talk are contained in Spoken English for academic purposes, pp. 193–7, this chapter.) Teachers may find that small literature study groups offer a more easily managed forum for focused talk.

A further challenge is the level of students' English. Realistically teachers will find that beginning and early intermediate learners of English have difficulty in joining in general discussion. Most teachers confine their spoken questions to L2 students at this level to simple matters of fact involving the sequence of a narrative or physical descriptions of a character or location. With L2 children who are advancing in their command of English, teachers need to act as models in the processes required to answer higher-order questions. They should spell out the steps in their own thinking and give examples from the piece of reading that lead them to make an inference or to arrive at a conclusion. They need to construct small group opportunities that enable L2 students to observe other children in the process of carrying out collaborative higher-order thinking activities.

L2 students who fail to make the leap from successfully answering questions of fact, to talking or writing in ways that involve higher-order thinking, may be reflecting the educational traditions of their own culture. Certain L2 students, usually including those from the Indian sub-continent and from some schools in Europe, the Middle East and East Asia, are not accustomed to engage in the analytical and independent-thinking modes required in most international schools. Their cultures place value on traditional knowledge and received opinions. Schools in these cultures tend to require students to learn and reproduce facts gained from the teacher and via textbooks. L2 students from these cultures in international schools frequently take time to change their accustomed ways of thinking. Teachers of such students need to spell out on each occasion what are the processes involved in reaching an answer to an open-ended question or one that requires analysis or inference.

Strategies for checking students' comprehension

Before L2 students are ready to write fluently and effectively in English they can be asked to show their reading comprehension via activities that are text-based but that do not require free composition of new language. Such activities include putting sentence strips in an appropriate order, completing cloze passages that require students to fill in gaps with appropriate words and phrases, and maintaining reading logs supported by graphic organisers.

Retellings of the content of a fiction or non-fiction text are a further effective and flexible strategy for checking L2 students' understanding of written material. This strategy is appropriate for use with all sorts of texts — narratives, biography, informational pieces and lists of instructions. It is ideal in a multi-level language arts classroom because the retelling can take forms that are accessible to L2 students at all levels of language competence. They include dramatic reconstruction, the creation of plans and maps based on descriptions in passages, making board games, designing graphs and charts to explain numerical and statistical text, and creating pictorial representations and comic strips. Retellings can be carried out independently or by pairs of students or small groups.

Use of the dictionary

Familiarity with the use of the dictionary is beneficial for L2 students. It is a helpful exercise for L2 children to create a personal dictionary incorporating new vocabulary as it occurs in the classroom. However, it is not desirable for the dictionary to be used to translate every unknown word in a reading passage. Good choices of texts for L2 students contain only relatively few unfamiliar words. Students are then in a position to

Textbox 8.2 Changing the way children think

The paragraphs on higher-level thinking-skills give rise to a question that troubles many reflective teachers in international schools. Are we really doing some of our L2 students a service when we educate them in ways so far removed from what will bring them success in their own cultures? Most international school students will eventually return home. Most expect to resume their place in home school systems and to reintegrate into the accustomed social life of their culture. For some L2 students the return home requires a major adaptation after their years in an international school.

Most long-term teachers in the international school system have had the experience of receiving letters from and about students who have recently returned home to find that they are ill-equipped or unable to cope with the profound differences in their home schools. Sometimes these differences concern social life and behaviour in class. In other cases children may have been unable to pass examinations to enter the schools that their parents had planned for them. Students from the Indian sub-continent fall into this group, in my experience, particularly when they return home at a young age. (Young students in India learn to decode texts and to carry out mathematics computation from the age of four.) An ability to think analytically, to offer opinions about a text, or to solve problems in mathematics are not what is needed to enable Indian students to succeed in their own system.

What is our responsibility as teachers, if any, to recognise and act in this matter? We can argue that parents choose to place their children in our schools and by so doing, must accept the differences in educational approach. Certainly, it is not possible to offer distinct programmes appropriate to the 50 or 60 nationalities to be found in many of our schools. The practical solution is to urge parents to keep their children in touch with their home language and school system. Sometimes this means that children are burdened with two sets of homework, or even that they are absent at times while they go to school in their own countries. At the very least parents should consider having their children tutored by one of their own nationals in the period before they return home.

It is a good policy, in general, for teachers to be open and non-defensive in talking to parents while acknowledging the practical difficulties of re-entry for some students. There are many benefits to be gained from the international school experience. Students from our schools are equipped to deal with all sorts of people from every nation. L2 students become competent users of English. These assets are of great benefit to students when they move into higher education, and eventually, when they seek employment.

employ independent strategies to unlock the meaning of a word. Such strategies include using illustrations as visual cues, gaining meaning from the surrounding context and the ability to make intelligent guesses based on prior knowledge. Dictionaries are for use when these strategies have been exhausted.

Encouraging L2 children to read widely

Wide reading in both languages has many benefits for bilingual children. Reading in their home language contributes to their emotional and cognitive development and leads to an increased understanding and command of their own language. This mastery is important in itself and is also effective in supporting L2 readers in their reading of English. Reading widely in English brings L2 students into contact with a level of language that is above their own ability to produce themselves. It gives them insights into how written English is constructed; they meet complex sentences and new vocabulary items in context. They are introduced to a range of reading genres and given insights about the customary use of English in these contexts.

A teacher's influence on the reading behaviour of all students is significant. With L2 students in particular, the time given in class to reading and talk about books gives a clear message of the importance attached to reading for personal interest and entertainment as well as to reading for academic purposes. Time for independent reading in the school day, and the weight attached to the use of the library, are influential factors in signalling the value placed on sustained and wide ranging reading.

Understandably, many students discover the ease and pleasure of reading stories from one of the series published by astute publishers. (The latest of these include the *Goosebumps* and *Babysitters* series as well as old favourites such as the *Hardy Boys*.) These formula stories contain the attributes that make easy reading for L2 students. They have a strong narrative line, the plots are repetitive, the characters are familiar and the language used is direct and colloquial. Thus, they represent one way of introducing L2 students to writing in English that allows them to read with fluency and ready understanding. Most teachers, however, will wish to ensure that L2 students make the leap to a more challenging range of reading.

A useful strategy to encourage L2 students (and all students) to read more widely is to make connections with a student's individual interests and enthusiasms. A single genre such as biography, for instance, offers subject matter that it potentially appealing to all students. Age-appropriate biographies exist that describe the lives of sports personalities, explorers, scientists and screen personalities. Experienced teachers take a broad view of what comprises appropriate reading material. Magazines concerned with sport, computers, animals or cars, children's novels on which the latest Hollywood movie has been based, and books giving instructions about making models or carrying out craft activities may prove the starting point for more broadly based reading selections. (See Chapter 11, pp. 255–7, for further suggestions.)

L2 students reading poetry and plays

Poetry, perhaps surprisingly, can be appealing to L2 students. It is important that the content is age-appropriate and that the poem has a strong rhythm and a degree of rhyme. Attractive illustrated poetry books now exist containing poems that answer these criteria. Many deal with topics and themes that appeal to today's children. These include comic poems about animals, food, dinosaurs and dragons, descriptive pieces about the weather and far away places, narrative poems about legendary heroes as well as more thoughtful pieces about the problems of childhood. Apart from the pleasure they give, poems of this sort are easy to memorise, give L2 children practice in English intonation, and introduce them to vocabulary words in easily accessible contexts. Choral readings are an enjoyable and supportive way of reciting poems in the classroom.

Appropriate published plays and student-created pieces of dialogue offer a similar mixture of pleasure and valuable teaching opportunities. Reading dialogue in role gives practice in authentic spoken English and provides L2 students with experience of linguistic elements such as intonation and appropriateness of language. Frequently the content of such dialogues, an amusing encounter, an angry exchange or asking for information, supplies valuable examples of the use of English in these situations.

There are exciting possibilities for teachers who decide to produce a play, however short, in a language arts class. Plays written by the students themselves that retell all or part of a story read in class are valuable to L2 students since they reinforce the use of previously heard structures and vocabulary. It is rewarding for L2 students to be included in all the backstage aspects of putting on a play as well as performing in the play itself. The numerous opportunities for students to take part in meaningful, contextualised conversation are an additional benefit.

L2 students who experience difficulty in reading English

Occasionally, eight- and nine-year-old students arrive in international schools unable to read or write in their own languages or with only minimal competence. This is sometimes due to the pattern of education in their home countries, where the teaching of reading and writing begins one or even two years later than in English-speaking schools. In other instances, the child's education may have been disrupted for significant periods of time through displacement or family upheaval. In these cases, there are grounds for requesting extra support so that such children can be provided with a carefully structured reading programme on an individual or small group basis.

L2 children who arrive with a history of difficulties in their own language, or who display unaccountable difficulty in transferring their reading skills from their own language to English, need careful monitoring by the classroom teacher. It takes time and continuing observation to establish whether the problem derives from the move into another language, or whether the student has a specific learning difficulty. (See pp. 86–9, Children with special needs, for a detailed discussion of this important area.)

The use of language arts reading textbooks

A new generation of published language arts materials offers a basic scope and sequence for the teaching of reading, writing and oracy to older students. (Textbox 7.1 on p. 150 deals more fully with the use of these publications.) Deriving chiefly from the United States, these materials include graded and themed selections of whole books, together with booklets and interactive CD-ROM packages that supply reading response and extension activities. The pedagogic basis for this material is the integrated, literature-based approach used in much of North America, Australia and New Zealand.

Teachers who work in international schools that have adopted these series will find that they must make adaptations to the materials in order for them to be of use with beginning and intermediate L2 students. Although some publishing houses include assignments and alternative content material for L2 children, these additions do not comprise an adequate programme for supporting L2 students in their acquisition and development of English. Frequently the language of the text is at too high a level, the follow-up activities are beyond their reach and the discussions and instructions are couched in language which is inaccessible to L2 students.

Teachers in these circumstances must supply supplementary reading materials at an appropriate level to meet the needs of L2 students. They must also utilise the strategies mentioned in the previous and following paragraphs to enable L2 students to participate in the mainstream language arts programme. In the case of reading, these include adequate pre-reading activity, a carefully tailored choice of reading material and adapted reading response and extension assignments.

Writing

An effective language arts programme for older L2 students builds on their existing writing skills in their own languages. It also teaches students the skills needed for success in all subject areas. Teachers help L2 students to achieve mastery of relevant writing skills if consistent strategies are used to teach writing across the curriculum, and if overt connections are made between the writing needs of subject areas and the standard content of the language arts programme.

Involving students in monitoring their own writing development

As older L2 students' oral skills in English increase, it is valuable to engage children in talk about their own writing. Teachers can guide children towards acquiring an ability to assess their own language development, where they feel confident and where they feel they need help. By asking children to evaluate their own strengths and weaknesses, teachers give students a greater sense of control over their own language learning. Talking about their strengths and weaknesses as writers also gives students valuable insights into the structure of the written language. Talk between teacher and student of this sort, followed by tuition in the specific areas of need identified by the student, leads to a profitable partnership between teacher and student.

The writing process and L2 students

The approach to writing known as the writing process, is found in many international schools. Other schools employ an approach similar in most essentials, but may use different terminology. Central to this view of teaching writing is the aim of encouraging children to concentrate on the content of their writing and to become fluent and reflective writers. Students move from extensive pre-writing activities to creating an initial draft. The writer then reflects on this draft independently and in collaboration with fellow students and the teacher. Changes are made to improve the content and construction of the writing and the work is edited for mistakes of grammar and spelling which are then corrected. Lastly, the student produces a final version that is read aloud or 'published' in some form.

The following headings relate to key phases in the process approach to writing. Teachers should note that few new L2 students are used to learning to write in this way. Most L2 students expect to create a piece of writing in which grammar, spelling and punctuation, as well as content, are written down in their final form. L2 students will therefore need tuition in carrying out the phases of the process itself. Teachers will also need to take into account the specific language learning needs of L2 children. The list of points under each heading below draws the attention of teachers to areas where L2 students need special consideration. Suggestions are made for adaptations that allow L2 students to engage effectively in process writing.

Pre-writing activities

- Pre-writing activities are essential for L2 students in connection with all types of writing. These include writing out of personal experience, responses to reading, third person narratives, poetry, letter writing, biography, and so on.
- Accessible examples of the target format should be read to students.
- In the case of beginning L2 students, it is a useful strategy to ask parents, where possible, to find a piece of writing in the target format in the home language. In this way, L2 students are given an understanding of the basic format that they can then transfer to their work in English.
- Teachers should discuss and show in detail how the author has communicated her or his ideas.
- The target audience should be agreed.
- In the case of a non-fiction piece of writing, arrangements for acquiring the necessary information should be made. This phase can usefully be carried out collaboratively. (Biography, empathetic pieces relating to characters in books and letter writing related to authentic issues are likely to need additional information.)
- Whole class discussion, independent research or small group activity are means of gathering factual information.
- Time should be given to discussing the construction and content of the intended writing. Ideas and outlines should be displayed in a symbolic or visual form in webs, trees or linear formats.
- Further support can be supplied to L2 students by providing an opening sentence and key words or phrases that move the writing along.
- Layouts and sentence patterns typical of the target writing format should be supplied. (E.g. the convention of laying out a letter in English.)
- Useful vocabulary can be discussed and displayed in an accessible form, using visual or other support.

Creating a first draft

- The notion of drafting is likely to be unfamiliar to new L2 children. Teachers will find it helpful to show students examples of drafts and how they are altered to produce a better piece of writing.
- Work in the draft phase should not be seen by L2 parents without an explanation attached. Most L2 parents will be uncertain about the value of allowing children to concentrate on content and fluency rather than on correct grammar and spelling.
- Explain at the first Open House, or earlier in an individual conference, the rationale behind each stage of process writing. L2 parents need to be reassured that the school is committed to high standards of accuracy in grammar and spelling.
- Examples of students' work from initial planning through to the finished version should be used to explain to parents how reflection and editing achieve writing of quality.
- L2 students who have difficulty in composing in English are sometimes helped by being able to dictate their thoughts to the teacher or a fellow student. The discussion that surrounds this exercise gives L2 students valuable information about creating a piece of writing.
- The word-processing application on the computer offers a supportive writing environment to L2 students, since the technology allows students to change and refine their initial attempts at expressing their ideas.

Reflecting on initial drafts

- Reflecting on their own writing is a difficult process for beginning and intermediate L2 students. Even advancing students will find the process of viewing their writing objectively in order to make changes to content, grammatical structure and spelling very challenging.
- The reflecting and editing stages are likely to be more effectively carried out by L2 students if the first draft has been created on the computer.
- It is a core part of the writing process in many classrooms that students read their drafts to a classmate or in a small group. These students then ask questions about the author's intentions and make constructive comments and suggestions about ways that the writing might be improved. Early learners of English are unlikely to find these sessions helpful or manageable.
- In most cases, teachers will have to guide L2 students in ways they can change their writing. They should concentrate initially on one

or two areas such as the ordering of the material or the use of opening and closing sentences.

- As L2 students' competence in English increases teachers can encourage children to vary their use of vocabulary, to add descriptive detail and to employ a greater variety of sentence construction.

Editing for mistakes of grammar and spelling

- Teachers will likewise find it more profitable with all but advanced L2 children to focus students' attention on one or two types of mistakes in grammar or spelling.
- This is an opportunity to give instant tuition relating to common confusions ('there' and 'their' and 'its' and 'it's') and to point out consistent types of spelling mistakes.
- Errors that relate to a student's level of English language development should be explained at the time or, if useful, taught in a short lesson to two or three students together. Common errors that occur include, for example, the inconsistent use of verb tenses in a narrative or failing to complete a sentence with a main verb.
- Classroom teachers should liaise with the student's ESL teacher concerning persistent errors of English usage.

Creating a final version

- Beginning and early intermediate L2 students may find that producing a finished version of their writing is an onerous task. This is especially true of children who are not used to the Roman alphabet. It is quite common for the final version to contain many, often different, errors.
- Creating a final version is a less weighty undertaking if the drafting and editing phases have been carried out on the computer.
- Classroom teachers may find it more effective to use alternative methods to obtain a correct piece of writing. These include asking volunteer parents to type out the piece and to 'publish' it in book form. Other possibilities are for the teacher to type it out, or for the L2 student to read out the writing to a friend who types it on the computer. In international schools, it is quite common to see this sort of help given willingly by one class member to another.

Creative writing out of personal experience

It is valuable for L2 children to be able to write about their life experiences. Such writing helps them to make sense of what they have experienced and allows them to recall and describe events and ways of living that relate to their home cultures and traditions.

However, the construction of a consecutive first-person narrative involving descriptions of thoughts and feelings as well as factual details is a difficult task for an L2 student. It is possible that new L2 students are unused to writing creatively out of their own experience. It is helpful if teachers read out examples of writing that describes the authors' experiences at a deep level. Novels in the first person written for children, diaries and short poems are possible sources of this type of writing in simple English. Published examples by classmates are effective models.

L2 students who are new to this type of writing should begin by using a more easily controlled format such as a daily journal. Journal writing provides the student with a framework in which the content and sequence of events are laid down. The student needs a mastery of only simple sentence structure to be able to express interesting and colourful events; personal reactions can be introduced as the student author's expertise increases. Books such as *Island of the Blue Dolphins* by Scott O'Dell, and *Anne Frank, The Diary of a Young Girl* by Anne Frank serve as compelling and useful examples at this stage. Many schools make a practice of asking 11- and 12-year-old students to describe their experiences and to write down their thoughts as they move on to the next stage of schooling. Some of the best of these graduation speeches are written by L2 students.

Writing poems and rhymes

Writing poetry is a rewarding activity with L2 students. It should be prefaced by reading examples of poems in the targeted format. L2 students tend to enjoy poems with strong rhythms, a good deal of rhyme and a compelling story line. Comic poems are very popular, especially limericks and rhyming couplets. These are formats, however, that L2 students may find difficult to reproduce owing to the demands of metre and rhyme.

Frames and patterns are one way of giving L2 students a degree of support in writing poetry. This strategy allows teachers to vary the quantity of original language students are required to insert for themselves. In this way students can be asked to write only alternate lines in a rhyming ballad or to supply the final words in a series of lines. Teacher and students can brainstorm together to produce lists of rhyming words or webs of ideas and vocabulary associated with a theme or subject. These give children a resource from which to construct their first poems. Later, L2 children are capable of writing poems that display humour, tell a story or reflect an original personal response.

Textbox 8.3 Second language students and writing biography

One of the chief challenges facing classroom teachers in international schools is to incorporate beginning L2 students in a meaningful way into the mainstream instructional programme. An effective strategy in the early days is to use the student's own language as a means to an understanding of a writing format or reading genre.

I have seen this approach used successfully to include a 10-year-old French-speaking student, newly arrived mid-year from Canada, in a unit on biography. The boy's parents were much involved; they understood the teacher's aims and co-operated with her at all stages of the process. The first step for the new student and the rest of the class was to read a varied selection of biographies. In this boy's case he read one greatly simplified biography in English from a range of ESL graded readers produced by a publishing house. He also read several biographies in French at a level appropriate to his age. The teacher then gave the parents an outline in English of the introductory work she intended students to carry out before writing biographies of their chosen subjects. This work consisted of constructing a list of questions and answers that would supply the content material on which to base their biographies.

The student and his parents discussed the content of the outline in their own language and he later constructed the required list of questions in French. The resultant biography of his grandmother, written in French, was well composed and showed a knowledge of the requirements of the writing format. A French-speaking teacher looked over his work and made some helpful comments. This is a successful strategy with beginner students. They learn some English, they remain in step with the mainstream instructional programme of the class and they can transfer their understanding of biography to later work in English. At the same time their self-esteem is maintained by being able to produce work at a similar level to the other students.

In reality it is more challenging for teachers when children are advancing in their language learning. At the stage when students are just about capable of battling their way through the mainstream instructional programme in English, the teacher may have to intervene extensively. They need to supply key word and visual support for each new text and to provide examples and outlines in the case of unfamiliar writing assignments. The efforts are worthwhile, however, when they enable L2 students to participate with their fellow students in a meaningful way, and to produce work of quality.

Co-operative writing possibilities

The use of varied grouping strategies in teaching L2 children is mentioned in many places in this handbook. Small groups and pairings are useful means of providing L2 children with support in the area of writing. The management issues associated with children working in groups are discussed in Literature study groups on pp. 171–3.

Co-operative writing activities take two broad forms: those in which each child contributes sections that are later combined into a single end product, and those in which students carry out separate writing activities relating to a core theme. For both these forms of co-operative writing it is necessary for the task to be divided into manageable units. Retellings are a form of writing that break down easily into parts. The original telling can be taken from a book or viewed on a screen and needs to be accompanied by the standard strategies for supporting L2 students. A successful format is for each child to take responsibility for retelling a chapter or small part of the original. These individual contributions are then bound together into one version. Biographies of explorers or the exploits of adventurers are good sources for this type of activity. Alternatively each child can be asked to describe the personality, appearance and place in the plot of one character in a story. This is an opportunity for illustration and story mapping.

Other schemes involve each child in an activity such as retelling a complete myth or folktale. These versions can be decorated with a repeated co-ordinating border or graphic device to give a feeling of unity to the final bound volume. It is essential that L2 children are supported in their writing in these circumstances. Key vocabulary, pattern sentences and structural outlines appropriate to the child's level of English are generally adequate to allow all but beginning learners to complete a simple narrative.

Teaching grammar, usage and punctuation

A feature of literature-based language arts programmes is the embedded teaching of grammar, usage and punctuation. One form of the embedded approach links the teaching of these areas to examples drawn solely from reading texts and arising out of children's writing needs. In many schools, this approach is adapted in order to ensure that certain material is 'covered' during the school year. In many international schools, it is common to find a grammar, usage and punctuation curriculum in place. Teachers are expected to deliver this curriculum using a mixture of explicit teaching and authentic practice exercises, making use where appropriate of thematically linked material relating to classroom reading or topics.

With L2 students, the emphasis placed on the teaching of grammar, usage and punctuation needs to be different. Explicit, distinct and repeated teaching of grammar, usage and punctuation is necessary for older L2 students at all levels. Embedded teaching alone is unlikely to be satisfactory with the majority of language learners since it requires L2 students to carry out two processes simultaneously. They must first isolate the language item in question from the body of the text, and must then try to understand the point of grammar or usage that is being taught. It is a more effective strategy with L2 learners to relate an embedded grammar lesson to a sequential programme of language teaching. A grammar and usage textbook at an appropriate level provides students and teachers with a useful common reference point. Explanations and exercises that relate to a consistent source are more likely to be assimilated and can be referred to on subsequent occasions. The security that such an approach provides for students offsets some of its disadvantages.

The limitations of teaching grammar, usage and spelling separately from authentic contexts are well known. It is essential that specific grammar teaching of this type is related to authentic use and practised through meaningful and relevant reading and writing tasks. With L2 students in mainstream language arts classes, the most effective strategy is to combine explicit, distinct teaching of grammar, usage and punctuation with extensive practice via authentic literacy activities.

Expanding the vocabulary of L2 students

These paragraphs relating to vocabulary might arguably be included within the section devoted to the teaching of reading. It is included in the writing section because the teaching of vocabulary is so often considered alongside the teaching of grammar, usage, punctuation and spelling. Valuable teaching opportunities are lost, however, if the teaching of these areas is restricted to single scheduled periods. An effective strategy with L2 students, (and with all students), is for teachers also to point out and expand on examples relating to the areas of grammar, spelling and vocabulary, as they occur, throughout the school day.

The strategy of supplying decontextualised lists of words and definitions to develop children's vocabulary has fallen out of use in most classrooms. Teachers now recognise that students retain an understanding of the meaning of unfamiliar words and acquire the ability to use them in their own speech and writing by associating them with a meaningful context and by practising their use in authentic literacy activities. L2 children need further support in grasping the meaning and in making use of new vocabulary they hear or read.

L2 students' active store of vocabulary derives chiefly from what they need to function in daily life. The basis of this active vocabulary is likely to be the spoken form, but as students become more accomplished in the classroom so they add basic words and phrases that they use consistently in their writing and meet in their reading. Besides this active store, L2 students have command over a larger store of passive vocabulary. These are words that they recognise in both spoken and written contexts, but do not themselves yet produce freely. The consistent aim of teachers is to increase L2 students' active vocabulary so that it can be used appropriately in a variety of contexts.

In approaching a new piece of fiction with L2 students, it is a useful strategy for teachers to distinguish between the areas of vocabulary that are vital to an understanding of the text. The first of these vocabulary areas involves words that are essential to an understanding of the main plot. This point can be clearly illustrated in the book, *I am David*, originally written in Danish by Ann Holm, and now widely available in an English translation. The story tells of a twelve-year-old boy's journey at the end of the Second World War from a camp in Northern Greece to his unknown home in Denmark. In order for L2 students to follow the basic narrative thrust of the story it is essential that unfamiliar words associated with the journey are introduced and explained. With an understanding of these vocabulary items, L2 students are able to read the book with relative fluency. In this book, and in many others, words of this type frequently comprise verbs of action and concrete nouns. In the case of *I am David*, words such as escape, compass, search-party, stumbled, staggered, crawled, poison, vagabond and dragged, fall into this category. Too many unfamiliar words of this sort signify that the book is not an appropriate choice for an L2 student's level of English.

Further areas of vocabulary may be related to specific settings or themes in the book. Thus, in *I am David*, an understanding of the words related to his time in Italy, words such as delicate, fine, gracious, gleaming and magnificent give L2 students access to a further rich layer of meaning. This type of vocabulary can be usefully presented via a format other than the purely verbal. Illustrations from the book, photographs and film offer other ways of conveying meaning related to settings and themes. A third area of unfamiliar vocabulary in many books is associated with the characters' thoughts and feelings. One of the signs of quality in *I am David*, and a fact that makes the book so valuable for work with advancing L2 students, is that the language in which his thoughts are expressed is generally straightforward and accessible. Nevertheless, the relatively few abstract words that express conceptual notions such as despair, suspicion, deception, ignorance and freedom, may present difficulties to L2 students. It should be emphasised once more that the choice of book is an important factor in ensuring that L2 students gain pleasure and confidence from their reading. Difficulty in understanding the basic story and too much unfamiliar vocabulary makes reading a chore for L2 students.

A useful strategy to help L2 students retain the meaning of a new vocabulary item, is for teachers to point out the root of a new word and to make connections with related words. It is also an effective policy to relate the discussion of a vocabulary item to its spelling and derivation. Abstract nouns, for instance, frequently end in 'ion' or derive from French roots. Teachers will find that students are more likely to retain both the meaning and the spelling of a new word if they are able to connect it with known words and familiar spelling conventions.

An overall aim is to develop in students the capacity to use independent strategies in working out the meaning of new words. The strategies involve inferring meaning from the surrounding context, making connections with known words and, where possible, making use of similarities with words in their own language. Mastery of these strategies aids students in reading a carefully chosen text with fluency and understanding. Some students find security in a two-way dictionary in English and their own language. As pointed out in Use of the Dictionary, pp. 175–6, however, students need to have exhausted other strategies in finding out the meaning of unfamiliar words in a reading passage before turning to a dictionary. To avoid over-use of the dictionary, it is important that L2 students are supplied with reading material that contains only a manageable number of new vocabulary items.

Many of the new words which L2 students encounter fail to become part of their active vocabulary or to be taken into their passive store, unless further work is done that involves active use of these words. Important items of new vocabulary can be emphasised in class discussions following the reading. Written reinforcement can take various forms; these include retelling all or part of the story, answering specific comprehension questions, or writing a piece about character or theme.

New vocabulary relating to themes and topics in science and social studies requires teachers to adopt similar approaches. The quantity of new vocabulary in those areas is liable, at times, to be greater than occurs in a carefully chosen work of fiction. Further suggestions for teaching vocabulary to L2 students in those circumstances are made in Chapter 10, pp. 226–7.

Teaching spelling

The teaching of spelling in most international schools is based on a combination of modified traditional approaches and features that derive from whole language programmes. This combination of embedded teaching relating to authentic literacy activities, and specific spelling instruction, offers an effective basis for teaching spelling to L2 students. Teachers in international schools need to add further strategies that take account of their status as L2 learners of English. The following points emphasise the areas that are significant in teaching spelling to L2 students:

General approaches

- L2 students display a range of spelling ability. L2 students, including those who are accustomed to a different writing system, may be effective spellers. It should not be assumed that all L2 students are poor spellers because they make initial mistakes in writing English. They need specific instruction in order to understand how English spelling works.
- Spelling and vocabulary building go hand-in-hand. Treat spelling as part of word study.
- Teachers should consult with the ESL teacher about students who display consistent misunderstandings about grammar-related spelling conventions. Examples of this type of error include the changes in spelling arising from the formation of different verb tenses and the comparative and superlative of adjectives. Keep the ESL teacher informed of vocabulary and spelling needs related to the mainstream programme.
- Integrate the teaching of spelling into all areas of the curriculum. Teach spelling in context; relate spellings to relevant content in the subject areas; avoid decontextualised lists.

Transfer from the first language

- Evidence of transfer from the speech and writing of L2 student's first language is likely to occur in the spelling of beginning and intermediate students. (See Transfer from the first language, pp. 81–2, for explanations of this feature.) Errors due to transfer take different forms. Typical instances are when students have difficulty in using the appropriate English letter symbols to represent sounds that do not occur in their first language, (when, for example, Japanese students write 'l' for 'r' in marry and cherry.) or when a letter symbol in an L2 student's alphabet is associated with a different sound from that in English (when, for example, German speakers write 'v' for 'w'.)
- Teachers in international schools come to recognise typical instances of transfer from the languages to be found among their L2 students. Experienced teachers recognise when a student's spelling errors may derive from more general difficulties.
- The ECIS publication, *Languages and Cultures in English-Language-*

Based International Schools, gives much useful information about instances of transfer.

Strategies that help L2 students to learn to spell in English

- L2 students do not have the same access to phonetic information as L1 children. In practice this means that early learners of English do not have an innate knowledge of how sounds in English are likely to be represented in writing. Older L1 students acquire this knowledge from visual memories of environmental print, from their reading and writing experiences and from specific spelling instruction.
- L2 students also have limited access to semantic information. Beginning and early intermediate students cannot depend on their knowledge of the meaning of a word to help them to spell it. L1 students use meaning to guide them in the spelling of the base roots of words and common prefixes, suffixes and grammar-related endings.
- L2 students benefit from being taught the common conventions of English spelling.
- Teachers help L2 students to spell unfamiliar words correctly when they build connections with known words and contexts.
- Lists of spellings can be useful if they relate to a known context. Involve students in making their own word lists related to classroom topics and themes. Display lists of high-frequency words. Make lists of words that conform to the same spelling pattern.
- Relate spelling to authentic reading and writing experiences. Use passages in reading texts to pick out words that connect to other words through meaning or spelling patterns.
- Create writing opportunities that allow L2 children to practise significant spelling areas. Retellings and first and third person narratives require students to practise the spelling of verb forms. Making out shopping lists, writing out cookery recipes and creating lists of instructions give students practice in the spelling of plural endings and imperatives.

Raising L2 students' awareness of correct spelling

- When correcting L2 children's writing, focus the students' attention on spelling errors of one type. Give the student instant instruction in the relevant rule or convention or give a small group lesson on a later occasion.
- Give L2 students practical hints about avoiding spelling mistakes.

Point out to them that questions based on reading passages contain most of the words that they need in order to give correctly spelt written answers. The same is true for proper nouns.

- L2 students have difficulty in recognising incorrect spellings. Their visual awareness is likely to be less developed than that of L1 children. This is especially true of students whose own languages use different writing systems.
- When giving spelling tests, give them twice. Allow the child to learn from the mistakes in the first test.
- Proof-reading and editing skills must be taught. Dictation can be a useful strategy to teach an awareness of spelling mistakes. Give students a piece of dictation; allow them time to evaluate their work for possible errors and to check their version against the final text. Daily 'edits' on the board are another means. The teacher asks the class to point out what is wrong with the spelling and punctuation of a short piece of writing on the board. This is an opportunity for teachers to include common words that are frequently spelt incorrectly.

The use of the computer in encouraging L2 students' writing

The computer is a potentially powerful means of encouraging L2 children to write. (A full account of the use of the computer with L2 students in all subject areas is included in Electronic Media, pp. 245–6.) As mentioned in the paragraphs above on process writing, the use of the computer allows L2 students to create and edit a piece of writing and to produce a final version, without the necessity of rewriting each draft. This is useful since most beginning and intermediate students make further errors when they write out their work a second or a third time. Programs designed to allow users to create greetings cards and invitations, or to write and illustrate magazine articles, offer further writing possibilities especially appropriate to L2 students. Such programs provide frames that guide students in creating a piece of writing that is correctly laid out in an appropriate writing format, and are highly-motivating to L2 students who are at ease with the technology.

The use of language arts textbooks to teach writing

The remarks made in Reading (p. 179), relating to the use of published language arts materials, apply also to the teaching of writing. Generally the content and instructions of textbooks designed for mainstream classes are at too high a level of English for use with beginning and intermediate

L2 students, despite the addition of material aimed specifically at ESL students. As with the teaching of reading, teachers will have to make modifications to the assignments and replace activities and exercises with tasks at a more appropriate level in order to use these materials to teach L2 students to write.

Teachers may find it useful to incorporate published materials specifically designed to teach writing to ESL students, into their work with L2 children in the mainstream classroom. These are to be found in the ESL catalogues of textbook publishers. Used with small groups these materials allow teachers to cater specifically to L2 children's language needs. Much of the material in books designed for the ESL market relating to writing now incorporates the approaches used in most international schools.

Spoken English for Academic Purposes — the Teaching of Specific Oral Skills to Second Language Students

In the upper grades of an elementary school L2 students are required to be competent users of spoken English for specific purposes related to the mainstream programme. These purposes are associated with two broad areas; working and rehearsed talk. Working talk includes the ability to participate in whole class discussions, to contribute in co-operative learning groups and to take part in discussions about student writing. Rehearsed talk includes the ability to give a speech, to carry out activities related to poetry and drama and to make oral reports.

Working talk

As was mentioned under the heading, Shared reading, Managing class discussion to include L2 students, pp. 144–5, many L2 students are not used to making the oral contributions expected in international school programmes. For many L2 students their expected role in home country classrooms is to sit quietly and listen to the teacher. When asked to speak, they are expected to respond either with a repetition of what the teacher has said, or with a factual answer based on the content of a book. Thus, L2 students in international schools frequently need to be encouraged to speak out and to offer opinions.

Whole class discussions

Successful whole class discussions with older children require the teacher to involve the students in the management of the group. Older children are capable of understanding the need for rules that allow each student to speak. Competent speakers of English appreciate the need for management strategies that allow L2 students to contribute. Various strategies exist that allow the group to function without constant teacher intervention relating to turn taking. One option is for each student in the circle to be called upon to speak in turn. Another effective strategy is for each child in the group to have one or two tokens. These tokens indicate their right to speak. When students have used up their tokens, they must wait for other children to contribute.

A further challenge is to create an atmosphere where L2 students feel able to take the time to formulate their thoughts. In most classrooms, however, it is not only L2 children who have difficulty in expressing themselves, or who have trouble in coming to a halt. Very soon, both the teacher and children in a class recognise the strengths and weaknesses of their peers as speakers. It takes diplomacy, humour and management skills on a teacher's part to keep a discussion on course without allowing the talkative students to dominate or the reticent children to go unheard.

Working talk in co-operative learning situations

In order for L2 students to contribute to oral activities in co-operative groups teachers should introduce each assignment with appropriate visual and text-based activities. In the early part of the year, it is helpful if teachers structure group activities to provide opportunities for explicit modelling of the oral language needed to take turns and to express points of view. Teachers need to ensure that L2 students are not left on the sidelines even in small groups. It is helpful for these students to be asked to contribute practically by providing graphic material for the final presentation if the level of their spoken English does not yet allow them to perform orally.

Strategies for providing the optimum means for L2 students to learn the language of working conversation include graduating the assignments given to the group. Tasks involving the creation of a series of instructions for a game, for instance, require a less advanced conversational interchange than comparing the differences between the book and film version of a story. The computer offers further concrete opportunities for small groups to use working talk together in successfully completing a task.

Making and responding to suggestions about writing drafts and contributing to whole class solutions of mathematics problems

There are occasions when students are required to make suggestions orally and to respond to spoken questions. This type of language production is challenging to L2 children until their level of spoken English has reached an advanced level. Such a situation occurs when students are called upon to share their own writing with peers or are asked to make suggestions about other children's work. Most teachers do not call on L2 students to contribute in this way until their level of competence in English allows them to cope linguistically and emotionally.

Rehearsed talk

Rehearsed talk can be divided into several areas: those such as poetry reading and dramatic activity that require memorisation or familiarity with the content, and those such as making an oral report or giving a speech that involve preparatory working using several language skills.

Reading poetry and taking part in dramatic activity

Poetry and drama require memorisation and familiarity with the content to ensure an effective reading. These skills are within the reach of L2 students when given the appropriate encouragement and direction, and provide a useful means of practising English intonation and reinforcing English spoken structure. Choral readings are an effective manner of including beginning L2 learners.

Giving a prepared speech or presenting an oral report

Giving a prepared speech or presenting an oral report to the whole class presents a considerable challenge to beginning and intermediate L2 students. As mentioned in the paragraphs on report writing in Chapter 10, Answering the Needs of Second Language Students in Social Studies and Science: pp. 231–2, creating a report is a complex task that involves effective management and a number of language skills. All but advanced L2 students require support to allow them to meet the challenge.

Strategies that are effective with competent English users are not necessarily appropriate for L2 children. The use of two or three word headings on cards as reminders to the speaker rarely gives enough support to L2 students when making a presentation to the whole class. As a result L2 students frequently copy out their speech verbatim and read every word when making their presentation. A useful strategy is to base an explanation of the process of constructing an oral report on examples of notes made on a previous occasion by another student. This gives teachers an opportunity to model the process step-by-step. As with the creation of written reports, it is essential when working with L2 students, to break down large tasks such as constructing an oral report, into a manageable form. Supplying a model or providing a practical outline is more effective than giving long oral or written explanations.

It is preferable in the early months of the year, for such reports to be created with a partner, or in a group of three or four students which

Textbox 8.4 A 5th Grade drama project

It is standard practice in books on teaching diverse classes to advocate dramatic activity as a useful strategy for involving L2 students in meaningful practice of English. Usually the suggestions are confined to role-play and dialogue. Drama, however, has the potential for offering children an enriching and memorable experience. With care and forethought on the teacher's part, the positive impact on L2 children is as great as on their L1 peers. In my school, the work of one of my colleagues has evolved in a fascinating way. Starting some years ago with an elective after-school Drama Club, her latest production included all the children in the 5th Grade and involved the integration of language arts, social studies and artistic themes. The shared element derived in part from a social studies unit on Ancient Civilisations, and in part from a myth and legend strand in the language arts programme. The emphasis throughout was on a co-operative approach to the process of creation.

The first phase involved the writing of a series of myths relating to a core theme. This was carried out using examples from a variety of cultural backgrounds including ancient China. The students were then divided into small groups to work on one section of the envisaged production. The task was to plan the physical movement and dialogue relating to one myth. The concentration on physical expression was a deliberate strategy to allow L2 students to make useful contributions. The nature of the talk required by the groups was also designed to extend students' use of language. Making decisions about movement involved discussing thoughts and feelings as well as what should happen next.

Work on the production was given a boost by the presence of two sets of adults. The first of these was the art teacher and a gifted parent. Together they led groups of children and parents in creating artefacts — masks, costumes, and large symbolic portable props — to enhance and expand the narrative. The second area of adult input was a weeklong stay by two talented young staff members from a major school of music in London. For the week of the production they worked with all the children to create music, chants, songs and percussion themes to accompany the stories. Even the super-cool dudes of the 5th grade became enthusiastic participators in this lively scene. The actual production was regarded as part of a still-evolving process by the students rather than a once-and-for-all version of the stories.

The total commitment and engagement of the L2 children at all levels of English competence was remarkable. The simple, powerful stories allowed them to gain an understanding from the start. The emphasis on physical expression alongside the creation of dialogue, the art work and, of course, the music workshops, allowed all the students to contribute. Not surprisingly, it was some of the L2 children who shone in these areas. As valuable was the social aspect. The discipline and hard work as well as the shared fun incorporated the L2 students at a deep level into the mainstream life of the 5th Grade.

includes some competent English speakers. In this way, the creation of the report can be divided between the members of the group according to their level of language competence. The presentation phase can be similarly shared out: some children speak while others manipulate the visual aids or manage the technology. Teachers need not be fearful that L2 children will shrink from contributing eventually. L2 students are almost invariably eager to contribute the moment their level of English allows them to do so.

Summary

The integrated literature-based approaches found in many international schools offer a sound framework for work with L2 students in the mainstream language arts programme. Teachers must, however, employ additional strategies if L2 learners are to benefit fully from mainstream teaching of English language skills.

Three features need to be in place to allow L2 students full participation in reading, writing and oracy assignments. Teachers should provide an extensive introductory framework, they should offer the degree of vocabulary and structural support that allows L2 students to carry out the assignment and they should construct a range of follow-up activities involving authentic language use and higher-order thinking skills.

A range of instructional groupings provides L2 students at varying levels of English competence with appropriate degrees of support in carrying out assignments. The specific teaching of grammar, English usage, spelling and punctuation, together with opportunities for authentic practice, supply the optimum circumstances for L2 students to increase their skills and understandings in these areas.

Finally, the making of cross-curricular connections and the use of consistent strategies in teaching the skills of reading, writing and talk, allow L2 students to apply their language skills effectively in all areas of the mainstream programme.

Chapter 9
Strategies for Supporting Second Language Students in Mainstream Mathematics Classes

Introduction

The aim of this chapter is to raise teachers' awareness of the need to adapt their teaching strategies for second language children in mainstream mathematics classes. It might be thought that mathematics is a subject area where second language children with varying competencies in English can participate with only minor adaptations on the teacher's part. Today's mathematics programmes, however, require students to master many skills besides the conceptual and computational. New approaches to the teaching of mathematics involve students in extensive uses of English. Areas where a knowledge of language is essential include word problems, co-operative problem solving and explaining mathematical processes verbally and in writing.

Teachers therefore have the task of creating a learning environment that enables second language children to negotiate the language of mathematics and allows them access to the content of the programme. As with other subjects, the content of the programme itself, via the use of appropriate adaptations to teaching strategies and to subject material, provides a powerful vehicle for language learning. Factors that significantly influence students' ability to decode the language of mathematics are their existing mathematical knowledge and their level of competence. Teachers will find that their work with second language students in mathematics classes is most effective if they take account of these individual differences and vary their strategies accordingly.

Four sections at the beginning of this chapter address underlying issues of importance in planning instruction for second language children in mainstream mathematics. These are followed by lists of suggestions relating to the teaching of mathematics language and content to diverse classes. Finally, four further sections discuss types of mathematics provision for distinct groups of second language children.

The Impact of L2 Students' Previous Educational Experiences and Individual Aptitudes

L2 students come from education systems where the teaching of mathematics may vary in methodology as well as content from what is normal in international schools. Like L1 students, they display a range of aptitudes. Teachers need to recognise these differences when they plan programmes for L2 students.

A significant group of students comes from certain European countries and East Asia where mathematics programmes are traditionally effective. Their strength is not solely in the area of computation. Most students are well trained in problem solving and in an understanding of mathematical process. Students from these countries are often limited in their learning only by their lack of English. For these students, their existing knowledge of mathematics is a potentially powerful tool to bring to bear on the language which modern mathematics teaching incorporates into every aspect of the programme.

Where a school has the policy of dividing children by ability for the teaching of mathematics, the placement of these students is problematic. It makes little sense to deny such students a higher-level programme of instruction as may be the case if L2 children are grouped according to their language ability alone. An appropriate instructional programme for these students supplies them with a basic mathematics vocabulary in English and carefully focused support. This in turn enables strong L2 mathematics students to bring their prior knowledge to bear on mathematics content in the new language. Suggestions concerning detailed teaching strategies are made in later paragraphs. (In practice, many schools who group children for mathematics by ability, place even beginning students of English from countries that are known to be strong in mathematics in a middle level group. Placement arrangements should be sufficiently flexible to allow such students to advance to a higher-level group as soon as the level of their English allows it.)

A second group of new children, which usually includes students from the Indian sub-continent, may be accustomed to mathematics teaching which is based largely on numerical computation. Such children are adept at carrying out relatively advanced computational exercises. However, when asked to make sense of words and numbers in the form of problems or to express mathematical principle through practical activities, such students may be at a disadvantage. Their programme should therefore include specific explanations and strategies for dealing with aspects of mathematics that are new to them.

This is an instance where differences in cultural expectations about educational practice need to be acknowledged and discussed. The parents of these students are frequently concerned that the mathematics programmes of most international schools prepare their children inadequately for competitive entry to home schools. They may question the amount of time given to work with manipulatives or the co-operative solving of word problems. These activities may appear irrelevant to the examination demands of their national school systems. (See Textbox 8.2, Changing the way children think, for further discussion.)

A third group of L2 children may have covered less ground in the area of mathematics than is customary for students of the same age in international schools. This group includes children whose home school systems start formal education at a later age than is usual in English-speaking countries, and children for whom a relocation has led to gaps in their learning. It is the teacher's task to take account of children's existing knowledge in planning instruction. Initial assessment should be designed to reveal where a student needs this type of teaching.

The fourth and final group of L2 students which teachers quickly learn to differentiate are those for whom mathematics presents difficulties in any language. They may have a documented history of specific problems with number, or a more general learning difficulty may be present. Such students do not have the advantage of a strong basis in mathematics to aid them in working out the meaning of mathematical language. For them English is an added barrier to the understanding of an already difficult subject. In many schools these children are given extra support from a resource teacher within the classroom, in a small group on a pull-out basis, or in a separate class where students at a year level are grouped by need and/or ability.

Key Elements in Effective Mathematics Programmes With L2 Students

Certain key elements have considerable impact on the effectiveness of instructional programmes for L2 students in mainstream mathematics classes. These include:

- The personal aptitude, educational experience and learning style of the student.
- The length of time given to the study of mathematics and the time of day when the classes are held.
- The nature and range of the resources available to the teacher.
- The use of appropriate modifications to content material.

- The use of language teaching strategies that allow L2 students access to the language of mathematics.

The length of time given over to the teaching of mathematics and the time of day at which the mathematics class is held have a significant impact on the success of L2 students. Ideally, mathematics classes should take place in the morning, and earlier rather than later. At this time of day L2 students are still relatively fresh. They have not begun to experience the build-up of fatigue that can occur during each day, and cumulatively over a week. They are able to give their best efforts to the exacting task of constructing mathematical meaning through the medium of English. The length of time spent on mathematics is also significant. Students need time to experience and practise the range of mathematics language. They need time to access the content of the subject in a variety of ways. A narrow programme of instruction does not supply enough opportunities for diverse students to negotiate a full understanding of content or the use of language. Time is needed for a variety of experiences.

The nature and range of resources available to teachers and students play a major part in the effectiveness of any mathematics programme. Most schools have a basic textbook in place that supplies the sequence and structure to the programme. However, a wider range of resource is necessary to offer an effective programme in international schools owing to the diversity of experience, aptitude and language ability among both first and second language students.

Experienced teachers collect over time a variety of manipulative materials including counters, construction kits, pattern blocks, geo-boards and an array of craft and print materials. Print materials include further textbooks, supplementary word-problem texts at all levels, books of mathematical puzzles and logic problems, and stories and non-fiction texts that contain a mathematical or problem-solving element. The availability of stand-alone and networked computers is a further potential source of effective mathematics teaching and learning opportunities for L2 students. Teachers should search out mathematics software of quality to provide practice and reinforcement at age-appropriate levels for L2 children to access independently or in small groups.

Many teachers build up a collection of theme-based material relating to year-level topics in social studies and science. These collections include printed texts and other media concerned with such topics as the Pyramids, the construction of castles, the design of environmentally friendly houses, the planets, sports rules and pitches, for example. CD-ROM titles and the Internet offer further sources of this type. Such topic-based materials give teachers a context on which to build a range of authentic mathematics activities. This context, in turn, supplies L2 students with further support in understanding and producing the language of mathematics.

Finally, the teacher's choice of strategies contributes to the effectiveness of a programme of instruction. These strategies included making modifications to the material and adjusting the means of presentation to take account of the students' level of English. They include teaching L2 students specific word-attack skills to unlock the meaning of language commonly used in mathematics word-problems. Varying the groupings in a class, supplying a range of activities and employing theme-based approaches give children further support and practice in gaining meaning and in producing language themselves.

Evaluating the Mathematics Competence of New L2 Students

A student's level of English has an impact on the initial assessment of new children. With non-speakers of English it is usually possible to gain at least some insights into a student's level of competence by means of a range of computation exercises. Problems involving the use of manipulatives may also provide a means of evaluation. With students who speak more English it may be feasible to introduce symbol and word problems into the assessment process. Notes from the former school and input from parents may be sources of information concerning a student's previous exposure to elements of mathematics such as geometry. Knowledge of the nature of mathematics teaching in a student's home education system is also useful to the teacher. Observation of the student's mode of working and ease in carrying out mathematical assignments is a significant factor in choosing effective strategies for later use with that student.

Enabling Students to Negotiate an Understanding of Mathematics Through the Medium of English

L2 students in mainstream mathematics classes have two major needs related to their lack of English. The first of these is to gain an understanding of the language commonly used in mathematics. This involves the relatively simple task of supplying students with a standard mathematics vocabulary plus the more difficult undertaking of equipping students with the strategies needed for decoding the language of mathematics problems and for carrying out a range of mathematics activities.

The second major need of students is to move forward in their learning of mathematics content. Here the teacher's task is to present new material in a manner appropriate to the needs of the range of L2 students. Strong mathematics students with a previous experience of the same material need carefully focused support to enable them to transfer their prior knowledge. Other students for whom the material is new need to acquire an understanding of the mathematics concepts involved. A further group may need teaching about the processes and outcomes associated with unfamiliar types of mathematics activities.

Strategies that cater to L2 students' needs in mathematics classes

Basic strategies to employ in explaining mathematics assignments

- Explain clearly, and explain again, what are the expectations associated with any new piece of work.
- Give step-by-step examples to show how it is possible for the student to achieve the desired outcomes.
- Guide the student through the practical resources that will enable her or him to carry out the task (manipulatives, tables, number grids, etc.).
- Make clear the support structure that will enable the student to move through the process with confidence (easily understood examples in a textbook, pairing with another student or small group).
- Explain with examples how the student should present the answer.
- Ensure students understand tasks by questioning and feedback.
- Have strategies in place for reteaching and/or further practice.

L2 students need time

- Remember, L2 students need time in carrying out any task containing an element of language.
- They take longer than competent speakers of English to complete assignments both in school and for homework.
- If they achieve less it is likely to be because of difficulty with language.

Homework

- During the first weeks in school, set new L2 students homework that requires them only to practise something mechanical and familiar in format; computational work is ideal.
- Save the practice of word problems for class time, or until the student's English is more advanced.

Approaches to teaching vocabulary

- Pick out mathematics terms in consistent use in the basic textbook.
- Make available display sheets showing symbols and associated vocabulary.
- Consider the possibility of asking L2 parents who speak English to supply translations of mathematics terms in the home languages of students.
- Do not attempt to teach vocabulary initially through decontextualised lists.
- Show meaning through practical explanations via manipulatives or computation or simple word problems.
- Give many opportunities for practising new vocabulary items in authentic mathematical contexts.
- Use lists as a resource and reminder for students when they have reached an understanding of the meaning of vocabulary items.

Skills for negotiating the meaning of word problems

- Equip students with word-attack skills by teaching them to focus on key words; these are the words that carry the weight of meaning. They include verbs and prepositions and conventional mathematics phrases.
- Show students how to use the glossaries that are included at the back of many mathematics textbooks.
- Teach students that they can look up the meaning of nouns later.
- Show students how to break down the problem into separate steps; get them to number the steps; model this process on the overhead projector.
- Ask students in pairs or small groups to express steps in words as well as numbers.
- Teach students to concentrate on process; if they speak enough English, ask them to describe how they intend to carry out a calculation or to solve a problem.
- Allow beginning L2 students who speak the same language to work together occasionally; this gives them confidence. The negotiation of meaning in English through their own language is a valid method of gaining understanding of a concept.
- Do not overdo this strategy; L2 parents are very sensitive about the use of home languages in what they feel ought to be an English-speaking environment.
- Use collections of word problems originally designed for younger

learners to provide simpler examples of word problems involving the target mathematical concept.

- Write a problem on the board. Talk about a problem together; ask the class to suggest solutions. Illustrate different ways of arriving at the answer.
- Use symbolic problems of logic as a means of varying the input.
- Require students to make simple drawings to illustrate the solutions to story problems.

Teaching new content

- Start with a whole class explanation of a new concept using manipulatives and practical demonstrations; move on to number and symbolic representation; give practice assignments at a variety of levels; reteach to small groups; organise extension activities for able L1 and L2 students; be prepared to present material in other ways if difficulties with English prevent L2 students from understanding.
- Use manipulatives to give a practical illustration of a concept, e.g. fractions.
- Always move from concrete/near at hand examples (giving change in shops, adding-up the cost of making a trip) to the symbolic and numerical.
- Accompany the introduction of new concepts or extension work by questioning, speculation, explanation and discussion.
- Build on what L2 students know about a concept at a simpler level to introduce the English required to explain a more advanced application.
- Only introduce new applications of a concept when the base vocabulary used with that concept is established.
- Ask students to practise new content in a number of ways; use games, puzzles and construction projects. Provide social studies and science topic-linked activities as well as formal mathematics assignments.
- Allow students to make choices in accordance with their preferred learning styles from a range of practice assignments.
- Allow L2 students to work with an English-speaking partner in carrying out initial assignments on new content.
- Realise that L2 students may be used to different methods of expressing and carrying out mathematical operations such as subtraction, multiplication and division.
- Be aware that mathematics notation varies around the world; e.g.

the decimal point may be represented by a comma or a full stop/period.

- Remember that in many countries numbers are expressed differently; this may lead to confusion in setting out calculations involving hundreds, tens and units; compare, for example, English twenty-one and German ein-und-zwanzig.

Mathematics activities

- Exploratory activities need to be carried out in small groups or in pairs.
- Mathematics games and open-ended construction tasks carried out in small groups enable tired L2 students to be involved in a valuable activity in a stress-free environment.
- Connect the activities to on-going topics or themes in social studies or science, e.g. Roman numerals, making charts or graphs of observations related to an experiment.
- Supply an element of choice; allow groups to make choices of activities from a range of cards.
- Ask groups of students to write poems with a number theme.
- Ask groups of students to create a mathematics game.
- Ask groups of students to design a building; ask them to calculate the materials needed.

Ways of working

Individual

- Working alone on computational exercises in a familiar form can be a motivating and stress-free activity for L2 students.
- Use the wide range of mathematics software available on the computer to give L2 students self-regulated practice in mathematics concepts at an appropriate level.

Pair work and co-operative groupings

- Co-operative groupings allow the social integration of students and the opportunity for students of mixed abilities to work together. Weaker L2 students have access to language models and mathematical content. Strong students are emboldened to take language risks in solving the problem collaboratively.
- Suggested make-up of a co-operative group: strong L1 math

student, confident English speakers, strong L2 math student, weaker L2 math student.

- Encourage all students, both L1 and L2, to make use of symbol and numerical computation in solving word problems. This allows L2 students to participate more fully.
- Sometimes put two speakers of the same language in a group together; this builds confidence and allows shared negotiation of meaning in English through their common language.
- Give strong L2 students the opportunity to work with a strong L1 student; this will allow the L2 child access to the use of English employed by capable mathematics students.
- Use computer software to allow small groups of students at varying levels of mathematics and English competence to problem-solve together.

Assessment

- With older L2 students carry out early assessment via computation.
- With young L2 children carry out early assessment via practical tasks and the use of manipulatives.
- Test L2 students' understanding of a concept by getting them to solve problems using manipulatives, pattern blocks, etc. Texts exist which give examples at various levels of difficulty and language.
- Investigate the possibility of carrying out later assessments of L2 students through unit tests in textbooks; criteria for suitability are the level of English and the student's understanding of the type of mathematics activity being used as the basis for assessment.
- Only ask students to carry out assessment tasks in the same format that they have practised in class.
- Be aware in correcting work that wrong answers or methods of working are shown in different ways in some parts of the world. (In Japan and Korea, for instance, correct work is picked out and incorrect work is left untouched.)

Advanced students

- Ask advanced L2 students to write about their experiences in mathematics during the year; how do they feel they learn best? What do they feel they have not yet properly understood?
- Ask advanced L2 students to describe their strategies in gaining meaning from a word problem.

Textbox 9.1 A checklist of terms used in writing down mathematics problems

- Terms associated with **addition**: add, plus, combine, and, the sum of, increased by, find the total, all together, in all.
- Terms associated with **subtraction**: subtract from, decrease by, less, take away, minus, difference, have left, how much change does he...? how much longer does it take to travel by road than to travel by...? how much greater is...than...? how much less is...than...? fewer/more than.
- Terms associated with **multiplication**: times, multiplied by, ...times as much/many..., find the product.
- Terms associated with **division**: divided into, divided by, how many in each...? how many times larger...?
- Ways of asking and giving **answers**: total, equals, makes, what is the result? how much is left when...? give the total.
- Terms involving **comparison**: high, higher, highest, higher than, large, larger, which is the larger? which is the largest? is the red apple heavier than the green apple? smaller than, greater than.
- **How much? how many?**
- **Commands**: Choose, choose between, build, find, explain, use, try, put, repeat, do, make
- **Questions**: How far did...? is it possible for...? what kind of...? what number did you use to...? into how many slices did Mum divide the pizza? what day of the week did...? how long did it take the car to...? how long did it take for ... to reach...?
- **Volume**: More, less, greater than, smaller than
- **Measurement**: Longer, shorter, how long is? how far is?
- **Weight**: How heavy is, how much does it weigh?
- **Estimation**: What do you think is...? what is the likely result? what do you think would be a good answer? approximately, roughly
- Illustrate vocabulary of **geometry** with names and simple definitions of shapes, angles and forms
- Provide vocabulary words for **weights**, **measures** and **currency** (do not assume that L2 children will understand the weight, measurement or money terms used in texts).
- Supply both **imperial** and **metric** terms if necessary in your school
- Do not forget to display a **list of common symbols and their definitions** for easy reference: Addition, subtraction, multiplication, division, equals, percent, greater than, smaller than etc.

Tricks and tips

- Have fun with mathematics; in the five minutes before the end of class ask students to do a number puzzle from the board, chant tables, play mathematics games such as fizz buzz, do number crosswords and word searches.
- Fill in short periods of time with mental arithmetic questions at varying levels of difficulty.
- Periodically give time to small group craft activities and art projects relating to mathematics: creating visual mazes, constructing geometrical shapes, surveying and mapping buildings and grounds.

Mixed ability classes or grouping by ability?

In the later years at the elementary level, some international schools group all students at a year level by ability for mathematics. Other schools prefer to teach mathematics throughout the elementary years to students in their home classrooms. There are advantages and disadvantages for L2 students in both approaches.

In mixed ability groups strong students give a lead to the other students and the level of motivation overall is likely to be high. Weaker L2 mathematics students benefit by contact with effective users of mathematics language. Strong L2 mathematics students do not suffer loss of esteem from being placed in a class for students of lower ability solely because of their limited English. On the other hand, the broad spread of mathematics ability may limit the time the teacher is able to give to making explanations in comprehensible English to L2 students. Teachers may feel that they cannot cater adequately either for students who need challenge or for children who need individual help.

In classes grouped by ability, teachers are able to target both the language and content of the programme more accurately owing to the narrower range of ability among the students. This means that teachers need to supply fewer assignments at varying levels of difficulty. On the other hand, the early placement of new L2 students in ability groups may result in an inappropriate choice. Strong L2 mathematics students may be demotivated by being placed in a group for less effective students. The placement of strong L2 mathematics students even in middle level groups may deprive these students of the opportunity to experience the full range of mathematics content and language-learning opportunities.

Young L2 students and mathematics

In young children's classrooms, the methodology in common use in teaching mathematics to L1 students lends itself well to the needs of L2 children. It is standard practice to lead young children towards an understanding of mathematical concepts via a series of practical tasks associated with familiar objects. This approach provides L2 students with the optimum circumstances for acquiring age-appropriate mathematics language together with an understanding of content. In a similar way, the standard practice of grouping students to carry out shared tasks, supplies L2 students with effective support for their language learning. Teachers should, nevertheless, be aware that L2 students are likely to need more practical explanation and practice activities to ensure that the language as well as the concept is firmly embedded.

The use of integrated topic areas to teach mathematics in young children's classrooms is helpful to L2 students. Common topics include shape, colour, the family, food and drink, transport and the home. The fact that these topics figure significantly in early vocabulary work with young learners provides them with valuable support in making sense of words related to these areas when they meet them in a mathematical context. Their prior familiarity with the language enables them to grasp the mathematical concept being taught. Children gain meaning and understanding from activities associated with counting, ordering, sorting, measuring, weighing and estimating when they meet them in familiar contexts in association with known language.

Second language students who experience difficulties in mathematics

In most groups of students, some children fail to make steady progress in mathematics. In the case of L2 children, a complex mixture of factors including language, mathematics aptitude and attitude may make it difficult to establish the reasons for an individual student's lack of progress.

Strong mathematics students are able to build on their understanding of mathematics concepts in working out the likely meaning of unfamiliar language. For students with a weaker grasp of mathematics, the presence of new language places an additional barrier in the way of their understanding. Their inability to make sense of the language detracts also from their ability to grasp the mathematical meaning of what they hear or see.

In the case of these students teachers need to supply further concrete examples to establish a basic understanding of the new concept. Such students may benefit from more co-operative activity with both L1 and L2 students. For other students regular one-to-one time with a teacher for a short concentrated period may be more effective in building a child's understanding and confidence. In most cases, an understanding of the process will go hand-in-hand with an ability to make better sense of the language. In serious cases teachers need to be aware of the possibility of a specific learning difficulty.

Differences in cultural expectations and modes of learning may be factors in other children's lack of steady progress. Some children feel a sense of unease at the content of mathematics programmes in international schools. They are unaccustomed to co-operative problem-solving and mathematics games or to carrying out activities involving the practical application of mathematics principles. Such students (and their parents) may not view these activities as 'real' work. In these cases, it may be beneficial to accommodate the child's expectations, at least in the early days while their grasp of English is limited. Such students may make better progress in acquiring the language of mathematics via a traditional computational approach. Later when their level of language allows, teachers can involve these students in a wider range of mathematics activities.

Sheltered mathematics classes for beginning learners of English

There are reasons why the provision of a flexible sheltered programme for new non-speakers of English is an effective strategy. The flexibility is an important element, since ideally students should be placed in an appropriate mainstream class as soon as the student's English competence and general ability to face challenge allow. In the case of confident students with a strong background in mathematics, this may be after a few weeks. For others, a class that offers a mathematics programme adapted to the language needs of beginning learners supplies an effective means of keeping such children in touch with the mainstream programme.

It is important for these classes not to be seen as a long term answer in themselves. The aim of sheltered classes is to prepare students for mainstream life as soon as possible. The disadvantage of a long stay in such classes is that L2 students are denied the possibility of learning from their L1 peers.

Summary

Today's mathematics programmes involve a considerable use of language. Teachers of classes containing L2 students should adopt teaching strategies and make content modifications that give these students access to content while teaching the language of mathematics. The content of mathematics itself is a powerful vehicle for teaching the language that students need in order to succeed in the programme.

Effective teachers acknowledge the different needs of distinct groups of students in planning their instructional approaches. Further factors such as scheduling and teaching time, and the quality and quantity of resources contribute to the effectiveness of the programme. An array of adjustments and variations in strategy and mathematical content offer ways of catering better to L2 students' needs. The integrated thematic approaches current in young children's classrooms provide an effective context for young students to acquire the language of mathematics.

Schools have a variety of models to choose from in catering for the needs of different groups of students. Grouping by ability, special provision for struggling mathematics students and sheltered classes for beginning L2 students are possible options.

Chapter 10

Answering the Needs of Second Language Students in Social Studies and Science

Introduction

This chapter offers suggestions relating to the teaching of social studies and science to second language students. Teachers can make the content of social studies and science accessible to second language students by appropriate modifications to instructional strategies and materials. These modifications enable students to gain meaning from the subject area material, which in turn gives a powerful impetus to language learning. A further advantage from relating language learning to subject content is that students gain opportunities to practise useful language skills in authentic contexts.

The strategies suggested in Chapters 7 and 8, relating to the teaching of language arts, provide a basis for the broad speaking, reading and writing requirements of social studies and science. Second language students respond positively to the consistent use of similar strategies and routines across the curriculum. The suggestions below offer teachers more specific guidelines related to social studies and science. These guidelines are based on two strands of teacher activity. The first strand deals with the adaptation of social studies and science materials for students at all levels of English competence, and the appropriate strategies for delivering this material. The second strand describes how teachers can use content area material to teach the English language skills required for success in social studies and science.

In this chapter, standard topics taught in international schools at the elementary level will be used to provide practical examples. The theme of ancient civilisations is used to provide examples related to social studies. The planets and the life cycle of plants are used to provide examples relating to science.

A final section deals at length with short and extended field trips arising out of units of study in social studies and science. Teachers can enhance second language students' experiences on field trips in a number of ways by the use of carefully targeted strategies. This is worthwhile since field trips offer second language students access to content material in concrete, authentic and interesting ways.

Strategies for Use With Second Language Students in Mainstream Social Studies and Science Classes

Second language students' previous experience of social studies and science

Previous experiences of social studies and science among new L2 students may vary widely. Teachers in international schools must be ready to adjust their expectations of L2 children in these subject areas, where necessary. In many education systems, history, geography and science are taught as separate subjects with a strong emphasis on the acquisition of facts. Hands-on experimentation and practical activities are not usual in this type of programme. In the case of history, much of the content may be confined to an account of the home country, perhaps with a political subtext.

With this range of experience among newly arrived L2 students, chronological social studies programmes based on published textbooks still offered in a few international schools, clearly present difficulties for both students and teachers. To minimise these difficulties, and to offer a more appropriate programme to a mobile multinational student population, many schools have opted for social studies and science curricula constructed on a modular system. Each module is complete in itself, although increasing complexity and the development of skills are introduced by means of a sequenced framework.

The International Baccalaureate Primary Years' Programme, (formerly known as the International Schools' Curriculum Project) is an initiative that aims to bring order to curricula at the elementary level in international schools. Groups of practising teachers have come together to design a series of consistent curriculum frameworks that allow the unique situation of each school to be taken into account. The aim is to enable a student to move from one school to another without repeating content or missing out important steps in skills acquisition. The IBPYP is in use in a significant number of international schools and is being piloted in individual curriculum areas by others.

Teachers cannot assume that L2 students will understand how to perform the tasks asked of them in social studies or social science. Assignments that involve searching for information, note taking and report writing, which are standard features of social studies programmes at the upper elementary level in international schools, will cause difficulty for many L2 students. Likewise, typical requirements of a science programme including speculation, hypothesising and drawing conclusions will leave many L2 students bewildered and at a loss.

The implication for teachers is the need to state explicitly at the beginning of each unit, lesson or individual task what is the desired outcome. Teachers must then provide students with step-by-step directions and support in achieving that end.

Modifying texts to make the content accessible to L2 students

Most social studies and science programmes involve the use of texts to convey part of the content. Whenever L2 students are required to gain and use information from text, it is likely that teachers will need to modify the material in some way for beginning and intermediate L2 students. With early learners of English the main priority is for students to understand the central message of the text. This is the case whether the chosen topic is theme-based or related to a single subject.

Whatever the topic, the teacher needs to decide if the layout of the book offers students enough visual and graphic content to carry the meaning. It is possible that good illustrations or photographs and charts and graphs may make the meaning clear. If not, teachers need to set out the information contained in the text in a way that makes it accessible to their L2 students. This may involve representing the content in a visual manner or through a simplified framework of key words. Often it will require the use of both approaches.

Visual adaptations

For teachers with a gift for drawing it is a natural way into a text to map out the main points with symbols or illustrations. Visual materials can also be gathered ready-made from many sources. It is worth a teacher's time to create photocopiable masters for use in teaching topics that are repeated each year. Most teachers regularly base part of their social studies programme on buildings or natural features in the neighbourhood. In this case it is relatively easy to collect together materials such as tourist brochures, guidebooks and information pamphlets. These can then be broken up and reassembled in a form, together with teacher-made materials, that carries students visually through the main points of the content.

Sets of materials about such standard topics in social studies programmes as ancient civilisations are not difficult to compile. Materials abound on ancient China, Egypt, Greece, and Rome and on the Aztec and

Textbox 10.1 Visual and textual outline designed to teach vocabulary and concepts relating to flowering plants. The outline as given here is directed towards improving beginners and early intermediate students at the sixth grade level. For younger students only the less complex information would be appropriate

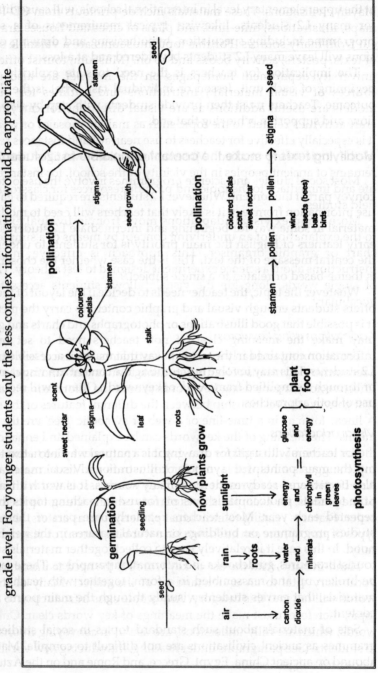

Mayan civilisations. These materials include printouts from CD-ROMs, maps, illustrations, time-lines and plans of cities and houses drawn or cut from many sources. For this topic museums are a valuable source of texts, posters, activity books and so on. (Museum, tourist office and university department homepages on the Internet are also useful sources of visual material.) Instructions and outlines for making models are useful additions as are visual directions for carrying out craft activities related to the topic such as making mosaics or weaving. It is especially effective for teachers to use near-at-hand instances relating to the topic being studied. Museum collections, vestiges and larger remains of ancient peoples in the vicinity of the school, for instance, give life and immediacy to the topic and provide resources for classroom and field studies.

More complex visual adaptations move from individual examples to the explanation of an underlying concept by means of a simple flow chart or graphic organiser. This approach is effective in giving instructions about a science experiment designed to test a theory. The use of single words alongside the visuals allows students access to key vocabulary.

Adaptations using keywords

For beginning and early intermediate students, the use of key words is a recommended means of leading students to an understanding of a topic. Effective adaptations using key words set out the information in a form that conveys the relationship between the different features of the study. A linear form as in a time-line or a web or symbolic 'tree' are the usual means. The meaning of the keywords can be explained and enhanced by the inclusion of illustrations or a graphic component. The nature of the topic suggests a helpful layout for key words and text in some cases. An effective visual representation of key words associated with a study of the planets, for example, shows planets orbiting the sun in the correct order. Features relating to individual planets, such as craters, rivers and types of atmosphere can be shown via a webbing format, or diagrammatically.

Hand-in-hand with the use of key words is the need to introduce new vocabulary vital to an understanding of the subject. Many of the key words will fall into this category. Any whole class introduction to a new topic, therefore, must make the meanings of key words clear. Only key words, which are fully understood, are useful in conveying information to students. (See paragraphs under heading, Introducing new vocabulary below, for suggestions.)

Textbox 10.2 Visual and textual outline for teaching key vocabulary and basic concepts related to planets to 11-year-old beginner and early intermediate second language students. See also material in picture dictionaries, illustrated topic books, CD-ROMs and on the Internet

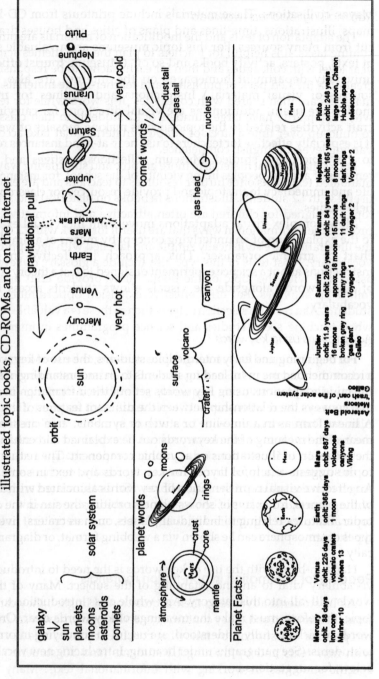

Rationalising teachers' workload

The adaptation of texts and the modification of materials are time-consuming tasks. It is helpful for teachers to plan the core themes across the year level with colleagues and then for each teacher to be responsible for creating a themed pack of published and teacher-made materials. These materials are then shared with colleagues. It is worthwhile for teachers who customarily have large numbers of L2 students in their classrooms to build up over time a stock of adapted materials that take account of varying levels of English competence.

Books that present material in more graphic and stimulating ways than mandated textbooks offer further resources to teachers and are especially useful with L2 students. Illustrations in books on historical and scientific topics designed for children are often attractive and informative. Many provide the information in ways that are useful for work with L2 children; the illustrations are stylistically simple and labelled with age-appropriate vocabulary. Most texts of this type also include a glossary of key words associated with the topic of the book. Many provide craft and other follow-up activities that offer effective extension opportunities for L2 students. As a result, a selection of texts such as these is a valuable resource when teaching social studies and science programmes in international schools.

Further resources for teaching topic areas are to be found among the picture dictionaries published for use in ESL classrooms. Those designed for middle school students frequently give labelled drawings or photographs associated with standard topic areas such as plant life and the planets. These are useful with L2 students in mainstream classrooms in the higher levels of an elementary school. Teachers can also make use of tactfully selected books directed at younger readers that give easier access to the content of a topic than school texts. Finally, teachers should not forget to make full use of the school library. School librarians are generally willing to create displays of books and other media associated with a class topic and to base regular library skills classes on material that links with the theme.

Reading for information in non-fiction materials

As L2 students advance in their acquisition of English they can work from the standard text. They continue to need support, however. Teachers can provide this support by following consistent procedures in working with new texts and by training L2 students (and all students) to use specific strategies in working with informational texts. Many of the

Textbox 10.3 Presenting Ancient Egypt to second language students

Ancient Egypt is an area of study where many L2 students have prior knowledge. Schools in the Middle East, for obvious reasons, frequently use this topic as a basis for study. Even if students have made no formal study of the topic, most children are likely to have seen illustrations of the Pyramids and of Egyptian paintings and hieroglyphs. Such familiarity makes the study of this and similar topics effective vehicles for early content study and language learning.

Ancient Egypt with its powerful visual associations cries out for the initial introduction to students to be given via the use of CD-ROM programs, film, material culled from information sites on the Internet, and slides taken on personal visits or bought at a museum shop. During the presentation and discussion of this material, teachers should make it a regular practice to establish students' existing knowledge and understandings.

In presenting the main body of new material teachers have a range of choices to make concerning their method of approach. School texts for older children frequently base their study of such a topic on a chronological account of significant events, in the case of Egypt, with a list of the Pharaohs. Texts with younger learners in mind tend to approach such topics via separate themes or areas of study. In classes containing L2 learners the second approach is more effective, although many teachers will feel the need to display a timeline showing significant events in order to ground the study in an historical framework. The thematic approach offers teachers greater possibilities in modifying the material so as to give all students a stimulating experience connected to the significant areas of interest. In the case of ancient Egypt, themes might include the following: the Nile, the role of the Pharaohs (this would include a study of significant names such as Tutankhamun and Ramses II), the Pyramids and tombs, Egyptian hieroglyphs, Egyptian painting, gods, goddesses and the underworld, and everyday life.

Each of these topics provides teachers with a relatively easy task in presenting accessible material, via visual adaptations and keywords, to L2 students at various levels of English. To take the topic of hieroglyphs as an example, a subject that most children in elementary schools enjoy, teachers have a choice of approaches. One strategy is to place the emphasis on codes and decoding by introducing the topic with a study of hieroglyphs and their meanings. Another approach places the emphasis on the historical context via authentic instances of hieroglyphs as they appear in original sources. In either case teachers can modify the content, via the number of words they present, or the complexity of the examples, to suit the level of students in the class.

A range of follow-up tasks gives L2 students enjoyable means of reinforcing their understanding. These tasks might include decoding a variety of hiero-glyphic texts, creating hieroglyphic accounts of events in school-life with appropriate drawings in the Egyptian style or inventing their own picture codes. How the Egyptians created a writing-surface from papyrus is a further area for exploration related to the Egyptian writing system. The process of

Textbox 10.3 (*cont.*)

---

making papyrus scrolls, from the reed to the finished article, can be clearly represented with illustrations and key words. Most textbooks and specialist books on Egypt contain this information. Some teachers may feel inspired to demonstrate practically how paper is made from plant sources. The aim for teachers is to search for classroom topics that give worthwhile content information and that lend themselves to presentation in an adapted form to L2 children.

Competent speakers of English can be asked to study more challenging topics that require a wider use of language. Such topics might include the opening of Tutankhamun's tomb, the personal history of Nefertiti, Tutankhamun's mother, and a study of the wonderfully illustrated papyri known as the Book of the Dead. Each of these subjects offers a strong visual component combined with possibilities for research and interesting methods of final presentations.

At the follow-up phase of a project, it is a helpful practice to place L2 students with an English-speaking partner or in a co-operative learning group. This reduces stress to a minimum and gives L2 students access to conversation about the topic in hand. Such conversation will no doubt involve the use of key items of new vocabulary and thus offers further reinforcement of these language items. A study on these lines gives even absolute beginners some significant understandings of the topic. It also provides all L2 students with opportunities to practise useful English skills in authentic settings.

---

reading strategies described in the language arts chapters are transferable to the reading of non-fiction.

(a) Pre-reading activities

With non-fiction texts as with fiction texts it is important to give students a context for the reading to come. An important part of the process is to find out what students know already about the chosen topic. It is an effective strategy to ask students to give examples from their own countries or region relating to the topic. Students from the Middle East, for example, may be able to contribute to discussions on ancient civilisations by referring to ancient Egypt or the civilisations on the Tigris and Euphrates.

In the case of science, most teachers make it an invariable practice to present the topic by including a practical demonstration or a filmed introduction. At the time of writing two significant events in connection with the topic of space and the planets were occupying the headlines. The Mars probe had arrived on the planet and pictures were being relayed via television, the newspapers and the Internet. The Russian space station, Mir, was experiencing significant difficulties. Pictures and dialogue could be seen and heard on the Internet via NASA and the Russian service, and the topic was headline news on CNN (the worldwide television news station watched by many international families). Such events provide teachers with a stimulating and relevant means of introducing a topic and of placing it in a meaningful context

Before expecting L2 students to read and gain information from a text, teachers need to provide a framework of prompts or headings that guide students through the material. The purpose of these prompts or headings is to enable students to focus on the parts of the text that provide essential information. Further strategies make the task more manageable for L2 students. Students should be reminded that paragraph headings and titles under illustrations often supply useful pointers to key areas of content.

Outlines that include a visual component are useful. The most helpful outlines are worded in language that reflects the wording of the text and emphasises key vocabulary items associated with the topic. When making outlines teachers should eliminate as a matter of course, detail, synonym, complicated grammatical constructions and subordinate clauses. Allow students time to read these outlines before they are asked to read independently.

(b) During reading

Students can be asked to read to themselves or aloud in small groups. There are good reasons for teachers to read parts of the text out loud themselves. By reading and explaining as they move through the text, teachers can indicate how to select useful information. This is also an opportunity to explain and give examples of making inferences and deductions.

After a first reading, teachers may wish students to make notes. Such note taking should be tied to an intended use such as a practical craft activity, creating a longer piece of writing or conducting a science experiment. (The section below on gathering information in writing from a text offers further detailed strategies in this area.)

(c) After reading

After reading is completed teachers need to ensure that students have extracted the required information. This can be done by a general question-and-answer discussion although a good level of English is necessary for students to participate fully. Straightforward verbal re-tellings of various sorts, either by individuals or in groups, are simpler ways of allowing teachers to evaluate the degree of understanding which students have of the text. Students' comprehension can also be assessed effectively by other means. These include asking students to create picture maps and flow charts, to construct models of houses, buildings and natural features (the order and orbits of the planets around the earth, for example), and to compose raps and rhymes. Such strategies not only provide teachers with assessment evidence, but also give L2 and other students further opportunities to practise subject-related English in stress-free and enjoyable ways.

It is a wise practice for teachers to check whether students' own notes or understandings are sufficient to enable them to work independently or in a group on follow-up activities or written assignments. It is likely that teachers will have to supply further support via text, illustration or personal intervention in order that L2 students can participate fully in further activity.

Use of visual media

Visual media of all sorts are useful in making social studies and science content accessible to L2 students. Visual components in a programme provide instant information at all stages of a unit. These stages include the introduction, citing of examples, gaining information from text, previewing an activity, carrying out the activity itself, summarising and reviewing.

Static visual materials include charts, maps, graphs, displays of data, photographs, slides, illustrations, paintings, illustrated family trees and time lines. Electronic media include pages down-loaded from the Internet, CD-ROM material, film loops and videocassette footage. These last are especially valuable because of the possibilities they offer for flexible usage. Teachers can choose to supply their own commentary and can use the pause button to allow time for explanation or to ask for student input. The use of authentic visual media allows the teacher to present material in a more immediate and vivid manner and gives opportunities to include references and examples from a wider range of countries and regions than are likely to be included in a standard textbook. (See pp. 243–52, Electronic media, for further suggestions.)

Modern science and social studies textbooks

Modern social studies and science textbooks designed for mainstream classrooms are attractively presented with a high ratio of illustration and photographs to text. They provide suggestions for a range of activities related to the topic including practical activities and writing assignments. Many of these textbook series also suggest assignments for L2 students.

Certain features of these textbooks tend to limit their usefulness with L2 students. Firstly, they contain too much material: L2 students are likely to be overwhelmed by the weight and density of the subject matter. Secondly, their terms of reference are often narrow: the illustrations and examples tend to reflect the global interests of the English-speaking country in which the series is published. It remains the responsibility of teachers to make the content adaptations and to supply the language skills teaching that allow L2 students access to the programme.

Teaching packages are now being offered by United States publishing houses, which provide content-based language teaching at every year level. The complete programmes include well-illustrated core textbooks with simplified text and an array of supplementary material designed to cover the four skills of language. The teachers' resource books include photocopiable graphic organisers and 'letters home' written in six languages. Hard-pressed teachers in international schools might reasonably hope that these series would serve as a valuable resource in their classrooms.

There are reasons, unfortunately, why these textbook series do not fulfil the needs of students in international schools. The languages in which the 'letters home' are written give an intimation of the anticipated use for these series. The languages are those of significant minority language communities in the United States. The series are intended for use in sheltered classrooms for L2 children from those backgrounds. They provide a structured programme based on the use of content area themes as vehicles for language learning. One new series is authored by some famous names in second language teaching and learning and would provide an effective means of giving L2 children in North America the general content knowledge and language support that are needed for success in local school systems.

The situation in an international school classroom varies significantly from that of teachers and students in national education systems. The aim for L2 students in international schools is to allow them access to the mainstream programme as soon as their level of English allows. Teachers are committed to a continuation of these students' education during the time that they are learning English and accept the responsibility of adapting the core programme so that L2 students have access to the subject matter. This is an area where general content-based skills series do not meet the requirements of L2 students in international schools. Teachers in international schools require a range of parallel adaptations that closely relate to the content work of the mainstream programme in their school.

One final point needs to be made relating to the teaching of science and social studies in international schools. International schools are uniquely placed to offer relevant and exciting teaching and learning opportunities to their students. This is done by drawing on the resources available in the host country and by accessing the array of diverse cultural experiences and talents in the school community. Textbooks may be of use in supplying basic skills teaching in specific areas such as geography. The most memorable and stimulating teaching, however, takes account of the possibilities offered by the make-up and location of each international school. (See p. 61, Cultural studies programmes, for examples of social studies approaches that make use of local resources.)

Using literature and music in social studies and science classes

Fiction texts, biography, poetry and music supply useful means of giving a further context to a unit of work in social studies and science. Rhythmic media such as raps and chants are also valuable since they tend to be simple and repetitive in their use of language. These resources can be used at any point during the study to provide variety and to deepen or enhance the students' understanding of the subject matter. (Tapes and compact discs containing selections of ancient music are effective in giving a sense of atmosphere to students when studying ancient civilisations.)

For L2 students it is necessary to search out written texts that are within their range of English competence. A careful search through material intended for younger readers is sometimes fruitful. The wide list of adapted readers available from ESL publishing houses may be useful in this context. Titles such as *A Journey to the Centre of the Earth* by Jules Verne, and biographies of the first astronauts for use in broadening a study of the planets, can be found in these series. (For addresses of publishers who specialise in these series, see Appendix A.)

Co-operative groupings in social studies and science classes

Co-operative groupings are a major strategy in supporting L2 students in social studies and science classes. Such groupings enable beginning students to observe authentic language in use in these subject areas and to gain an understanding of the skills needed. Intermediate and advanced students gain the interim support they need as they move towards making greater contributions to the success of the group. Careful management of such groups as suggested in the language arts chapters is equally necessary in these subject areas.

In science, arranging students in pairs or small groups is the customary method of organising the setting up and carrying out of science experiments. Subsequent writing up can be carried out co-operatively or individually. In either case the L2 student gains from general discussion during the experiment. Major projects, such as making presentations before or following visits to planetaria or space centres, or creating a display for a science fair, are likewise more profitable and less daunting if L2 students share the task with classmates.

All stages of a social studies unit can usefully be carried out as co-operative ventures. This includes the early gathering of information. This is a time when L2 students can be encouraged to contribute examples and references from their own cultures. Each group can be organised to collect information from different sources and then to report back to the whole class on their findings. These sources can include reference materials, magazines, newspapers, electronic media and interviews. Follow-up and extension activities likewise lend themselves to a co-operative approach. L2 students are supported in this way to contribute effectively in completing such tasks as group presentations and joint craft activities involving modelling or constructing a relief map.

Introducing new vocabulary

Teachers need to use a range of strategies to introduce and reinforce new vocabulary for L2 students in science and social studies. These are areas where there are likely to be words unfamiliar to L2 students. Many of the strategies are described in the earlier chapters on language arts. Some further ideas are useful in teaching science and social studies where the density of new vocabulary words is likely to be higher than in a piece of carefully targeted fiction.

- An understanding of the keywords that carry the weight of meaning and lead the student through the text is an essential first step.
- In the case of science these key words are likely to include both conceptual and naming words.
- New vocabulary should be presented in a context. Lists of isolated words with definitions are not an effective means of introducing a number of unfamiliar words.
- Pictorial flow charts are one way of illustrating the meaning of new vocabulary words in both science and social studies. A flow chart allows the naming words, the verbal phrases and the conceptual words to be given a context.
- When students are asked to carry out a practical task such as a science experiment or craft activity it is helpful to provide a visual representation alongside the essential key words.

- Carrying out practical activities, preferably with a partner or in a small group, confirms and reinforces the meaning of new vocabulary.
- It is a helpful practice to use the same words consistently to name objects and concepts and to describe processes.

Approaching content in English through students' first languages

Teachers will find it helpful to remember the value to L2 students of negotiating meaning in English through their first languages. Reading about a topic in their home languages enables L2 students to approach a study topic in social studies or science with a basic understanding of the facts and of any conceptual elements. It is likely also that reading in the home language will reactivate details of prior knowledge. Many L2 students, for instance, will have previously studied aspects of the example topics chosen for this chapter: ancient civilisations, the planets and the life cycle of plants. When study topics are unfamiliar, students should be encouraged to search for relevant material in their home languages. For this reason the choice of global topics with broadly applicable vocabulary is a wise move for teachers in international schools. In order to give students and parents time to gather material, if necessary from home country bookshops, it is worthwhile letting L2 families know in advance what are to be the major areas of study during the year in social studies and science.

An understanding of the topic gained through their home languages makes it easier for L2 students to recognise the meaning of new vocabulary and to follow the course of a discussion. They will then be better able to take part in activities that require higher-level thinking such as making connections and deductions from a range of facts. Teachers should let students and parents know that they encourage this approach. Some families imagine that teachers frown on students carrying out work in their own languages.

A further effective strategy is for L2 parents who are fluent in English to provide translations of key words in the study topic. Teachers find it a valuable resource to build up lists of vocabulary related to the topics they regularly study in science and social studies. Useful as they are, these lists should not be used as the sole means of explaining new vocabulary items. Direct translation is time-consuming for students and rarely supplies the full meaning of words as they are used in context. The value of these lists is to provide a reference once the meaning of unfamiliar words in English is understood in the context of the topic being studied.

Textbox 10.4 Teaching social studies and science to very young second language children

Much of the content of this chapter relates to teaching social studies and science to older L2 children in the upper grades of elementary schools. This weighting reflects the type of material and learning tasks customarily found in those classrooms. The complexity of the subject area material and the advanced nature of the English language skills needed for participation in social studies and science programmes at that level require teachers of diverse classes to make extensive adaptations.

Providing learning opportunities for young children that incorporate the distinct content and skills associated with social studies and science takes a different form. Early education is devoted to teaching young children to observe the world about them, to making sense of what they see and to giving them the skills to talk, read and write about their experiences. These are aims that relate closely to the desired outcomes of social studies and science programmes designed for young students. Thus, topics that are standard in young children's classrooms such as shape, size, light, the weather, the seasons, the natural world and living in communities provide ideal teaching and learning situations for the integration of social studies and science within the core literacy and numeracy programmes.

Today's methods of teaching young children allow L2 students access to the content of these topics in an ideal way. They are introduced to new uses of language and the meaning of unfamiliar vocabulary while they investigate the nature of things in a practical and hands-on manner. Thus young L2 students are able to join with their English-speaking peers in making observations, in collecting those observations in a useful form and in drawing conclusions from the evidence. Teachers can make the means of systematising and displaying the knowledge that has been gained similarly accessible to young L2 students. Such means include the construction of large-scale models, the representation of data with blocks and counters and the creation of wall-friezes.

Electronic technology designed for young users is a further means of introducing L2 students to the content and language of social studies and science topics. **Trudy's Time and Place House**, for instance, a program from **Edmark**, teaches a range of geographical concepts in a way that is motivating and accessible to young children. What makes this program especially appropriate for use with international school students is that it is possible for children to click on a map of the world in order to call up graphic images and sounds associated with chosen countries and regions.

Young L2 students benefit from the opportunities and stimulation provided by exciting extension activities and special events. In my own school, parents, administration and teachers work together to organise an annual Science Fair solely for the very young children. Small groups of children move from exhibit to exhibit, and in each case watch a demonstration before trying out a similar activity themselves. The atmosphere is welcoming and colourful. The topics range from growing crystals using common household products to the

Textbox 10.4 (*cont.*)

---

properties of natural dyes and the creation of vacuums. Parents use only equipment familiar to young children and that is part of their everyday world. Children are encouraged to comment and ask questions and to draw conclusions. It is noticeable that the child-friendly content and approach lead to a high level of engagement among all the students, L1 and L2 children alike. Happily, the approaches that make science and social studies fascinating and accessible for all young children are also effective in promoting second language learning.

Specific language skills associated with social studies and science

The study of social studies and science involves the use of specific reading and writing skills. It is standard practice to ask students in international schools to select and summarise information from text in their own words, to produce reports and to write up science experiments. Some L2 students will already be familiar with these activities. Many students will not have observed these skills in use or practised them. Teachers need therefore to recognise the extent of the support that L2 students are likely to require in order to participate in the mainstream programme.

A core strategy when asking L2 students to carry out an unfamiliar task is to provide examples of the target format. These examples should be explained in detail and the task broken down into manageable stages. Students will also need to be taught the specific English structures and specialised usage associated with the target format and provided with a frame or pattern to follow. Explanation and practice is more effective if it relates to an on-going study in the classroom than if presented as a separate language-learning exercise.

Selecting and writing down information from written text

Students in the upper levels of elementary schools are sometimes asked to write about a topic using information they have gained from textbooks or from books in the library. Activity of this type is required in order to produce a social studies report or to supply information for a science project. This is a challenging task for elementary school students who are competent English speakers, and it is certainly unrealistic for teachers to expect beginning and early intermediate L2 students to function at this level. It is likely that many students, both L1 and L2, will copy out whole paragraphs and reproduce them verbatim in their writing. Teachers therefore need to be flexible in their approach to this type of assignment when working with L2 students. Their expectations may have to be modified so that the task is more appropriate to the level of students' English competence, and they should be prepared to offer a high degree of support to all but the most advanced students.

Approaches that support L2 children in extracting and writing up information from text

- Teachers need to vary their approaches according to students' differing levels of competence in English.
- They should ensure that students approach the text with a clear understanding of the information they are required to select.
- It is essential first to establish an overall understanding of the text from which the information is to be taken. An effective introductory phase involving the use of visual material and key words allows prior knowledge to be applied to the text in question.
- The teacher should guide beginning and intermediate L2 students through the text picking out the key pieces of information. (L2 students typically have difficulty in extracting essential information from the mass of text. Students who have been asked to write an account of slavery in Ancient Greece, for example, frequently include information about everyday life in Greece, the typical plan of Greek villa, and so on, because they lack the skills to discriminate between essential and background information.)
- An overhead projector supplies a useful means of working through a piece of text with students.
- With beginning and early intermediate students the required information should be summarised in single words and short phrases and written down by the teacher in an outline form. This outline can then be used to carry out an extension activity at an appropriate level such as completing a graphic organiser or filling in the gaps in a cloze passage.
- With more advanced L2 students these words and phrases can be written down by the children themselves and used later to guide them in carrying out the writing task.
- The outline giving key words and phrases relating to the target theme can be used by the teacher to demonstrate how these notes are formed into sentences in a consecutive piece of prose.
- More advanced L2 students will benefit from tuition in the use of link words to make factual or causal connections.
- Collaborative groupings can be used for the early phases of

information gathering. Facts can be assembled in a list or web form by the members of the group.

- It can be a useful exercise for L2 children to observe how competent speakers of English make use of these short notes. In general, though, it is difficult to gain a profitable writing experience from working in committee.

Report-writing

Report writing has been introduced at ever earlier stages in elementary schools and now it is not uncommon for eight- or nine-year-old children to be asked to produce reports. Writing a report constitutes a challenge for L2 students of all ages even when provided with support. One of the chief causes of difficulty is the size of the task together with the number and complexity of the different language skills required to produce a satisfactory report.

Students are frequently required to choose their own subject within a broad area of study, and to plan the content of the report. They are expected to carry out research in books and other media and to summarise the content. They must organise their material into a first draft and, finally, produce a polished piece of work containing illustrations and other graphic elements and a bibliography. The demands of writing a report of this type often cause L2 students to feel stressed and panicky. They and their parents spend anxious hours trying to achieve a finished piece of work that answers the teacher's specifications.

The element of choice is often difficult for students to manage. It is more satisfactory if teachers join with students in choosing a topic based on their interests and language capability. The research phase should be similarly tailored. An appropriate assignment might involve students finding out the answers to a stated list of questions from only one or two listed books. For beginning and early intermediate students this is a more manageable assignment than asking students to search for unspecified information from a large number of books and other media. Advancing students can be asked to write a limited number of paragraphs under designated headings. Teachers should make it clear how L2 students are to obtain the necessary books. They should be readily available. L2 students tend to be shy in asking for the necessary material, or fail to borrow books from the library soon enough to allow them adequate time to complete the task.

A piece of work in a report format can be created out of even a limited amount of written information. In addition teachers can suggest other ways of conveying facts and opinions. These include graphs, maps, students' own reproductions of craft and artistic features and the use of downloaded pages from the Internet. L2 students at all levels of English competence can thus produce a finished piece of work that resembles in type and purpose that of the rest of the class.

Teachers might question whether it is useful to ask beginning and intermediate L2 students to carry out such large and complex tasks. Other related activities may offer a more appropriate degree of challenge. Such activities include the making of detailed picture maps, the collection and charting of data, the drawing-up of questions for a series of interviews and the charting of replies. Suitable assignments for beginning and early intermediate L2 students involve the completion of a small number of clearly specified tasks, rather than the production of a complex and interlinked piece of work.

Writing up science experiments

The writing-up of science experiments is an area of difficulty for L2 students. This is certainly the case when the writing involves the use of the passive voice. (Three beans were placed in the soil. Water was poured on the soil and the jar was placed in the sun.) The passive voice is rarely used in children's spoken English and modern English language programmes for young students defer teaching the passive until learners are quite advanced. Nowadays, descriptions of science experiments in an elementary school tend to be written in a more natural, less prescribed style. Writing up science experiments does, however, require students to write precisely and to use a specified formula and layout.

Prior to the writing phase, most science classes move through a series of stages. These stages include an introduction by the teacher to the topic of study, the possible use of informational text and an explanation of the experiment to be carried out by the students. The most effective forms of teaching science to L2 students (and all students) involve practical demonstrations and concrete examples. This approach gives students effective opportunities to gain an understanding of the basic concept and to meet new vocabulary in real use. Teachers should supply further support relating to the understanding of concepts and the meaning of new vocabulary in a graphic form.

During the experimental and writing-up phases, working with a partner or in a small group provides valuable support for L2 students. Teachers should give clear directions, in writing and orally, concerning the purpose, method, means of displaying results and the drawing of conclusions associated with the experiment. They should give L2 students examples of how experiments are written up. It is useful to supply standard phrases that recur in writing laboratory reports. They need to explain to students the precise usage that is customary in writing about science. This is an area where ESL teachers can offer valuable support to both classroom teachers and students. Providing detailed language teaching and offering appropriate opportunities for practice enables students to approach the writing up of science experiments with greater confidence.

Increasing the range of follow-up and extension activities

The presence of L2 students in social studies and science classes stimulates teachers in planning follow-up activities. Initially this effort is designed to allow L2 students to join with their peers in carrying out meaningful extension work in these subject areas. Experienced teachers soon recognise that a range of activities enriches and deepens the experience and understanding of all the children in a class. A number of options are also valuable in allowing children to chose according to their preferred learning styles.

Follow-up activities that best serve the needs of L2 students typically contain certain elements. They move from the concrete to the conceptual. They offer a supportive environment for practising new language skills in a variety of instructional groupings. They reflect as far as possible the cultural and home backgrounds of all the students in a class. They make use of the near-at-hand resources in the school and host country community.

Several of these elements are included in the standard extension activities to be found in young and older children's classrooms. These include illustrated and cartoon retellings of historical events and the construction of friezes, murals, models, large-scale constructions, puppets, mobiles and relief maps. The creation of stories, poems, play scripts and empathetic pieces are additional means of challenging competent users of English.

Many international schools derive a good part of their social studies and science curricula from the historical and environmental resources in the host country. It makes sense from all angles for students to study a rich period in the history of the region or to use a nearby river or mountain range as the basis for a long-term geographical or environmental study. Myriad extension activities are open to teachers in this situation that also answer L2 students' language learning needs. Field trips, museum link-ups or involvement in a local environmental project offer L2 students experiences that connect language skills to real use and practice.

Creative teachers are continually thinking of new ways to broaden children's experiences related to subject work in the classrooms. The tradition has evolved in many schools of holding an annual event

Textbox 10.5 Re-creating the Bayeaux tapestry: A social studies project accessible to all students

During the time I was writing this chapter I was able to observe the evolution of a project on my own corridor which fulfilled many of the criteria for successful work with L2 students in curricular areas. Two classes of 4th Grade students joined together to study a social studies unit on Mediaeval Europe that culminated in the re-creation of part of the Bayeaux Tapestry. During the period of this work all the students, both L1 and L2, were filled with enthusiasm. The classrooms buzzed with focused talk and I often had to make my way round small groups of absorbed children on the floor engaged in measuring, cutting and sticking. Their work is now proudly displayed in our lunchroom.

This exercise was the final stage in a study of life in mediaeval castles of which there are many in Belgium. Several field trips to nearby castles were an integral part of the unit. Video, CD-ROM material, illustration and photos were used to present the content along with a variety of written materials. A range of retelling and vocabulary activities was followed by the creation of small groups across both classes with the aim of completing an agreed section of the Bayeaux Tapestry. (This famous tapestry — in fact an embroidery — tells the story of William the Conqueror's invasion of England in 1066. It fits in well with the theme of life in mediaeval castles since it portrays many homely as well as mighty incidents. It is immediately accessible to children because of the lively and direct manner in which the story is told and the figures presented.)

The groups were selected by the teachers and generally comprised at least one strong L1 student, an L2 student and a balance of boys and girls from both classes. The social contact across the classes was an important aspect of the arrangement. The children were required to copy and enlarge to scale their part of the Tapestry. They studied the significance of colour and placement in the original embroidery. They worked on the actual cutting, placement and sticking, which involved measurement and working to scale. The art teacher and the two classroom teachers supervised the work of the groups in rotation. At each stage the children were required to keep a record of the procedure in writing.

One of the classes had recently been joined by a complete non-speaker of English. I followed with interest his involvement in the project. The fact that he spoke French (although not from France) gave him access to the French context of the project. This connection was built on by the class teacher to enable the student to make a unique contribution to his group. For all the L2 students the activity worked well on a number of levels. They met new keywords in context. New vocabulary and phrases were repeated and practised through real use in association with concrete activities. They could clearly see the need for the information they were asked to gain from text. This information was made available in a variety of accessible forms. The co-operative nature of the activity provided the supportive environment that allowed students to contribute at their own language level. Finally, the experience of working together led to the formation of new friendships.

Textbox 10.5 (*cont.*)

Several further elements were present that led, I felt, to the success of the project. These included the allocation of an extended period of time and the careful organisation and management of the groups. Throughout the project there was a continuing awareness of the need to make provision for the varying levels of English among the students. Lastly, the imaginative choice of the Bayeaux Tapestry to act as a focus for the wider study of mediaeval Europe inspired the children and ensured their engagement.

connected with key themes in social studies and science. Roman banquets, re-creations of ancient Olympic Games and Chinese New Year festivities bring life to social studies programmes. Science fairs on designated topics and harvest meals using produce grown or picked by the children bring relevance and immediacy to science programmes. Such activities allow L2 students to be involved in a manner appropriate to their level of English, individually or in groups. Their parents can be asked to contribute with support at home or by practical activity in school. Dressing up may be included in the fun and the whole school buzzes with excitement. It is almost incidental that these participatory activities provide L2 students with the optimum environment for gaining meaningful practice in subject-related English.

Providing a challenging programme in social studies and science for competent speakers of English

Teachers in international schools sometimes express concern about the level of challenge they deliver to competent speakers of English in diverse classes. They are aware that they fight shy of introducing difficult concepts when the class contains a high number of beginning and intermediate L2 students, and consciously limit their vocabulary to simple and common words. They may feel under pressure from some parents to deliver a sequenced course of study involving more extensive formal written assignments such as many children receive in their home schools.

There are grounds for teachers' anxiety if a relatively narrow view of what comprises education is adhered to. In most international schools it is not possible, (or appropriate) to replicate the academic atmosphere that exists in the selective schools that some children in international schools attend in their home countries. The nature of the student body in international schools, however, as well as the background and education of their parents, enriches life in the classroom in many ways. Students bring to their work in school a range of experience and general knowledge that is rare among children in national schools, and teachers can refer to a wider range of references and examples to expand and deepen the programme. The resources of the host country are available to offer stimulating experiences and fresh examples.

There are various strategies available that enable teachers to enlarge the range of challenge for students, and to address parental concerns about the nature and quality of the programme. Teachers should feel free to modify the content of the programme to suit the needs of varying groups of children. On occasion it is appropriate to group together children who are capable of very challenging work. (L2 children may be quite at home in this type of group, depending on the language level required by a specific task.) The variable factors that make material more or less challenging include the degree of learner independence built into the task as well as the nature of the activities themselves. Allowing a group of able L1 and L2 children with a high level of competence in English to assess a learning task, to plan the means for carrying out the assignment and then to choose the form of the final presentation is an effective method of incorporating challenging activities into the classroom.

Appropriate activities that involve a high degree of challenge are discussions on the pros and cons of an issue that are followed by a presentation to the whole class using visual aids and other media. Such topics can involve an historical perspective: 'What would happen if we lost the use of the wheel?' or be related to a science theme: 'Why should we continue to explore space?', Environmental studies offer further challenging activities for small groups that involve looking at two sides of an argument. Topics of this sort include the difficulty of conserving endangered animal species when it is contrary to the interests of the people who live nearby, and the advantages and disadvantages of keeping animals in zoos. Effective and challenging activities in diverse classrooms should involve global issues that allow all children to contribute out of their own knowledge and experience. The Internet offers a valuable resource in providing-up-to-date input relating to this type of topic.

Team teaching with a colleague may allow flexibility to be built into the programme to take account of differing student needs. Permanent division by ability is not the intention, nor does it provide the answer to catering for varying levels of competence in English. Working with a colleague does, however, allow greater variety in grouping and in providing varied levels of assignments. The presence of CD-ROM facilities and access to the Internet, together with varied homework assignments and a range of suggestions for private reading offer further opportunities to stretch each student academically.

Field Trips Relating to Social Studies and Science: Ensuring a Valuable Experience for Second Language Students

The value of field trips to L2 children at all levels of English is enhanced if teachers take specific steps to ensure that materials and tasks are adapted to their needs. If extended field trips are a traditional part of a school's programme then the wider practical and social issues need to be addressed as well. (See Life in the Classroom — Management Issues: Residential field trips, pp. 111–12.)

Prior to the trip

- Articulate and write down for yourself, the administration, parents and students, the reasons for taking students on the field trip.
- Decide on a limited number of specific objectives and outcomes for the trip.
- Establish whether any students have made the same visit before; ask for their input at all stages.
- Ask children to describe their experiences of trips to somewhere similar. How had they set about deciding what to do? Had they used maps or plans? What happened on their trip?
- Introduce themes and topics through appropriate pieces of fiction, non-fiction and poetry.
- Ask the librarian to set aside a range of non-fiction and fiction media related to the objective for the trip. Books with a high proportion of illustrations in relation to text are useful for L2 children.
- Enlist help from ESL teachers in presenting new vocabulary and content in an age-appropriate manner.
- Supply illustrated vocabulary lists where necessary; ask for parental co-operation in translating lists into their own languages.
- Make a collection of guidebooks concerning the place to be visited in as many languages as possible. (Parents can help with this too.)
- If the trip is to an area with a different language, introduce students to simple vocabulary and survival structures.
- Provide visual introductions to the subject matter of a field trip via maps, posters, tourist brochures, photos and visual organisers.
- Access tourist home pages on the Internet to gain information about the places to be visited.
- Present material in video and film form if possible.
- By means of a plan take children along the route in advance; draw attention to specific buildings, details and features to be seen

first-hand later. (Check to see whether there is material available in CD-ROM format.)

- Present text in a modified form via keyword summaries, short sentence outlines, informational texts originally aimed at a younger age group.
- Send a note home or ensure that students write down what items they need to bring on the trip; these may include clip-boards, drawing paper, pencils, rulers, coloured markers, cheap cameras, a small dictionary, money for postcards and so on.
- Make absolutely clear to L2 students and parents (in writing) what are the food and cash requirements for the trip, and whether transport arrangements before and after school will be different from usual.
- In the case of residential trips give adequate written information in advance about all aspects of the trip. Get this information translated if necessary or put the parents in touch with the parent of a child who went on the trip in a previous year and who speaks their language.

Suggestions for field trip assignments and follow-up in school after the trip

Young children

General Note

Young L2 students will need one-to-one or small-group adult support on field trips. The move outside the familiar environment of school, particularly in the early months, may make too great a demand and result in children becoming bewildered and confused. It is helpful if a simple practical task is required of L2 children during the trip to give them a near-at-hand, concrete focus. The new vocabulary and use of English required for participation in this activity can profitably be built upon and reinforced during follow-up activities in the classroom.

- During or after the trip ask children to draw some examples of the focus of study — zoo animals, buildings, seaside objects, etc. These can be used later to illustrate a class book, to make a frieze with labels, or to construct a mural.
- During the trip ensure that children take note of key features. On return involve the class in making models of buildings, people and landscape elements to bring the plan to life. An effective form of this strategy is to construct a walk-through plan or relief model on the floor.

- Guide children in observing and counting an array of objects and people; these can include animals, types of transport, boats, types of buildings or policemen. Involve them in recording the results.
- On return these can be used for a mathematics activity such as constructing a coloured block graph or collecting tokens and counters in appropriate groups.
- On return involve the class in a language experience exercise to create and illustrate an account of the day's outing. Use photographs taken during the trip to illustrate the writing.
- Use the library to expand on what was seen. Both fiction and non-fiction texts may be used to confirm the children's experiences and to expand their understandings. This is an excellent way to reinforce new vocabulary.
- Suggest that students' families revisit the site of the field trip and get their children to act as guides.

Older children

General Note

Field trips are times which emphasise the social groupings in a class. They offer fluent English speakers chances to socialise, share jokes and to spend time with their friends, activity that may leave L2 speakers on the fringe. This can be avoided if small working groups are set up beforehand to include a spread of children. This is also a time when L2 children should be allowed to sit with friends on the bus and at lunch in order for the trip to be as positive an experience for them as it is for fluent English speakers. It is important that there are enough adults on the trip to talk in comprehensible language to the L2 students, and to be the centre of a sociable group if necessary.

- Create a questionnaire concerning a specific aspect of the trip. Consider providing a list of questions with yes/no answers for L2 students.
- On residential trips have students keep a daily journal. Model the use of possible sentence structures beforehand.
- Give clear directions for the research and writing of a report on one aspect of the study topic. (This type of assignment is a daunting undertaking for L2 students. It should only be required of L2 students if teachers give support at every stage.)
- Ask students to prepare oral reports before or during the trip. L2 students will need help with this. For many students it is an ordeal to speak out loud in this way, and the collection of information is an

overwhelming task for all L2 students except the most advanced. (See pp. 195–7: Spoken English for academic purposes, for further detailed suggestions.)

- Involve the ESL department in the research phase and construction of L2 students' written or oral reports.
- In the case of L2 students, consider replacing extensive written and oral assignments with activities that involve a visual or graphic element. These might include illustrated time-lines, illustrated and labelled walking plans of the trip, botanical and zoological diagrams, graphs and charts of observable events and features or a simple diary.
- On a residential trip involve the students in a dramatic recreation or role-playing exercise connected with the topic of the visit.
- Suggest that students' families make the same visit and ask their child to act as guide.

Summary

Teachers of diverse classes cannot assume that L2 students will be familiar with the demands of social studies and science programmes in international schools. Many L2 students will be unused to the tasks that are asked of them in these subjects. Teachers must expect to make modifications in the content so that it is accessible to L2 students and to give students support and guidance in carrying out assignments that may be unfamiliar in nature. They must also teach L2 students the English language skills that are necessary for success in social studies and science. The content of the subject areas themselves provides a powerful vehicle for language teaching and learning.

Teachers can achieve these objectives by consistently employing effective strategies and making adaptations to the content of the programme. Modifications by means of visuals and keywords make the content of social studies and science accessible to L2 students. A range of strategies enables students with differing levels of English language competence to select information from texts. Targeted teaching approaches and graphic organisers allow students to gain an understanding of new items of vocabulary. A variety of instructional groupings supports students in their learning. The teaching of specific language skills in authentic contexts allows L2 students to participate, according to the level of their English competence, in reading and writing activities such as gaining information from text, report-writing and writing-up science experiments. Care and forethought in preparing L2 students for day and extended field trips ensures that they gain the most from these learning experiences.

Teachers can enrich and enhance social studies and science programmes in many ways. These ways include the appropriate use of modern social studies and science textbooks and other reading material. Further means include the use of visual and technological media, the resources available in the host country and stimulating and varied extension activities. Finally, teachers can supply a challenging programme to all students by using a variety of grouping strategies and by offering a selection of assignments.

Chapter 11
Further Resources Available to Teachers of Second Language Students

Introduction

Electronic technology and the library or media centre offer rich resources to teachers of second language children in international schools. Books and print media, for most teachers and children, continue to occupy a central position in providing information and pleasurable reading experiences. Teachers are familiar with the process of incorporating such elements into their teaching. Electronic technology offers a different sort of challenge since teachers have the wider responsibility of preparing students for the technologically based working environment they will meet outside school. Teachers should therefore make use of this valuable tool with second language learners for two reasons: first, electronic technology provides unique possibilities for language teaching and learning; second, a need exists for all students to become proficient users of the applications of electronic technology.

Teachers need to ask three questions in relation to these resources:

- How can they be used by teachers to extend their professional knowledge and to augment their teaching?
- What are effective ways for teachers to use these resources to enhance teaching and learning experiences in the classroom?
- How can students who are unfamiliar with electronic technology and an integrated use of the library be brought to incorporate these resources into their academic and recreational activities?

Teachers of diverse classes will discover varying degrees of familiarity with electronic technology and libraries among their second language students. Some children come from education systems where the provision of books and other print media is limited and there is no access to electronic technology. Other L2 students are accustomed to school libraries, but the use of these facilities takes a different form from that in international schools. In some national education systems, in parts of East

Asia for instance, schools have moved directly to the extensive provision of electronic technology. In other countries, books and computers in children's homes supply resources that are not generally available in national schools.

The discussion in this chapter about these areas is divided into two parts. The first deals with the uses of electronic technology in catering to the needs of L2 students. The second is concerned with the use of the library or media centre. (Information relating to individual software titles and CD-ROMs is to be found in Appendix A, pp. 259–63, together with addresses of e-mail networks mentioned in the text. The addresses (URLs) of Internet Websites are to be found in Appendix B.)

Electronic Media

Many large international schools and some well-endowed small schools have by now invested in a range of electronic media. Among these schools, at the elementary level, it is usual to find stand-alone computers, printers and scanners housed in a computer laboratory, as well as at least one computer accessible to students in each classroom. Software generally includes word-processing, graphics and data collection applications, and subject related titles. The largest schools may have a designated computer teacher, although all teachers nowadays are expected to be familiar with the functions and classroom uses of electronic technology. In other schools, the provision is less extensive, although most schools own some computers and perhaps one or two CD-ROM drives.

Other electronic media include audiocassette players, televisions, videocassette recorders (VCRs) and screens. In order for teachers to make full use of electronic media it is essential for there to be easy access. Ideally each classroom should contain an audiocassette player and at least one computer linked to a printer. There should also be convenient access to further computers as well as to a VCR and television.

No doubt, very soon, every classroom in larger schools will contain facilities for incorporating CD-ROM material into the regular programme. At present, the high cost of the multimedia hardware packages necessary to ensure reasonably rapid and effective use of CD-ROM material dictates that this resource is located only in the library or is shared among several classrooms. At the time of writing, most elementary schools give students only limited access to e-mail and the Internet.

Audiocassette players

Audiocassette players are a useful tool for work with L2 learners. As listening centres, with several sets of headphones, they allow students to listen to tapes of stories while following the written text. This can be done without disturbing other students after the teacher has introduced and read the story. Listening centres allow L2 students to become familiar with the story in their own time, and to listen to another English-speaking voice. Teachers can use tapes more generally to bring sounds, music and songs into the classroom. Young children, especially, enjoy listening to familiar songs and rhymes.

The recording function of an audiocassette player has a variety of uses. One method for L2 students to gain information for a report without the necessity of taking notes is to record interviews on tape based on their own written questions. In this way they can play and re-play the tapes in order to gain the necessary information. This can then be collated using a chart or graph, or slotted into a prepared outline. These tapes can also be used at home so that their parents can help with the assignment. Other uses are mock radio interviews to a pre-arranged format, taped retellings round the class and choral recitations, dialogues and short plays.

Language laboratories and other taped language-learning devices are not in widespread use in elementary schools. They have the advantage of allowing students to work at their own pace through the material. One of their disadvantages, however, is a tendency to isolate the student and this is the main reason why such methods are little used except with highly motivated older learners. Children thrive on human interaction, and their language learning progresses best through real communication with their teacher and peers.

Videocassette recorders

Taped television programmes as well as professionally produced videocassettes offer many possibilities for work with L2 children. Professionally produced programmes for schools include material on early literacy, stories, historical and geographical topics as well as up-to-date sport and social comment at an age-appropriate level. These programmes offer the sort of visual, immediate approach that helps L2 students to gain meaning. The advantage of taping programmes is that teachers can turn down the sound and give a commentary themselves using simplified English. They can also stop the tape in order to explain and to establish understanding. Programmes that relate to on going work in the classroom and which lead into profitable extension work are the most useful.

Taped programmes made for a general audience can be put to good use with more advanced and older L2 students. Environmental topics, documentaries about the natural world, sports events, current events in the host country such as festivals or national celebrations provide all sorts of introductory and follow-up possibilities. Again, the teacher may prefer to provide the commentary. The use of this type of material has two benefits: the wider world is brought into the classroom, and children, attuned as they are to the visual medium of television, gain a high degree of support in working out the meaning of new language.

Professionally made videocassettes offer further possibilities. Filmed versions of stories intended for child viewers provide introductory or follow-up material related to the written text. L2 children gain much from seeing characters and narrative brought to life on the screen. The moving image engages them completely and bridges any gaps in understanding. Some teachers have concerns about using filmed versions of stories in the classroom. They prefer children to make the acquaintance of modern and older classics through a written text. However, filmed versions have their uses with L2 children during the time that their level of English does not allow them easy and pleasurable access to the original book.

Stand-alone computers

One or two computers in a classroom, as well as computer laboratories themselves, provide opportunities for teachers to enrich and develop L2 students' use of language. This is particularly true of the L2 student for whom the computer is an absorbing passion. Students of this type who have difficulty in writing at length, or in reading a simple text, willingly spend time in reading and writing on the computer. Neither does working alone at the computer seem to have the effect of making students feel isolated and demotivated. The interactive nature of the technology generally ensures a high degree of motivation and engagement.

A note of caution should be introduced at this point. However valuable and motivating, work at the computer should not replace the need for the student to engage in real interactive communication with classmates and teachers. Neither should reading and writing at the computer entirely replace the need for students to experience the physical process of searching and recording information from a number of print media sources.

The computer offers much flexibility to teachers. It allows individuals or small groups of L2 students to work separately from L1 students on occasion. At other times, computers allow L2 students to participate positively in small groups of both L1 and L2 children. The language of the computer is quickly learnt, and suggestions and contributions to group discussions can be readily demonstrated in a practical way on the computer itself. It is remarkable how this technology liberates some children from their inhibitions and enables them to take risks with language to get their point across.

Word-processing and other standard applications

General application programs such as word-processing and data collection and display, as well as simple publishing and graphics programs, provide teachers with a basic resource for use with L2 students. Word-processing applications, in particular, provide motivated students with the means to produce attractive, correct work without the sometimes painful effort of creating a series of hand-written drafts. Students from language backgrounds with different writing systems, or who are used to writing from right to left, benefit especially from the reinforcement provided by such applications. Word-processing allows beginning L2 students to produce work by dictating to a teacher or another student, or enables small groups of students to compose a piece of writing co-operatively. On other occasions, parent volunteers can be asked to produce a typed 'book' from manuscript drafts. (See Teaching Language Arts to Older Second Language Students in Mainstream Classrooms: Writing, pp. 180–3, for a fuller discussion of process writing.)

Educational programs published for school use

In the early days of computer assisted language learning (CALL) educators at all levels hoped that computer software would supply a rich resource for teaching languages. Unfortunately, many of the early programs were of the drill and review variety, involving little use of meaningful language. Gradually, the specific language-learning programs have improved in quality. However more effective programs for use with L2 students are probably to be found among those designed for L1 students. These include programs for the practice of language arts skills and mathematics at all levels.

The growth of the whole-language movement has ensured that many of these programs require the creation of meaningful pieces of writing, as well as providing patterns and frames for practising specific skills. Many of the major textbook publishing houses have produced software that expands and embellishes their printed material. Other programs are readily available for teaching and practising spelling, punctuation and vocabulary, and for improving typing skills. These have their uses with some students.

CD-ROMs

The effective use of CD-ROMs with L2 students depends on the degree of access. If multimedia facilities are available in the classroom then a variety of uses can be incorporated into the regular programme. CD-ROMs that offer re-tellings of familiar stories together with graphics, sound and interactive additions are helpful in making challenging material more comprehensible. In the areas of social studies and science, there are numerous enticing pieces of software. Students can now walk round museums or through famous cities before they visit them. Software incorporating high quality interactive graphics enable children to learn more about dinosaurs, the lives of animals, famous painters and so on. For L2 students who feel comfortable with the technology the ability to manage their own learning is highly motivating. They can work their way through the material in their own time and at their own pace, and have the feeling of making independent discoveries.

As mentioned on p. 179, textbook packages in those subject areas now commonly included related material on CD-ROMs. This is also the case with the latest language arts packages where interactive literature materials are included in the base programme. One American educational publishing company has produced an interactive system on CD-ROMs, designed to offer learning opportunities in all areas of early literacy. (See Appendix A, p. 262, for details of *Wiggleworks*, produced by **Scholastic Inc.**)

The CD-ROM format also offers the possibility of bringing more life and meaning into material expressly designed to teach a language. *The Rosetta Stone*, produced by **Fairfield Technologies**, presents a living textbook centred on life in the home, at school, in the playground and so on. The language content can be delivered at a variety of levels, and thus the program is valuable for use in the classroom with a range of L2 students.

Versions in CD-ROM format of series of encyclopaedias, (e.g. *Grolier Multimedia Encyclopaedia* produced by **Grolier Interactive)** and encyclopaedias created for that format (e.g. **Microsoft's** *Encarta Encyclopedia*) offer all students a valuable resource. The search capability makes it especially useful for L2 students required to write a report involving independent research. By typing in key words, L2 students are able to call up relevant information complete with graphics, sound and video clips. Information is presented in such a way that students can quickly understand what are the major items in a piece of text. Children needing to make an oral presentation about an aspect of their social studies or science work can likewise search through a range of CD-ROM titles for the required information in a manageable form.

It is fair, at this point, to qualify remarks about the advantages of CD-ROM materials with some comments about their use. Few people would dispute the attractive and stimulating nature of the graphics, sound and video elements. They bring the topic to life and engage the interest of today's children. Many educators and reflective parents are, however, troubled by what they see as the slight nature of much of the content to be found on CD-ROMs. Short paragraphs presented in a user-friendly manner should not be viewed as a replacement for a deeper study of a topic from a variety of points of view. For L2 children, in particular, it is possible that the over-use of CD-ROM material removes the need for these children to develop the essential higher-order English language skills. It is also the case that the cost of delivering CD-ROM material remains relatively high. Administrators question whether CD-ROMs are a cost-effective method of providing information.

Children's librarians have also begun to reassess the place of CD-ROM materials in schools. Topic-related CD-ROM materials may be more appropriately used as an introductory and browsing facility. They allow children an easy and engaging route into a topic. This has valuable uses for L2 students. Later work in depth involves books and appropriate use of the manifold possibilities and resources of the Internet. The latest CD-ROMs combine the advantages of both technological and print resources. CD-ROMs are linked to specific textbooks and other printed material and offer expansions and follow-up assignments. Two clicks on the mouse take the user into related Internet sites, to regularly updated databases and to contact points with the author. These approaches offer both challenges and opportunities to L2 students and their teachers.

Networked and other communicating computer systems

Electronic-mail and the Internet allow a degree of local and worldwide communication that has potential for teachers in international schools, especially in their work with L2 students. Students in national systems, in particular from East Asia, are already accustomed to the integrated use of electronic communication in their schoolwork. At present in many international schools the use of e-mail and access to the Internet at the elementary school level is limited for students. This is a pity, since the Internet and e-mail offer teachers a flexible, enriching, dynamic and cost-effective resource for their own use and for use with L2 students.

Teachers who are accustomed users of the Internet recognise that knowledge of the capacities and strengths of the various 'search engines' gives effective access to good quality material. It is a worthwhile exercise to acquire this knowledge from an experienced colleague since it allows teachers to search quickly and effectively for sites on the World Wide Web that are relevant, appropriate to children, and useful for their purposes. (In sections, that follow, sites are described by name. Teachers will find the Internet addresses (Universal Resource Locators, 'URLs') under those names, together with an extensive list of further useful sites, in Appendix B: Internet Sites of Use to Teachers.)

Professional resources on the Internet for teachers in international schools

The Internet and e-mail offer teachers in international schools many possibilities for enhancing their professional lives. Being a teacher in an international school is sometimes an isolating experience. The Internet allows teachers to share ideas with colleagues facing the same professional challenges in other international schools across the world. The management of professional committees and the organisation of conferences are facilitated by this instant and cheap means of sending messages.

A second important use of the Internet for teachers is to supply them with access to a range of professional services. These include lists of resources, indexed extracts from research papers, subject-based discussion groups and recruitment possibilities. ECIS, (the European Council of International Schools), has its own e-mail network, known as **ECISnet**, so that member schools can communicate cheaply and with ease among themselves and with ECIS offices. The **ECIS** Website offers a **Professional Development Bulletin** relating to the ECIS subject area committees, the **ECIS On-line Directory of International Schools** and news about ECIS conferences. Other international school recruitment and professional development organisations are contactable on e-mail and some have their own sites.

A further range of professional resources is available to teachers. For no payment (or for a small outlay), teachers can subscribe to sites designed for educators such as those of the **Association for Supervision and Curriculum Development** and those under the heading **Teachers.net Web Services**. The **Education Index** offers access to a selected list of Websites indexed by curriculum subject and schooling level. Other resources include Website packages such as the **Education Resources Information Center (ERIC)**. This series of sites provides search mechanisms that allow users to access book lists, research abstracts, comment on educational topics and suggestions related to classroom practice. The book lists, abstracts and commentaries related to teaching L2 children are extensive.

Two provisos should be noted. The greater part of the material on L2 children and teaching in diverse classrooms is concerned with teaching immigrant children in national school systems: very few references are made to the needs of mobile children in international schools. Secondly, much of the material included in the ERIC sites and in the Education Index relates to the Western Hemisphere. To track down Websites that refer to other parts of the world, teachers need to access sites such as the **National Library of Australia**.

Two further groups of sites offer teachers practical resources related to their work with L2 students. The first comprises the home pages of major educational publishers listed under their commercial names. These sites offer a range of information and resource for teachers to use with students and for students to access directly. They supply not only up-to-date lists of their publications and educational materials, but also practical resources in the form of reproducible lesson plans and suggestions for extension activities in all subject areas. Most useful, perhaps, are the Websites of publishing houses that issue extensive lists of fiction and non-fiction books for children. These sites supply textual material, together with graphics relating to their major authors and best-selling series of books.

Use of the Internet for teachers in their work with L2 students

Electronic mail and the Internet offer potentially valuable resources to teachers of all students. For L2 students e-mail and the Internet have further advantages. To quote one international school teacher of L2 students: 'It works because the computer is a neutral object — it isn't going to show them up when they get things wrong, which is very important to our kids. They do things for the computer in a much more engaged way than they would for a teacher.'

Focused use of the Internet brings benefits to L2 students in their learning of English. While working at the computer, students face the continual need to read and act on authentic instances of written English in order to access the desired material and to carry out subject-related tasks. The students' understanding of the background content matter and related key vocabulary allows them to infer the meaning of unknown words and to predict the likely meaning of new pieces of text. Children who write on paper with reluctance feel freed by the technology to take risks with their writing. It is worth emphasising, also, that the benefits arising to L2 students from the use of the Internet are similar for children working together in groups. Many introductory and extension activities that make use of the Internet can profitably be carried out as collaborative exercises. This approach brings the added advantage to L2 students of the need to engage in content-related, contextualised uses of spoken English.

Incorporating the use of Internet material and electronic mail into the mainstream programme is most usefully described on a subject-by-subject basis. Suggestions have been made in Chapters 6 to 10 about uses of the Internet related to specific activities in the curriculum areas. The following suggestions give an overview

The resources of the Internet can supply valuable material for use with L2 students in language arts lessons. At present, jointly published magazines, with features pages managed by schools on each continent, exist only at the middle and upper school levels. Before long, no doubt, an international school publication will serve, and be created by, the upper grades of elementary schools. As mentioned above, there is material available relating to children's authors and illustrators. This can be used by teachers to create opportunities for independent research by individuals and in co-operative groups relating to author studies and the work of illustrators. The same information, together with publisher's extensive book lists, is valuable in encouraging children to search out titles about their favourite subjects or in connection with school work.

Internet material allows the teacher to construct a range of independent, active and authentic learning opportunities in the area of social studies. The value for L2 children in using the Internet is the possibility of incorporating references and instances that derive from all parts of the globe. Thus, studies of ancient civilisations and modern communities can be based on the regions from which students come. In a similar way, the study of geography topics such as habitats, natural features and the weather can be based on real-life instances from around the world and can include the latest data. At the time of writing, the Soufrieres volcano is in a state of continuous eruption on the Caribbean island of Montserrat. The earth's crust, earthquakes and volcanoes are standard topics in science programmes. An in-depth classroom study of these areas could be enlivened and made relevant and memorable by accessing the home page of the **Montserrat Volcano Observatory**. The direct and jargon-free language employed on this type of page, together with the accompanying graphics, allows L2 students ready access to the meaning.

Further resources relate to history topics and cultural studies programmes. The search engine known as **The Virtual Tourist Map** allows teachers to access guide books, plans, photographs of buildings, cultural events and museum exhibits located in countries and cities around the world. Thus, it is possible to enhance a classroom-based study in an effective manner or to use such material before making a residential field trip.

The Internet offers the possibility of involving children in interactive conversations with explorers and scientists as they venture into unfamiliar environments and carry out experiments. Students are able to communicate via e-mail with astronauts in space, and with world travellers. At the time of writing a small subscription to the author of the **Trike Trek** Website allows children to participate in all aspects of a world wide journey. The **National Geographic Society** was the one of the first users to offer children opportunities to explore the world. Further valuable science resources are to be found on the Websites of *Nature* magazine and *The New Scientist* (under the name, **Planet Science**).

Many environmental agencies and organisations offer extensive material on the Internet for children, although teachers should take care that information from these sources is objective and accurate. Children can join in worldwide co-operative undertakings such as collating sightings of birds and butterflies and documenting the numbers of endangered species. Such activities are ideal for international school students. L2 students, in particular, benefit from carrying out tasks that involve a global perspective.

The Library or Media Centre — Print Media

Collections of print media in international schools vary in quantity and variety. The facilities in which they house their collections also vary. Some facilities are purpose-built and attractively furnished, with large collections of fiction and non-fiction books, reference materials and magazines. Many libraries or media centres contain collections of audiotapes, videocassettes and filmed material as well as facilities for viewing CD-ROMs and working with the Internet. Some schools have sufficient funding to provide separate libraries for different age groups. Some libraries are fully computerised. Other schools are in the early stages of building-up a library; their print and media collections are small and their technological facilities limited.

Whatever the size and sophistication of the building, from the children's point of view it is important that the library is an inviting and friendly place where books are attractively presented and easily accessed. It is ideal if young children and older children have their separate spaces, with books and other media laid out in ways that are appropriate for their ages.

The following paragraphs offer suggestions for acquainting L2 students with the use of libraries in international schools. They also suggest ways that teachers can make the optimum use of the library as a rich resource for work with L2 children.

Young children

Young children's introduction to library use

The most effective libraries for young children (known as literacy centres in some schools) provide contact with books in a way suited to their needs and interests. They are attractive and welcoming places with cushions, low chairs and friendly objects on display. The presentation of the books tends to be planned with young children in mind and is suited to the nature of the books themselves. That is, many of them are presented with the illustrated cover showing, and arranged by reading level or by theme. There is likely to be a selection of Big Books (books in large-sized format for shared reading) as well as a choice of magazines for young children. Many libraries for young children contain a story corner and facilities for showing video film. Librarians stage events and activities in the library connected with work in the classroom or happenings in school. Some schools have a classroom attached to the library where children can work with books and other media connected to on-going classroom themes. The library is an area where trained parent volunteers can offer invaluable support to the librarian in carrying out the routine tasks involved in maintaining a library collection.

The first task of teachers in relation to new young L2 children is to introduce them to the use of this type of library. Some young L2 students may be unfamiliar with the presence of such a facility in school. The only books they have previously used in school are textbooks and sets of readers. They may be unacquainted with the notion of reading for entertainment or pleasure. With such students the teacher and the librarian must show the child in practical terms what the library is for, how to withdraw a book and the reasons for reading it.

Other children come from school systems that offer only restricted access to the library. Children in these systems usually visit the library once a week for 30 minutes during which time they may take out two books. They may be unused to the idea of a library as a continuing resource or as a place of relaxation and enjoyment. These children need to be introduced to the notion of browsing for pleasure, as well as to the possibilities of visiting the library to search out non-fiction books concerned with an on-going classroom project.

Helping young L2 children to make book choices

New L2 students, whatever their previous experiences of libraries, if left to themselves, frequently choose books that are beyond their reading ability in English. Understandably, they may be overwhelmed by the wide choice of unfamiliar and incomprehensible books. In this situation, they prefer to choose any book rather than to be different from their classmates.

The librarian and teacher need to guide L2 children in choosing books, so that they take out books that they will understand and enjoy. It is an effective strategy to offer the child non-fiction as well as fiction books. These non-fiction books should contain a wide range of realistic illustrations, photographs and references to many cultures and regions. L2 children frequently find such books more accessible than an imaginatively illustrated story.

It is a beneficial strategy to ask parents of new L2 children to join the class at library time or after school. This allows parents and children to enjoy choosing a book together, and allows parents who are unfamiliar with the library provision customary in international schools to observe how the library is used. Often this approach leads to new parents becoming involved in the library as volunteers.

Teachers need to pay special attention to the student from a family where it is not usual for parents and children to read together. Stories told solely through illustration, books with repetitive text, or information books with good quality photographs and limited text, are most accessible to children reading alone. In this circumstance, teachers should find time to read the book with the child before it is taken out of school.

The role of mother tongue books in an international school library

Young L2 students may be learning to read in their own language (through attendance at Japanese, Korean or other schools), as well as learning to read in English. Even if they are not engaged in formal reading lessons they usually recognise some words in their own language.

The role of so-called 'mother tongue' libraries in international schools is a subject for discussion. Most schools cannot attempt to supply complete collections of print media in a wide range of languages. Usually schools limit themselves to books in the host country language or languages, together with books in languages in frequent use among the student body. Bilingual programmes and the presence of large numbers of students from one nationality warrant this type of provision. There is a place, however, for representative examples of the languages and scripts of all the L2 children in the school.

Librarians and teachers should make it known to parents and the wider school community that they are keen to acquire books in L2 children's home languages. Attractive children's books are published in most languages, and large bookshops in children's home countries usually have a selection. The most useful items are traditional and modern stories in students' languages, together with illustrated wordbooks. Further valuable additions are translations into other languages of stories first written in English by well-known children's authors. Museum shops and famous places in the countries concerned are possible sources of children's books in the local language. Such books are valuable resources to teachers since their subject matter tends to relate to historical, geographical and cultural features. Embassies and cultural centres are possible sources of donations.

The presence of a limited number of books in L2 children's languages cannot offer students a full bilingual experience of reading. Their value is to provide a sense of security and familiarity to L2 students and to give librarians and teachers an opportunity to incorporate print materials from other cultures into their talk about books and reading. The presence of books in their home languages underlines L2 children's rich experience and language competence outside school.

Further strategies connected with books can similarly enhance the awareness of L2 children's cultures. As mentioned in Chapter 4, it is the practice in some schools for older children to visit young children's classrooms to take part in the story sessions. This practice is made even more effective if an older student reads a story to a young L2 child in their common language. Another enjoyable and effective strategy is to invite parents of L2 children to read a story to the class in their own language and to give explanations in English.

Older children

The mechanics of using a library

Older L2 children, as well as young children, arrive in international schools with a variety of experiences connected with the use of a library. Some may be used to a rich array of print media. Others may have had restricted access to books and print media. Many have no experience of the use of computers in accessing and cataloguing books, or of library skills instruction in carrying out personal research and information gathering. Most L2 students are unaccustomed to the dual role of the teacher librarian that is usual in international schools.

Where necessary, therefore, L2 students need to be taught the system for checking out books. They need to understand the nature and possibilities of cataloguing and how to search for books under thematic headings. They should be introduced to listening centres and how to access CD-ROM material. They must be encouraged to visit the library to pursue topics of interest connected with schoolwork and for the pleasure of browsing through the books and of reading magazines.

Teaching research skills to L2 students

Many L2 students, even from highly developed and academically challenging home school systems, are unused to carrying out independent research or to writing assignments that require information-gathering. (See Answering the needs of second language students in social studies and science, pp. 229–31, for a discussion of information gathering related to those subjects.)

The aspect of report writing that relates to the library is the collection of information. Teachers need to indicate to L2 students the range of choices that are involved in searching out what they need to know. First, they must choose between the available media. They must then decide on subject headings to guide their searches in book catalogues, in encyclopaedia or in electronic media. Finally, they need to decide how to display the information.

As mentioned in Chapter 10, it is preferable with beginning and early intermediate L2 students to adapt the nature of the assignment. It offers a more manageable experience if the assignment involves students in searching and recording accurately a limited amount of information. The results do not need to be presented in written form; graphs and charts may show a students' understanding just as effectively. (See Electronic media on p. 247 for suggestions concerning the use of CD-ROMs and the Internet in information-gathering.)

An effective way of supporting L2 students in their learning of research skills is to give them a competent English speaker as a partner, or to place them in a larger group. This requires careful monitoring by the teacher, and the allocation of feasible tasks among the members of the group.

The ESL section

Many international school libraries contain a collection of books known as the ESL section. This section usually contains simplified tellings of classic and modern stories as well as high-interest, low reading-level material designed for the L2 market. The quality and quantity of this type of material is steadily improving. Publishers' lists now offer well-illustrated books in a variety of genres at various levels. A broad collection provides teachers with additional resources for work with different literature genres in their language arts classes. These books allow students to visit the library along with their classmates and to choose books that they are able to read. They save L2 students from the embarrassing situation of having to choose from books written for younger students.

The classroom teacher, the librarian or the ESL teacher needs to be on hand to help L2 students in their selection of books. Students need positive support and guidance about choosing books for both academic and recreational purposes at an appropriate reading level.

Materials in L2 students' home languages

The provision of books in the home languages of older children generally reflects the language profile of the student body. In the case of bilingual schools, libraries generally provide an extensive selection of books and other media in the principal languages of the school. (See pp. 254–5, The role of mother tongue books in an international school library)

In international schools with students from a wide number of language groups, the provision of books in children's home languages necessarily takes a different form. For older students the most useful mother tongue books are dictionaries and encyclopaedias, as well as guidebooks and materials that relate to regular field trips and report-writing projects. The presence of this material allows L2 students to carry out research in their home languages. This understanding allows them access to similar material in English.

The library as a focus for multi-cultural activity

Librarians in most schools initiate activities that involve school-wide collaboration such as arranging author visits and writers' fairs. It is frequently the librarian who organises a visit from a professional storyteller. In international schools, this is an occasion when stories and poetry from many cultures can be shared.

Most librarians are happy to offer the library as a venue for events that relate to the international nature of the school. These events include displays relating to the history, geography, science, literary or artistic traditions of one culture, the telling of traditional stories or the demonstration of arts and crafts. Many librarians sponsor national weeks, when the parents and wider community pool their resources to celebrate the culture and language of a group of students in the school.

Summary

Electronic technology enriches teachers' professional lives and extends the possibilities for their work with children. Audio and video cassette players are generally available in international schools and can be readily incorporated into the mainstream programme. They provide a useful resource to L2 children in their language learning and they allow teachers to draw their material from the world outside the classroom.

Computers, CD-ROMs and the Internet are major resources for all teachers and students. They are of especial value in international schools since they allow the cultures and geographical regions from which the students come to be included in the mainstream programme in a real way. Teachers and students need no longer be limited in their subject matter or references. CD-ROMs and the Internet allow them to include material related to all parts of the world.

Modern librarians act as the link between the resources of electronic technology and print media. Books remain essential to the lives of modern children. They provide a depth and range of subject matter that is unique. Children need to learn to use books effectively in their schoolwork and to experience the profound pleasure to be gained from reading with ease every type of fiction and non-fiction. It is essential that L2 children in international schools acquire a level of competency in their prime languages that gives them access to the world of books.

Libraries should be attractive and lively places. L2 children should be quickly introduced, where necessary, to the procedures and possibilities of using the library. Their parents should be made welcome and encouraged to become involved in their children's reading experiences. In bilingual schools, adequate stocks of books should be made available in both languages. In international schools with students of many nationalities, it may not be possible for a library to hold collections of books in all the languages. However, schools should supply basic reference materials in as many languages as possible and libraries should contain well-illustrated examples of well-loved stories and topic-based non-fiction. The presence of this material acknowledges the existence of literary traditions other than those of English-speaking countries. Finally, the library is an ideal space to celebrate the cultures and traditions of all the children in the school. Story-telling, arts and crafts demonstrations, exhibitions related to world-wide environmental topics and displays of literature in many languages are some of the events that can usefully take place in international school libraries.

Appendix A
Resources for Teachers

(1) Organisations that offer services to the international school community:
International and Overseas Schools Directories: (updated annually)
The ECIS **(European Council of International Schools)** *International Schools Directory*, ECIS, 21 Lavant Street, Petersfield, Hampshire, GU32 3EL, UK. See Website in Appendix B
ECISnet: e-mail: 100412.242@compuserve.com
The ISS **(International Schools Services)** *Directory of Overseas Schools*, Order from Peterson's Inc., Department 1SS7, 202 Carnegie Center, PO Box 2123, Princeton, NJ 08543–2123, USA. See Website in Appendix B.

(2) Publishing Houses whose lists relate to the needs of teachers and students in international schools:

(a) The catalogue of **Intercultural Press, Inc.** offers a selection of books that deal with the circumstances of expatriate living and cultural adaptation. Books on the list are published by Intercultural Press or chosen from a wide range of publishers in the English-speaking world.
Intercultural Press, Inc., PO Box 700, Yarmouth, Maine 04096 USA
Phone: (207) 846–5168
Fax: (207) 846–5181
e-mail: intercultural@mcimail.com

(b) The catalogue of **Multilingual Matters** offers a wide range of books both practical and theoretical related to the areas of bilingualism and bilingual education.
Multilingual Matters Ltd, Frankfurt Lodge, Clevedon Hall, Victoria Road, Clevedon, North Somerset BS21 7HH, UK
Phone: (00 44 (0) 1275 876519
Fax: 00 44 (0) 1275 343096
E-mail: multi@multilingual-matters.com
The Bilingual Family Newsletter offers news and help for intercul-

259

tural people. The editor is Marjukka Grover and the newsletter is published by **Multilingual Matters**. It is available from the same address as above and Multilingual Matters will send a specimen copy on application.

(c) **Times Books International** of Singapore and Kuala Lumpur publish a series under the general heading, *Culture Shock!*, written by expatriates living in the countries concerned. The series is rather uneven. Some supply similar information to that found in guidebooks. Others contain useful insights into the culture of the country and the adjustment issues for expatriates who live there. Among the most useful are: *Culture Shock! Israel, Culture Shock! Japan, Culture Shock! Korea* and *Culture Shock! China*. This series can be found in specialist travel bookshops together with guidebooks.

(3) A further valuable source of information for ex-patriate teachers are handbooks published by organisations such as the local **American and British Chambers of Commerce** and the ex-patriate women's clubs. These are usually very practical, relevant to the interests of international school teachers and give useful insights into the lives of expatriates in the location.

Information sources of this type used in this handbook are **The American Chamber of Commerce in Korea** (1995) *Living in Korea* and **The American Women's League** (1992) *Orientation Book, 'Getting to know Kuwait'*.

(4) Publishing houses that specialise in high interest/low reading level material and graded versions of classic and modern texts:

English Language Teaching, Addison Wesley Longman, Sales Department, ELT Division, Edinburgh Gate, Harlow, Essex CM20 2JE, UK, or see Website in Appendix B.

Oxford Bookworms, Oxford University Press, English Language Teaching Promotions Department, Oxford University Press, Walton Street, Oxford OX2 6DP, UK, or see Website in Appendix B.

(5) Publishing houses that offer a range of thematically linked texts at varied reading levels for use with second language students in mainstream classrooms:

Raintree/Steck-Vaughn, *Library catalog*, Raintree/Steck-Vaughn Publishers, POBox 26015, Austin TX 78755, USA.

Scott Foresman Addison Wesley, 10 Bank Street, Suite 900, White Plains, NY 10606–1951, USA, or see Website in Appendix B.

(6) Reading schemes:

Oxford Reading Tree, **Oxford University Press**, Educational Division, Walton Street, Oxford OX2 6DP, UK.

Ready to Read, published for **Ministry of Education** by **Learning Media Ltd**, Box 3293, Wellington, New Zealand. Distributed in the USA by **Richard C. Owen Publishers Inc.**, Box 585, Katonah, NY 10536, USA.

Sunshine Readers, **Heinemann Educational Books Ltd**, 22 Bedford Square, London WC1B 3HH, UK.

(7) Reading material appropriate for young children's classrooms in international schools:

African Books Collective, Ltd, The Jam Factory, 27 Park End Street, Oxford OX1 1HU, UK.

Heian International Inc., PO Box 1013, Union City, CA 94587, USA.

Kane/Miller Book Publishers, PO Box 8515, La Jolla, CA 92038–8515, USA.

Scholastic Big Books, Scholastic Inc., Box 7502, Jefferson City, MO 65102, USA, or see Website in Appendix B.

Shortland Publications Ltd, 2B Cawley Street, Ellerslie, Auckland, NZ. Distributed in the USA by **Rigby Elsevier Inc.**

SOMA Books Ltd, 38 Kennington Lane, London SE11 4LS, UK.

Sundance Publishers and Distributors, a Division of Pharos Books, a Scripp Howard Company, PO Box 1326, Newtown Road, Littleton, MA 01460, USA.

Sunshine Science, Investigating Our World, published in the USA by **The Wright Group**, 19201 120th Avenue NE, Bothell, WA 98011–9512, USA.

PM Starters One, **Rigby, a division of Reed Elsevier, Inc.**, 500 Coventry Lane, Crystal Lake, IL 60014, USA.

(8) Individual titles or publications mentioned in the text:

Coerr, Eleanor (1977) Sadako and the Thousand Paper Cranes. New York, USA: G.P. Putnam's Sons.

Frank, Anne (1967) Anne Frank: The Diary of a Young Girl. Garden City, New York, USA: Doubleday.

Hertz, Ole (1984) Tobias. Minneapolis, USA: Carolrhoda Books Inc.

Hoban, Tana (1988) Look, Look, Look! New York, USA: Scholastic Inc.

Holm, Anne (1965) I am David. London, UK: Mammoth.

Hutchins, Pat (1968) Rosie's Walk. New York, USA: Scholastic Inc.

Martin Jr, Bill (1983) Brown Bear, Brown Bear, What Do You See? Illustrations by Eric Carle (1992). New York, USA: Henry Holt and Company Inc.

O'Dell, Scott (1960) Island of the Blue Dolphins. Boston, USA: Houghton Mifflin.

Steck Vaughn Writing Dictionary, see above for address.

(9) New series offering content-based English language instruction for use with second language children:

Cummins, J., Wong Fillmore, L. *et al., Accelerating English Language Learning*, Scott Foresman, 1900 E. Lake Avenue, Glenview, IL 60025, USA, or see Website in Appendix B.

(10) Photocopiable resources for teaching higher-level thinking skills: *Classroom Challenges*, **Media Unit, Cricket Road Centre, Cricket Road, Oxford OX4 3DW, UK.** The material from this source is based on Bloom's categorisation of thinking skills. The activities are particularly suited for use with L2 children, since they engage students in a variety of cognitively demanding tasks, by means of graphically supported step-by-step instructions in basic English.

(11) Software catalogues:

Cambridge Early Learning and Primary School (US Elementary School) CD-ROM Catalogue, Cambridge CD-ROM Ltd, Combs Tannery, Stowmarket, Suffolk 1P14 2EN, UK, Fax: 01449 677600 or e-mail: cdbooks@anglianet.co.uk

Edmark Software and Print Catalog, PO Box 97021, Redmond, WA 98073–9721, USA, Fax: 206–556–8430 or e-mail: edmarkteam2edmark.com or see Website in Appendix B.

(12) Individual software titles:

Bailey's Book House, created by Edmark, see Edmark Catalog above.

Grolier '97 Multimedia Encyclopaedia, Grolier Interactive.

Encarta Encyclopedia '97, Microsoft Corporation.

The Rosetta Stone, an interactive CD-ROM teaching program available in English and other languages, created by Fairfield Language Technologies, 122 South Main Street, Harrisonburg, VA 22801, USA.

Thinkin' Things, created by Edmark, see Edmark Catalog above.

Trudy's Time and Place House, created by Edmark, see Edmark Catalog above.

Wiggleworks, Scholastic Inc., see Website in Appendix B.

(13) Universities, colleges and other organisations mentioned in the text that offer advanced degrees and in-service opportunities in areas associated with international education:

International Schools Services: see heading, p. 259.

Michigan State University, Office of Admissions and Scholarships, Michigan State University, 250 Administration Building, East Lansing, MI 48824–0590, USA.

Oxford Brookes University, MA in Education for International Schools, Course Leader: Maggie Wilson, Wheatley Campus, Wheatley, Oxford OX33 1HX, UK.

The **British Council**, International Seminars, 1 Beaumont Place, Oxford OX1 2PJ, UK.

The College of New Jersey, Office of International Studies, Hillwood Lakes, Trenton, NJ 08650–4700, USA.

University of Bath, Academic Departments, Study and Research, University of Bath, Claverton Down, Bath BA2 7AY, UK.

Appendix B
Internet Sites of Use to Teachers

The Internet addresses (Universal Resource Locators: 'URLs') given below were correct at the time of going to press. It is common for URLs related to the same Website to be changed over time, however. The purpose of giving the list below is to indicate the range and nature of Websites. Teachers may find that they need to make use of an appropriate search engine to locate their chosen site.

Internet Search Engines

http://www.albany.net/allinone/	All-in-One
http://altavista.digital.com/	Alta Vista
http://www.ebig.com/	Brittanica Guide
http://www.euroferret.com/	Euroferret
http://www.excite.com/	Excite
http://guide-p.infoseek.com/	Infoseek
http://www.isleuth.com/	Internet Sleuth
http://www-english.lycos.com/	Lycos
http://kapow.bam.com.au/	Kapow
http://www.mckinley.com/	Magellan
http://www.xs4all.nl/~mbaan/	Marco's World Map
http://www.aaa.com.au/	Matilda
http://www.muscat.co.uk/	Muscat
http://www.northernlight.com/	Northern Light Search
http://index.opentext.net/	Open Text Index
http://guaraldi.cs.colostate.edu:2000/	SavvySearch
http://www.west.net/~jbc/tools/search.html	Search Plex
http://www.vtourist.com/webmap/	Virtual Tourist World Map
http://www2.webwombat.com.au/	Web Wombat
http://www.infospace.com/submit.html	Who's Who on the Internet?
http://www.hitbox.com/wc/world.html	World 1000
http://cuiwww.unige.ch/meta-index.html#TOP	WWW Search Engines
http://www.indiana.edu/~librcsd/ resource/search-list.html#gen	WWW Search Tools
http://www.yahoo.com/	Yahoo
http://www.mcp.com/	Yellow Pages

Publishers & Suppliers

These sites offer information about the books on publishers' lists. In many cases they also offer biographical information and the possibility of interactive communication with authors and illustrators. Many sites include reproducible lesson plans and extension activities for teachers related to published texts.

http://www.awl-he.com/	Addison Wesley Longman
http://www.cup.org/	Cambridge University Press
http://www.dkonline.com/dkcom/	Dorling-Kindersley
http://www.edmark.com	Edmark
http://www.harcourtcollege.com/	Harcourt Brace
http://www.helt.co.uk/	Heinemann ELT
http://www.multilingual-matters.com	Multilingual Matters
http://www.osborne.com/gaws/	Osborne/McGraw-Hill
http://www.oup.co.uk/	Oxford University Press
http://www.penguin.com	Penguin
http://www.reed-elsevier.com/	Reed Elsevier
http://www.scottforesman.com/sfaw/	Scott Foresman
http://www.scholastic.com/	Scholastic
http://www.waterstone.co.uk/	Waterstones

Daily News

http://www.abcnews.com:80/	ABC News
http://www.bbc.co.uk/	BBC Online
http://www.cnn.com/	CNN Interactive
http://www.centraleurope.com/	Central Europe Online
http://www.discovery.com/	Discovery Channel Online
http://www.glostart.com/	GloStart
http://www.reuters.com/	Reuters
http://www.online.ru/	Russia Online
http://www.sciencemag.org/	Science Online
http://dailynews.yahoo.com/headlines/top_stories	Yahoo: Top Stories

World-wide Organisations

http://europa.eu.int/index.htm	European Union
http://www.house.gov/	House of Representatives
http://www.gdn.org/parliaments.html	Parliaments of the World
http://www.ups.edu/polygov/oneil/index.htm	Political Science Resources
http://www.undp.org/popin/popin.htm	Population Information
http://www.ifrc.org/	Red Cross & Red Crescent
http://thomas.loc.gov/	Library of Congress

http://www.un.org/   United Nations
http://www.unesco.org/   UNESCO
http://www.unicef.org/   UNICEF
http://www.whitehouse.gov/   White House
http://www.who.org/   World Health Organisation

Educational Resources

This section includes an array of Websites that provide resources for teachers. Certain of these URLs offer access to a range of educational materials and professional writings. Other sites are owned by professional organisations such as ECIS and TESOL. Teachers can, in many cases, use these sites as means to access further material of use in international schools.

http://194.159.248.110/aardvark/   Aardvark's EFL Resources
http://www.ascd.org/   ASCD Association for
                                               Supervision &
                                               Curriculum Development
http://www.neat-schoolhouse.org/awesome.html Awesome Library: K–12
http://www.redmundial.com/ben.htm   BEN Bilingual ESL Network
http://www.britcoun.org   British Council
http://www.cisco.com/edu/   Cisco Education
http://www.euroschool.com/   Cisco Euroschool
http://www.eslcafe.com/   Dave's ESL Cafe
http://www.gakkos.com/   Gakkos Global Network
http://www.ecis.org/   ECIS
http://www.mathclub.com   Edmark Mighty Math Club
http://www.educationindex.com/   Education Index
  education_resources.html
http://www.education-world.com/   Education World
http://www.ilcgroup.com/books/ih-books.html ELT Mail Order Catalogue
http://www.geocities.com/Athens/   EFL Resources
  Delphi/2127/
http://www.wfi.fr/est/est1.html   English for Science and
                                               Technology
http://www.aspensys.com/eric/   ERIC Educational Resources
http://spot.colorado.edu/~youngerg/eiesl.html ESL on the WWW
http://www.lang.uiuc.edu/r-li5/esl/   ESL Home Page
http://www.educ.wsu.edu/esl/   ESL Links & Resources
  professionallink.html
http://www.prairienet.org/community/   General ESL Resources
  esl/GenESL.htm
http://globalnomads.association.com/   Global Nomads
                                               International

http://www.iac.net/~blenius/index.html	Global Nomads Virtual Village
http://www.harvard.edu/	Harvard University
http://his.rerf.or.jp:8080/#menu	Hiroshima International School
http://www.reading.org/	IRA International Reading Association
http://www.kidlink.org	Kidlink
http://www.isd77.K12.mn.us/resources/ staffpages/shirk/k12.music.html	K–12 Resources Music
http://www.ecnet.net/users/gdlevin/ home.html	Learning@Web.Sites
http://www.ncte.org/	NCTE National Council for Teachers of English
http://www.nctm.org/	NCTM National Council of Teachers of Mathematics
http://www.niss.ac.uk/education/index.html	NISS Educational Resources
http://www.nsta.org/	NSTA National Science Teachers Association
http://www.vni.net/~mcl/osb/osbmain.htm	Overseas Brats Online
http://www.fishnet.net:80/~karenm/ k3.bil.res.html	K-3 Resources: Primary
http://teachers.net/teachtalk/	TEACHTALK Mailing List
http://tefl.com/	TEFL Network
http://www.aitech.ac.jp/~iteslj/	TESL Journal Online
http://www.zait.uni-bremen.de/ wwwgast/tesl_ej/	TESL-EJ Online
http://www.aitech.ac.jp/~iteslj/ESL3.html	TESL/TEFL/TESOL/ESL/EFL Links
http://www.tesol.edu/	TESOL Online
http://www.thesis.co.uk	Times Higher Education Supplement
http://www.iteachnet.com/esl.html	TIPS ESL Department
http://scitsc.wlv.ac.uk/ukinfo/uk.map.html	UK Academic Institutions
http://sunsite.unc.edu/cisco/schools/	US Schools & Universities
http://www.comenius.com/	Virtual English Language Centre
http://www.wfi.fr/volterre	Volterre ESL Resources
http://web66.coled.umn.edu/Schools.html	Web 66 School Registry
http://www.scholastic.com/wiggleworks/ index.htm	Wiggleworks

Other Reference Material

http://www.cc.columbia.edu/acis/ bartleby/bartlett/	Bartlett's Quotations

http://www.barstow.cc.ca.us/referenc.htm	Basic Reference Volumes
http://opac97.bl.uk/	British Library OPAC
http://portico.bl.uk/	British Library PORTICO
http://www.ntu.ac.sg/ntu/lib/dic.html	Dictionaries, Reference & Language Guides
http://www.bibliomania.com/Reference/ PhraseAndFable/	Dictionary of Phrase and Fable
http://www.emap.com/ons97/	Office of National Statistics
gopher://odie.niaid.nih.gov/77/.thesaurus/ index	Roget's Thesaurus
http://the-tech.mit.edu/Shakespeare/table.html	Shakespeare
http://work.ucsd.edu:5141/cgi-bin/ http_webster	Webster's Dictionary
http://sunsite.unc.edu/lunarbin/worldpop	World Population

Science & Environment

http://sunsite.doc.ic.ac.uk/netspedition/	Amazon Netspedition
http://www.onestep.tandem.com/	Antarctic Expedition
http://www.astronomynow.com/	Astronomy Now On-Line
http://www.birminghamzoo.com/	Birmingham Zoo Alabama
http://web.ukonline.co.uk/bornfree/index.htm	Born Free Foundation
http://res.agr.ca/brd/poisonpl/	Canadian Poisonous Plants
http://www.auburn.edu/beetles/	Coleopterist's Society
http://planet.net.org/	Computer Museum Network
http://www.eso.org/	European Southern Observatory
http://www.vrsystems.com/everest/	Everest Online
http://sln.fi.edu/	Franklin Institute Science Museum
http://www.gsfc.nasa.gov/	Goddard Space Flight Center
http://www.cs.cmu.edu/~mwm/sci.html	Hands-on Science Centers
http://www.stsci.edu/	Hubble Space Telecope
http://curry.edschool.Virginia.EDU/go/frog/	Interactive Frog Dissection
http://www.netvision.net.il/~sci_muse/	Israel National Museum of Science
http://www.wcsu.ctstateu.edu/ cyberchimp/homepage.html	Jane Goodall Centre
http://www.mars.sgi.com/	Mars Pathfinder Mission
http://www.mtwilson.edu/	Mount Wilson Observatory
http://www.nasa.gov/	NASA
http://www.nasm.si.edu/	National Air & Space Museum
http://www.nationalgeographic.com/main.html	National Geographic
http://www.nlm.nih.gov/	National Library of Medicine

http:/www.ran.org/ran/	Rain Forest Action Network
http://www.ast.cam.ac.uk/RGO/	Royal Greenwich Observatory
http://chemistry.rsc.org/rsc/	Royal Society of Chemistry
http://www.nhm.ac.uk/	Natural History Museum
http://www.newscientist.com/	New Scientist Planet Science
http://www.sandiegozoo.org/	San Diego Zoo
http://www.cais.net/publish/voyage.htm	Science & Environment
http://www.nmsi.ac.uk/	Science Museum London
http://www.si.edu	Smithsonian Institution
http://www.skypub.com/	SKY Online
http://www.ex.ac.uk/tnp/	The Nine Planets
http://www.5tigers.org/	Tiger Information Centre
http://www.actwin.com/WWWVL-Fish.html	Virtual Library: Fish
http://www.astro.uva.nl/michielb/ sun/kaft.htm	Virtual Sun
http://www.soest.hawaii.edu/hvo/	Volcano Watch Hawaii
http://whyfiles.news.wisc.edu/	Why Files
http://www.ex.ac.uk/~gjlramel/six.html	World of Insects
http://www.panda.org/	WWF World Wildlife Fund

Museums & Galleries

This list of museums and galleries is by no means complete. Teachers should search for further sites that are likely to contain materials relevant to their needs. Many museums, galleries and university departments in countries all over the world provide material for teachers of elementary-aged children.

http://www.art.net/	Art on the Net
http://www.british-museum.ac.uk/	British Museum
http://www.nol.net/~nil/dali.html	Dali Museum
http://www.thinker.org/index.shtml	Fine Arts Museums of San Francisco
http://users.ox.ac.uk/~humbul	HUMBUL Humanities Resources
http://www.metmuseum.org/	Metropolitan Museum of Art
http://www.paris.org.:80/Musees/Louvre/	Musée du Louvre
http://www.sirius.com/~dbh/mummies	Museo de las Momias
http://www.moma.org/	Museum of Modern Art
http://www.msichicago.org/	Museum of Science & Industry Chicago
http://www.nmaa.si.edu:80/	National Museum of American Art
http://www.tate.org.uk/	Tate Gallery
http://www.uffizi.firenze.it/welcomeE.html	Uffizi Gallery

http://www.leonet.it/   Virtual Leonardo da Vinci
http://sunsite.doc.ic.ac.uk/wm/   Web Museum
http://wwar.com   World-wide Arts Resources

Typical National Sites

The list below gives the URLs of a selection of sites related to national
and cultural material. Many more exist that are of use to teachers in
international schools. Most cities, as well as national tourist offices, now
have homepages and teachers will find it rewarding to search for sites
relevant to their needs before planning a classroom activity or field trip.

General

http://www.city.net/   CityNet
http://travel.cm-net.com/   CM Travel Gateway
http://www.lonelyplanet.com/lp.htm   Lonely Planet Online
http://www.roughguides.com/   Rough Guides Online
http://www.travelchannel.com/   Travel Channel Online

Africa

http://www.africaonline.com/   Africa Online
http://www-tm.up.ac.za/   Transvaal Museum

Arabia

http://www.arab.net/cuisine/   ABC of Arabic Cuisine
http://www.arab.net/arabart/   Arab Art
http://www.arab.net/   ArabNet

Asia

http://www.asia-online.com/   Asia Online
http://www.jaring.my/   Malaysia
http://www.newasia-singapore.com/   Singapore
http://www.straitscafe.com/   Straits Café

Australia & New Zealand

http://www.csu.edu.au/education/   Australia Guide
  australia.html
http://www.erin.gov.au/life/tour/tour.html   Australian Biodiversity Tour
http://www.austmus.gov.au/   Australian Museum
http://osprey.erin.gov.au/anbg/index.html Australian National Botanic
                                          Gardens
http://www.nla.gov.au/   Australian National Library

http://www.enzed.com/net.html   New Zealand Internet Guide

Caribbean

http://sei.org/impacts.html   Montserrat Volcano

China

http://www.chinascape.org   Chinascape

Egypt

http://www.idsc.gov.eg/culture/cop_mus.htm   Coptic Museum Cairo
http://egypttoday.com/   Egypt Today
http://eyelid.ukonline.co.uk/ancient/   Temple of Karnak
karnak1.htm

France

http://www.france.com/   France Online
http://www.jde.fr/   Le Journal des Enfants
http://www.paris.org   Paris Online

Germany

http://www.bundesregierung.de/ausland/   Facts about Germany
index_e.html
http://www.rz.uni-Karlsruhe.de/   German Resources
Outerspace/VirtualLibrary

Greece

http://www.geocities.com/Athens/   Athens Online

India

http://www.webindia.com/   India Web
http://chandra.astro.indiana.edu/isongs/   ITRANS Song Book
http://www.timesofindia.com/   The Times of India

Japan

http://www.embjapan.org.uk/   Japanese Embassy in the UK
http://www.core-ad.co.jp/genshi/   Genshi
http://www.ntt.co.jp/japan/JNTO/Kyoto/   Kyoto Tourist Guide
http://www.ntt.co.jp/japan/JNTO/Nara/   Nara Tourist Guide

Korea

http://bora.dacom.co.kr/~gta/   Good Teacher's Centre
http://www.knto.or.kr   Korea Tour Guide
http://www.dongguk.ac.kr/Tour/Kyongju/   Kyungju Tour Guide
  map.html
http://www.kcna.co.jp   North Korean News Agency

Spain

http://www.spaintour.com/   Spain

Taiwan

http://www.gram.com.tw/   Gram English Centre
http://www.hess.com.tw/   Hess Language School

UK

http://www.royal.gov.uk/   British Monarchy
http://www.number-10.gov.uk/   No 10 Downing Street

Hobbies, Sport & Light Relief

Lists under these headings tend to reflect the interests of the compiler.
Sites relating to a range of sports and leisure pursuits can be located via
an appropriate search engine.

http://www.beeb.com/   BBC Online
http://www.cricket.org/   Cricket on the Internet
http://www.unitedmedia.com/comics/dilbert/   Dilbert Zone
http://www.doonesbury.com/   Doonesbury
http://netvet.wustl.edu/e-zoo.htm   Electronic Zoo
http://www.genhomepage.com/world.html   Genealogy Resources
http://www.imdb.com/   Internet Movie Database
http://www.napoleon.org/home_us.html   Napoléon
http://www2.mousehouse.com/rejoyce/palin/   Palindrome Generator
http://www.petstation.com/   PetStation
http://www.rps.org/   Royal Photographic Society
http://www.unitedmedia.com/comics/peanuts/   Snoopy's Dog House
http://www.squash.org/   Squash Federation
http://www.ncl.ac.uk/~nnac   Tony Hancock Society
http://www.snopes.com/   Urban Legends
http://www.disney.com/   Walt Disney
http://www.braine-lalleud.com/waterloo/en/   Waterloo 1815
  histor.html
http://www.dlcwest.com/~obustill/   Winnie the Pooh

Bibliography

Source Books on Issues Associated With Bilingualism and Bilingual Education

The following books cover every aspect of bilingualism and bilingual education (although with few references to international schools). They differ in focus according to the nationality of the author or authors. Each of them contains extensive bibliographies of the latest publications in the fields of bilingualism and bilingual education. The book by Colin Baker supplies the most up-to-date findings. It draws its data from Australia, Canada, Continental Europe, the UK and the USA.

Baetens Beardsmore, H. (1982) *Bilingualism: Basic Principles*. Clevedon: Multilingual Matters.
Baker, C. (1996) *Foundations of Bilingual Education and Bilingualism*. Clevedon: Multilingual Matters.
Baker, C. and Prys Jones, S. (1998) *An Encyclopedia of Bilingual Education and Bilingualism*. Clevedon: Multilingual Matters.
Cummins, J. and Swain, M. (1986) *Bilingualism in Education*. New York: Longman.
Skutnabb-Kangas, T. (1981) *Bilingualism or Not: The Education of Minorities*. Clevedon: Multilingual Matters.

Topics Associated With Bilingualism and Trilingualism

The following articles and books contain further reading on individual topics such as the maintenance of the mother tongue and cultural identity, effects of bilingualism, the silent period, comprehensible input, acquisition versus learning of a language, the length of time L2 learners take to reach competency, and so on.

Baetens Beardsmore H. (ed.) (1993) European models of bilingual education: Practice, theory and development. *Journal of Multilingual and Multicultural Development* 14 (1–2), 103–20. Clevedon: Multilingual Matters.
Baetens Beardsmore H. and LeBrun, N. (1991) Trilingual education in the Grand Duchy of Luxembourg. In O. García (ed.) *Bilingual Education: Focusschrift in Honor of Joshua A. Fishman*. Amsterdam/Philadelphia: John Benjamins.
Cenoz, J. and Valencia, J-F. (1994) Additive trilingualism: Evidence from the Basque country. *Applied Psycholinguisitics* 15, 195–207.

273

Collier, V.P. (1989) How long? A synthesis of research on academic achievement in a second language. *TESOL Quarterly* 23 (3), 509–31.

Cummins, J. (1976) The influence of bilingualism on cognitive growth: A synthesis of research findings and explanatory hypotheses. *Working Papers on Bilingualism* 9, 1–43.

Cummins, J. (1984) Bilingualism and cognitive functioning. In S. Shapson and V. D'Oyley (eds) *Bilingual and Multicultural Education: Canadian Perspectives.* Clevedon: Multilingual Matters.

Krashen, S. (1981) *Second Language Acquisition and Second Language Learning.* Oxford: Pergamon Press.

Krashen, S. (1982) *Principles and Practices of Second Language Acquisition.* Oxford: Pergamon Press.

Krashen, S. (1985) *The Input Hypothesis: Issues and Implications.* London: Longman.

Singleton, D. (1989) *Language Acquisition: The Age Factor.* Clevedon: Multilingual Matters.

Raising Bilingual Children

Arnberg, L. (1987) *Raising Children Bilingually: The Pre-school Years.* Clevedon: Multilingual Matters.

Baker, C. (1995) *A Parent's and Teachers' Guide to Bilingualism.* Clevedon: Multilingual Matters

De Jong, E. (1986) *The Bilingual Experience. A Book for Parents.* Cambridge: Cambridge University Press.

Harding, E. and Riley P. (1987) *The Bilingual Family: A Handbook for Parents.* New York: Cambridge University Press.

Saunders, G. (1988) *Bilingual Children: From Birth to Teens.* Clevedon: Multilingual Matters.

ESL Programmes

The following books provide further information on current thinking about ESL provision and ESL methodology.

Carasquillo, A.L. (1993) *Teaching English as a Second Language: A Resource Guide.* New York: Garland Publishing Inc.

Cummins, J. (1986) Empowering minority students: A Framework for intervention. *Harvard Educational Review* 56 (1), 18–36.

Murphy, E. (ed.) (1990) *ESL: A Handbook for Teachers and Administrators in International Schools.* Clevedon: Multilingual Matters.

Oxford, R. (1990) *Language Learning Strategies: What Every Teacher Should Know.* New York: Newbury.

Richards, J.C. (1990) *The Language Teaching Matrix.* Cambridge: Cambridge University Press.

SCAA Discussion Papers (1996) *No. 5, Teaching and Learning English as an Additional Language: New Perspectives.* London: School Curriculum and Assessment Authority.

Special Needs Second Language Students

Cummins, J. (1984) *Bilingualism and Special Education: Issues in Assessment and Pedagogy*. Clevedon, UK: Multilingual Matters.

Learning Styles, Higher-order Thinking and Gifted Children

Bloom, B. (ed.) (1956) *Taxonomy of Educational Objectives*, Vol. 1, Harlow: Longman.
Eyre, D. (1997) *Able Children in Ordinary Schools*. London: David Fulton Publishers.
Grigorenko, E.L. and Sternberg, R.J. (1997) Styles of thinking, abilities, and academic performance. *Exceptional Children*. Reston: The Council for Exceptional Children.
Prashnig, B. (1997) *Diversity is Our Strength*. Auckland, New Zealand: Creative Learning Systems.

Writing Systems and Language Transfer

Meakin, S (1987) *Languages and Cultures in English-Language-Based International Schools*. Petersfield: European Council of International Schools.

Spelling

Gentry, J.R. (1987) *Spel ... is a Four Letter Word*. New York: Scholastic Inc.
Gentry, J.R. and Gillet, J. W. (1993) *Teaching Kids to Spell*. Portsmouth, New Hampshire: Heinemann.

General Issues and Strategies Associated with Teaching Classes of Diverse Students

These books include discussions on general topics associated with L2 learning as well as chapters on specific teaching strategies in subject areas. The topics include maintaining the mother tongue and cultural identity, differences in learning and cognitive styles, and students' expectations about learning and being taught.

Carrasquillo, A.L. and Rodriguez, V. (1996) *Language Minority Students in the Mainstream Classroom*. Clevedon: Multilingual Matters.
Genesee, F. (ed.) (1994) *Educating Second Language Children: The Whole Child, the Whole Curriculum, the Whole Community*. Cambridge: Cambridge University Press.
Rigg, P. and Allen, V.G. (eds) (1989) *When They Don't All Speak English: Integrating the ESL Student into the Regular Classroom*. Illinois: National Council of Teachers of English.
Richards, J.C. and Lockhart, C. (1994) *Reflective Teaching in Second Language Classrooms*. Cambridge: Cambridge University Press.
Short, D.J. (1991) *How to Integrate Language and Content Instruction*. Washington, DC: Center for Applied Linguistics.

Strategies for Teaching Language Arts in Diverse Classrooms

Au, K. H. (1993) *Literacy Instruction in Multicultural Settings*. Orlando: Harcourt Brace Jovanovich College Publishers.

Clay, M. (1991) *Becoming Literate: The Construction of Inner Control*. Portsmouth, New Hampshire: Heinemann.

Clay, M. (1993) *An Observation Survey of Early Literacy Achievement*. Portsmouth, New Hampshire: Heinemann.

Fountas, I.C. and Pinnell, G.S. (1996) *Guided Reading: Good First Teaching for All Children*. Portsmouth, New Hampshire: Heinemann.

Heath, S.B. and Mangiola, L. (1991) *Children of Promise: Literate Activity in Linguistically and Culturally Diverse Classrooms*. Washington, DC: National Education Association.

Hester, H. *et al.* (1992) *Stories in the Multilingual Primary Classroom*. London: Harcourt Brace.

Milner, J. O. and Pope, C. A. (eds) (1994) *Global Voices: Culture and Identity in the Teaching of English*. Papers originally presented at the 1990 IFTE Conference held in Auckland, New Zealand. Illinois: National Council of Teachers of English.

Routman, R. (1991) *Invitations: Changing as Teachers and Learners K–12*. Portsmouth, New Hampshire: Heinemann.

Spangenberg-Urbschat, K. and Pritchard, R. (eds) (1994) *Kids Come in All Languages: Reading Instruction for ESL Students*. Newark, Delaware: International Reading Association.

Index